Other Books by Ian Southwell

(Stairways Series, Published by Salvo Publishing, Melbourne, Australia)
www.salvationarmy.org.au/supplies

Born of the Spirit:
Helping Seekers Enter and Grow in God's Family (2009)

Prayer:
The Communication of Love (2010)

Giving to God:
A Response of Love (2011)

Holiness:
A Radiant Relationship (2012)

SAFELY LED TO SERVE

A Joint Biography

IAN AND SONJA SOUTHWELL

BALBOA. PRESS
A DIVISION OF HAY HOUSE

Balboa Press books may be ordered through booksellers or by contacting:

Balboa Press
A Division of Hay House
1663 Liberty Drive
Bloomington, IN 47403
www.balboapress.com.au
1 (877) 407-4847

Print information available on the last page.

ISBN: 978-1-5043-0609-6 (sc)
ISBN: 978-1-5043-0610-2 (e)

Balboa Press rev. date: 09/24/2018

Contents

Dedication

To our family
and to all who are seeking to find God's will
and purpose for their lives.

Preface

In the Bible, God promises to guide and protect his followers. Jesus said that his disciples would produce fruit for him as they stay connected to him. He also promised that through the power of the Holy Spirit some of them would serve him by taking his message of salvation to the ends of the earth (Acts 1:8).

We have found that God has been faithful to his promises. In fact, when preparing for the public recognition meeting of our official retirement from Salvation Army active officership in 2007, we included the worship song 'Faithful God' by Chris Bowater. God has been so faithful to us. 'Faithful God' could almost have been the title of this book. Some early drafts of these chapters were commenced not long after that event.

The fresh reminder of the fragility of human life demonstrated by the operations that Ian needed to have during 2013 and 2014 (see Chapter 17) provided an additional spur to writing this account while physical strength and memory were still more or less intact.

While recovering from the last of his operations in August 2014, Ian was particularly encouraged by the presentation of *Songs of Praise* on the ABC—a repeat of a BBC broadcast from September 2012. As anyone who has experienced major surgery knows, about three days afterwards can be a particularly difficult time. At that stage, the anaesthetics wear off and every part of the body is struggling to return to a degree of normality. The lines the vocalist was repeating again and again when Ian tuned in halfway through the programme were:

And though the pain is strong and it is hard to carry on,
I know that this is true, my God cares for you…
My God cares for you.

The vocalist and composer of the song, Lou Fellingham, may not have thought of herself as an angel, but she was God's messenger to Ian that day—and so were the musicians of the group Phatfish who supported her. Although deeply committed to Christ for many years, as you will read, and having maintained his times of personal Bible reading and prayer plus experiencing pastoral ministry from Sonja and others while in hospital, Ian had 'felt lost' that morning. What an additional blessing and reassurance came as the congregation of the Church of Christ the King in Brighton, UK, concluded the programme by singing verses of the Francis Harold Rowley hymn 'I will sing the wondrous story'! Verse two reads:

I was lost, but Jesus found me,
Found the sheep that went astray,
Threw his loving arms around me,
Drew me back into his way.

He did it for Ian that day. And the contents of the final verse Ian knew so well from *The Salvation Army Song Book* spoke to his condition then, had done so in the past and will do so in the future:

Days of darkness still come o'er me,
Sorrow's path I often tread,
But the Saviour still is with me,
By his hand I'm safely led.[1] (our emphasis)

In the circumstances, and with prayerful reflection afterwards, *Safely Led to Serve* seemed to be a suitable title for this book. We have been wonderfully led by God in our service as his messengers.

What we outline in the following pages is not just our story. It is his (God's) story of his faithfulness to us and the way in which he has chosen—and we have allowed him—to use us over the years as his servants. He has prepared us and led us safely to serve him.

We have chosen to write this account in the third-person (often plural) style of the annual letters we sent to family and friends since we

[1] Francis Harold Rowley (1854-1952) *The Song Book of The Salvation Army* (2015), Song 855.

commenced our joint international service in Zambia in 1970. Anything that has been achieved is because of the support of each other and our mutual dependence on Christ. Our desire is that this story will encourage young and old alike as we share with you our distant, and more recent, past. We have taken the liberty of including some suggestions springing from our own experiences over the years in the Reflections and Appendix 1 after Chapter 17 on pages 233–243. This material is applicable both to readers who are already Christians and those not yet committed to Christ.

Because most of our service for God has been within the context of The Salvation Army, we have included a Glossary of Some Salvation Army Terms and Abbreviations at the conclusion of the book as Appendix 3 (pages 251–255) as well as occasional explanations in the main text. We hope these will serve to assist those not familiar with some terminology we may take for granted.

On the basis of what we share with you in this account, we recommend our Lord Jesus Christ to the reader. He has been a wonderful friend and guide to us. May this story encourage you to trust God's faithfulness! He can be depended upon as a reliable guide even when our feelings may be distorted by pain, sleeplessness or sorrow.

Our prayer is that you, too, may experience his Spirit's guidance and direction as you daily place your life in his hands!

Acknowledgements

We are grateful to each other for the mutual encouragement and love we have experienced over almost 50 years of Christ-centred married life. Ours has been a wonderful joint ministry with Christ. Three is not a crowd with him.

As you will sense from this account, we are abundantly grateful to God for our parents and the examples of godly living they set before us. They taught us God's Word, how to pray and how to have a natural relationship with him. We are also grateful to The Salvation Army for providing us with opportunities for service not only in Australia but also around the world. On the way, we have been blessed by many who have encouraged us, seen potential in us and were guided by the Lord to deploy us in ways in which we could bring God's blessing and help to other people.

Many others with whom we worked have been very precious to us as well. We would like to have mentioned each of them by name, but that would have produced a volume too large to handle. With human frailty, we may well have missed somebody important. Your love and prayers have been deeply valued. Thank you for the contributions you have made to our lives at various stages.

Copies of our annual Christmas letters and some of our other letters to family and friends, lovingly kept by them and returned to us later, have prompted our memories for this account. So have copious photo transparencies, plus printed and digital photos taken throughout the years. Some significant ones are included in this book.

We appreciate the willingness of those actually named in the captions of the photographs in the book, who are still living and who we could contact, for permission to do so.

In collating this material and endeavouring to ensure its accuracy, we want to acknowledge Lindsay Cox, the Territorial Archivist at The Salvation Army Australia Southern Territory Archives and Museum in Melbourne. Lindsay made available copies of *The Disposition of Forces* volumes from 1940 through until 2015, and copies of *The Salvation Army Year Book* spanning the same period. These books have helped to ensure that we have recorded as accurately as possible the ranks and appointments of officers who were especially influential in setting us along the path of service and encouraging us as we did so. Major Donna Bryan and Brother George Ellis have also supported our research by providing copies of relevant materials from Army publications.

We are also grateful for the support of a number of readers who have looked at the material and made helpful comments. Amongst these are Commissioner John Clinch who served as Field Secretary and Territorial Commander in Australia Southern Territory in the 1980s and 1990s; and also Lieut-Colonel John Jeffrey with whom we served in Western Australia in 1992–93 and who also conducted our retirement service in 2007. Our daughters, Sharon, Jenni, and Cathy, who were part of this story with us and witnessed significant parts of it from inside the family, have aided in the review process and helped ensure accuracy.

We are deeply grateful to our friend, Ms Dawn Volz of Ringwood Corps and the Literary Department of The Salvation Army in Australia, who undertook extensive editing and several reviews of the material and proofs. We deeply appreciate the work of Alexa Codia and Corina Palmer, publishing consultants; the content evaluator; design team members, especially Louie Romares the cover designer; and other members of the team from Balboa Press, for their patience with this material and for producing an attractive volume.

Ian and Sonja Southwell, Lieut-Colonels
Melbourne, Australia; January 2017

Illustration Acknowledgements

Cover Photograph:

Representation of the nail-scarred, guiding hand of Christ by Ian Southwell (2016)

Authors' Photograph (back cover):

© 2006 Photography courtesy of Tony Isbitt, Bromley, Kent, UK, used by his permission (October 2016)

Other Photographs

Most were taken by the authors, their relatives or colleagues, mostly on the authors' own cameras. Others are part of the authors' private collections with known sources recognised as noted below:

Northcote High School Band (top left, page 82): Taken in 1966. Permission granted for use by the Principal, Northcote High School, Vic., Australia, October 2016

Wedding photographs (middle row left and right, page 82): Taken by Geoffrey Baker Studios, Box Hill, Vic., Australia in 1967 (Company now out of business)

'Messengers of the Faith' Session 1967–69 (bottom, page 82): Taken in 1968. Permission granted for use by The Salvation Army Australia Southern Territory, October 2016

'Cadets commissioned in Zambia in 1973' (middle, page 84): Permission granted for use by The Salvation Army Zambia Territory, October 2016

'Delegates to the 1974 Training Principals' Conference' (bottom, page 84): Taken by Les Kirby Photographic Studio, 1974. Permission granted for use by The Salvation Army International Headquarters, October 2016

"Ian as producer/conductor of 'Jesus Folk'." (bottom row page 146): Taken in 1976 by The Salvation Army Editorial Department, the Philippines. Permission granted for use by The Salvation Army, the Philippines, October 2016

'The Clean Life March, Seoul, 1998' (bottom row, page 149): Taken in 1998. Permission granted for use by The Salvation Army Korea Territory, October 2016

Delivering supplies to an earthquake survivor, Puli, Taiwan, 2000 (bottom row, right, page 209): Taken in 2000. Permission granted for use by The Salvation Army Taiwan Region, December 2016

Photographs of inauguration of The Salvation Army in Macau, 2000 (top row, page 210): Taken in 2000. Permission granted for their use by The Salvation Army Hong Kong and Macau Command, October 2016

Cutting Pentecost Celebration birthday cake 2015 (bottom row right, page 212): Taken in 2015 by Sonja Southwell. Permission granted in 2016 for publication of this photograph by Sandra Gifford, the mother of the boy featured while helping Ian Southwell

Chapter 1

Sonja's heritage and early life

That Sonja survived the first seven years of her life is something of a miracle.

Her parents, Ryer and Johanna van Kralingen, were Salvation Army officers (ministers) who had been born in the city of Vlaardingen, the Netherlands. Ryer was the second youngest of 17 children and came from a Dutch Reformed Church background. He made his personal decision for Christ at The Salvation Army. Johanna was the talented daughter of The Salvation Army bandmaster at the Vlaardingen Corps. They eventually married and served together as corps officers (Christian ministers) in Holland.

In those years, the Netherlands East Indies was a colony of Holland and The Salvation Army was endeavouring to establish work both amongst those who had come from the Netherlands to the East Indies and the indigenous population. Ryer, his wife and their one-year-old daughter, Joan, travelled to the Netherlands East Indies in 1935 in response to God's call to minister in that area. They were given several corps leadership appointments before the Army leaders discovered Ryer's special gift was working with the men of the Dutch military. Having been a fisherman before training as a Salvation Army officer and knowing something of the tough life of the fishermen on the North Sea, he was ideally fitted to bring the Gospel and provide care for the troops protecting the colony. Johanna was also gifted in caring for people. They eventually developed an excellent partnership running Salvation Army rest and recreation facilities for military personnel known as 'The Open Door' during their service in the central part of Java.

Sonja was born on 4 November 1939 at the Turen Hospital in Yogyakarta while her parents were in charge of 'The Open Door' in that city. The Dutch colonial troops, away from family and friends in Holland, often needed spiritual counsel and wholesome activities whilst on leave. The Army's military homes were designed to provide for this. Sonja's parents received a change of appointment to the Malang 'Open Door', further to the east in Java, during 1941.

With war having been declared against Germany in Europe, and the threat of a Japanese invasion increasing in the peripheral islands of the Dutch East Indies, much uncertainty and fear pervaded the island chain. Obviously, the oil-rich island of Tarakan would be one of the first targets of the Japanese who would need its oil supplies to fuel their ships and planes in the event of a war. The colonial government was concerned for the welfare and morale of the Dutch and national troops stationed in Tarakan to protect the oil refineries and repel any invasion. Away from their wives and families, some of these troops were finding 'recreation' in some unsavoury situations. Could The Salvation Army do something about this? Would the Army supply a military chaplain? The Salvation Army leaders in Bandung had already established a military clubhouse in Tarakan, but this was rundown and no longer functioning. They looked around for someone to help. So they asked if Adjutant Ryer would go to Tarakan for about six months to reopen the recreational centre and to provide spiritual support to the troops.

After thinking and praying about this, Ryer and Johanna agreed that he should undertake this assignment.[2]

The military home in Tarakan was reopened late in November 1941, just before the first bombing by the Japanese a month later and invasion in early 1942. Ryer had the opportunity to leave on the ferryboat departing from the island for Java, but chose to remain with the men whom he had grown to love over those past few months. This was a providential decision because the ferry was torpedoed by the Japanese en route to Java. There were no survivors.

---

[2] We have agreed that Sonja will give a much more detailed account of God's wonderful guidance to her family members and herself during that period and through to the 1960s in the book she is currently writing, tentatively titled, *A Safe Arrival*. What follows in this chapter is a brief summary.

Before long, the Japanese troops invaded Tarakan and the Royal Dutch Shell Company employees set about destroying all the refinery equipment and stored oil so that the Japanese would not be able to use them. Obviously, the Japanese were furious that this happened and took revenge by executing large numbers of the employees and the troops who were protecting the facilities. Ryer was able to minister to those who were about to die and also to the others who were understandably distressed about what was happening. Thus began four and a half years of separation between Ryer, and Johanna, Joan, and Sonja.

After the Japanese troops also landed in Java, Dutch expatriates—men, women and children—were collected and housed in protected villages surrounded by barbed wire—the precursor of a formal prisoner of war camp.

In the case of Mrs Adjutant Johanna van Kralingen and her children, the initial protected village was 'The Wijk' in Malang. The transition to formal prisoner of war camps did not take long. Many families spent the remaining years of the war in such camps, although the able-bodied men were moved to work on projects such as the Burma–Thailand Railway. Large numbers of women and children who were interned died during those years. Johanna very carefully cared for the children and did everything possible to protect them. She also served as a leader amongst the women in the internment camp in Solo (Surakarta) before being moved with many others to Banyu Biru[3] (to the south of Semarang near Ambarawa) in central Java. Wherever she was, Johanna worked to secure the best conditions possible for all prisoners she could help, although her own health was declining by then. Sonja still remembers some of her own fears during that time. As a result, she was unable to watch war or other violent movies for many years because the memories were still so vivid in her mind.

When World War II ended in August 1945, a civil war of independence erupted. Indonesian nationalists wanted to control their country now that Dutch influence had been so severely diminished as the result of the Japanese occupation. Dutch nationals and former prisoners of war were not safe. The opened gates of their prisoner of war camp were closed again for safety as the nationalists fired shots into the camp to assert their authority in the area. More fear! Three and a half months were needed for British Gurkha troops to arrive and make reasonably safe the road from Banyu Biru to Semarang.

---

[3] Sometimes written Banju Biru.

For almost four years, the family had no idea whether Ryer was still alive after the invasion of Tarakan. Through God's protecting mercies and guidance, and the international networks of The Salvation Army and the Red Cross, information filtered through to Johanna that Ryer was safe in Australia. The first indication was a letter from Ryer given to them on arrival at Semarang in December saying he was alive and in Australia. How relieved they were! So repatriation plans were changed. Red Cross officials decided Sonja, her mother, and sister were to be sent to Australia rather than to the Netherlands—their homeland. They were moved from Java to Singapore to commence the journey by ship to Sydney.

So what had happened to Ryer? A few months after the invasion of Tarakan during which time he ministered to fellow prisoners of war as their chaplain, he had been shipped from Tarakan south to Balikpapan, south-east Borneo (Kalimantan) and, in 1945, on to Banjarmasin, further south. After being route-marched with other prisoners north toward Purak Cahu, he was found and released by Australian troops during their attacks to drive out the Japanese toward the conclusion of the war. Through a wonderful series of events that Sonja relates in her account, Ryer was repatriated to Australia, eventually coming to Melbourne, Victoria.

Having arrived in Sydney, Johanna and the girls journeyed south by train via Albury and met Ryer at the then Spencer Street Railway Station (now Southern Cross) in Melbourne in April 1946. As Ryer had left Malang when Sonja was just 22 months old, it was quite a transition for her to now have a father to whom she could relate.

After a period of recuperation at a Salvation Army rest home in Healesville, Victoria, the family was permitted to travel to the Netherlands again to meet with family members. Almost 13 years had elapsed since they had left their homeland, and Ryer and Johanna were well overdue for furlough. The visit to Holland provided opportunities for them to meet cousins, aunts, uncles, and other relatives who were all pleased that the family had been so wonderfully preserved during the war. The Netherlands itself, of course, had been badly affected by the invasion of the German troops. Much damage had taken place during those years and life was not yet back to normal.

Because of the need to re-establish Salvation Army work in the Dutch East Indies, Ryer indicated his desire to return to the islands in order to help in that process. The conditions in the archipelago were not stable due to the drive toward independence by the indigenous population mentioned earlier. Women and children were not permitted to return due to the state of the civil war that was still taking place. So another six months of separation took place.

Ryer had great credibility with personnel from the Royal Dutch Shell Company and the authorities in Jakarta especially due to his selfless service during the war years. He was able to garner many resources for the work of The Salvation Army. Most significantly, he managed to secure possession for the Army of a deserted Dutch colonial home at 55 Jalan Kramat Raya in Jakarta. Ryer set this up to be a military clubhouse for the remaining Dutch colonial troops stationed in and around the capital city. This site would also house the Jakarta 1 Corps, of which Ryer became the corps officer.

When independence came at the end of December 1949, the Dutch troops returned to the Netherlands and the military home became the training college for Salvation Army officers. The separate building on the left of main block (as viewed from the road) became the Jakarta 1 Corps and the pavilion on the right hand side the quarters for Ryer, Johanna, and family after they re-joined him in November 1947. Later some of the buildings provided office accommodation for Ryer's work as a public relations officer as he did the best he could to magnify the work of God and The Salvation Army in that part of the world. His work spanned the period both before and after the country gained independence from Holland, the Dutch troops left, and the country was officially renamed Indonesia.

Schooling at a local school in Jakarta followed for Joan and Sonja, together with many other children whose education had been delayed or disrupted over the war years. Sonja had received some classes of elementary schooling in the Netherlands whilst the family was on holidays, including a period when one of her uncles was the primary school's headmaster. Always an energetic child, Sonja admitted she did not always concentrate on her studies at that time, but did well enough to move up through the various levels.

Whilst Ryer was often away in connection with public relations work and her sister was busy with her studies, Sonja found that there were very few books to read and little activity available. Her dog named Siep provided some companionship and a sense of protection. Sonja became involved in The Salvation Army corps that had been established at the site in Jakarta. The heat and humidity in Jakarta were often oppressive, however. During the school holidays she would sometimes be sent to stay at a senior citizens' residence in Bandung where the weather was much cooler.

As she recorded in the account of her call to officership[4], Sonja made her personal decision for Christ sometime in 1948 during a young people's meeting at Jakarta 1 Corps. Her father, who was the corps officer at the time, later enrolled her as a junior soldier[5].

In about 1952, the then Captain (later Commissioner) Gijs (Herman) Pattipeilohy asked Sonja to give her testimony at a youth councils series of meetings to be held in Jakarta. She asked him why. 'You're a junior soldier and a corps cadet[6],' replied the captain. 'Just tell them why you love Jesus.' Sonja was the only corps cadet in the corps, but the young Norwegian woman officer who led the corps cadets made the weekly class exciting. Sonja felt the Old Testament came alive as they looked together at the prophets and their messages. The words of the prophet captivated her imagination for some time. 'A voice of one calling: "In the desert prepare the way for the Lord; make straight in the wilderness a highway for our God"' (Isaiah 40:3). As a child Sonja had seen the frantic preparations made when the president of the newly-independent Republic of Indonesia or other high government officials visited Jakarta or distant villages. Rubbish was removed and potholes filled, walls were whitewashed and pots of flowers placed near homes. So, she recorded 'I felt it was important that the way for the Lord's coming was equally well-prepared. I felt I wanted to be a voice for Jesus.'[7]

In retrospect, Sonja didn't feel that she had said much of significance in her testimony. After the youth councils session in which she participated, however, Captain Pattipeilohy came to her and said, 'One day God will call you to be an officer and you must say "yes".'

---

4 Sonja Southwell in Judith Soeters (ed.) *Where Jesus Leads* (Melbourne, Salvo Publishing, 2013) pp.127ff.

5 A boy or girl who, having accepted Jesus as their Saviour, has signed the Junior Soldier's Promise and become a Salvationist.

6 A young Salvationist who undertakes a course of study and practical training in a corps with a view to becoming effective in Salvation Army service.

7 Sonja's personal notes submitted for J. Soeters, *op. cit.* but not included in the book.

'Oh no!' she replied. The captain repeated his words: 'When he does, you must say "yes".' That day a 'seed' was dropped in the garden of her heart. As she reflected on the matter of 'preparing the way', this 'became the unspoken theme of her life'. She was convinced that God calls his followers to prepare the way to make it easier for others to respond to Jesus.

Sonja began to observe how her parents helped people respond to Jesus. They believed God called them to serve him and that he would take care of them. She observed their early morning times of prayer and Bible reading; prayers at meal times and their gratitude for daily provision. In uncertain times, they would assure Sonja and her sister that 'God will provide'—and he did!

When her parents' six-year term of service was coming to an end, they requested to be transferred to Australia, the country in which they had been so warmly welcomed and well cared for during 1946. Sonja arrived in Melbourne, Australia, at the age of 14. She was granted a place in the form two (year eight) at Collingwood Girls Secondary School and was the only student there who spoke no English. The first three months were a struggle, but caring teachers supported her and friendly classmates spoke slowly. The school was conveniently near the Anchorage Men's Home in Abbotsford. Her parents had been appointed there initially in the hope that they would pick up the English language quickly in a relatively casual setting. The Territory's leadership hoped Major and Mrs van Kralingen would be able to provide support to immigrants from the Netherlands who were arriving in Australia, linking them up with Salvation Army worship and service. Territorial Commander Commissioner Charles Durman had been involved in post-war relief work for The Salvation Army in Holland and had a high regard for Dutch resilience. During those first few years the family attended the Fairfield Corps, just a short train ride away from the Anchorage.

Eventually their accommodation was changed to Port Melbourne, close to the port where most migrants would be arriving by ship in the mid-1950s. This move provided another opportunity for Sonja to change school and to complete her secondary schooling at Mac.Robertson Girls' Secondary School in South Melbourne. The family also attended the South Melbourne Corps at that time.

The Salvation Army's Bethesda Hospital in Richmond was then available as a nurse-training school and Sonja was accepted for training in

January 1958. Sonja saw nursing as one of the caring professions through which she could help people.

So much of her concentration was on nursing and some Army activities that she did not give much specific attention to God's calling. Her three-year general nursing studies, with postgraduate work qualifying her as a midwife and infant welfare nursing sister, meant she could work anywhere in these fields in Australia. Subconsciously, she had an awareness of a 'voice calling: "in the desert prepare the way for the Lord…"'

She found life was exciting and she was ready to spread her wings. 'Perhaps I was trying to escape that call and move out of home at the same time. I applied with the Commonwealth Government for a position and was accepted for the hospital in Katherine, the Northern Territory as from January 1964,' she recorded later.[8] During that year, she was positively influenced by the fine examples of Majors (later Brigadiers) Vic and Olive Pedersen. Vic was the flying padre in the northern part of Australia and Olive led the Katherine Corps while he was visiting outback stations. 'Both genuinely cared for the people amongst whom they worked and reached out to them. They were living examples of God's grace in their community,' Sonja recalled.[9]

After 12 months of exciting work in the intense heat of the Northern Territory, Sonja's health deteriorated and her weight dropped to 45 kg. She returned to Melbourne in 1965 with a sense of urgency, convinced that God had something special for her there. After some needed rest at her parents' home in Croydon, she undertook a six-month postgraduate course at the Royal Victorian Eye and Ear Hospital. On completion of this course, she applied and was accepted for work in the operating theatres specialising in eye and ear surgery. Accommodation was provided in a staff residence adjacent to the hospital. When duty rosters allowed, she attended the Box Hill Corps and sang in the songsters.

Having learned to drive before travelling to the Northern Territory, and using this knowledge in ambulance work around the Katherine area, Sonja decided to buy her own car in Melbourne. From the excellent salary she had received whilst working in Katherine, she had the resources to pay cash on the spot—just less than 1000 pounds. This small Volkswagen

---

8 Sonja Southwell in J. Soeters *op. cit.* p. 130

9 Sonja's personal notes submitted for J. Soeters, *op. cit.* but not included in the book.

1300 sedan gave her great mobility, allowing her to regularly visit her parents in Croydon and also move around Melbourne.

Sonja decided to use her car to visit the recently completed Snowy Mountains Hydroelectric Scheme in New South Wales. Taking a friend, Anna (not her real name), they explored the wonders of this project for several days. One night they stayed at a relatively cheap hotel in one of the towns. After dinner, the dining room was expanded into a dance floor and a crowd of people from the township also entered. Anna stayed there for some time while Sonja went to her room for an early night.

The following morning, three very smartly dressed men with suits and ties asked Sonja if she could give them a lift to a certain place in the general direction in which they were travelling. Sonja wondered how they knew that she had a car, but perhaps Anna had mentioned this to them. Some 52 years later, Sonja would have been much more cautious. However, she agreed to their request and these three quite tall men clambered onto the back seat of the Volkswagen. They were not carrying any luggage with them—not even a bottle of water. Sonja thought this was very strange.

When they asked to be let out of the car, there was no obvious building or sign of life in the area—not even a tree. And after she had turned the car to travel back to the main route of their journey, Sonja looked back through the rear vision mirror. She could not see them. They had simply vanished from sight. To this day she wonders if these three were God's angels sent to protect Anna and herself from staying in that township any longer than simply overnight.

Increasingly, she sensed the pressure of the Holy Spirit over the matter of officership. At the age of 26, naturally, she was looking for a marriage partner. Marriage now seemed to be unlikely, especially if she became an officer, and she made this a matter of prayer. God had it all in hand. Very wonderfully, God was again preparing the way for her. He would lead her safely for service.

Sonja's sister, Joan, and her husband George Stolk, attended the Fairfield Corps in the inner north of Melbourne in 1966. They invited Sonja to attend occasional Sunday morning or night meetings when she was not on duty at the hospital and 'recommended' that she pay some attention to one of the trombone players in the band, Corps Cadet Counsellor (and Junior Soldier Sergeant) Ian Southwell.

Chapter 2

Ian's heritage and first 12 years

Ian's parents, David John Southwell and Florence Burgess Southwell (nee Lonnie), were, like Sonja's, thoroughly committed Salvationists.

David John's parents, Field Majors David and Sarah Southwell, were also Salvation Army corps officers who served in many appointments around Victoria. Such appointments were generally not of long duration, and conditions for officers were challenging. The growing family eventually numbered nine children plus an aunt, Hannah Southwell, who helped the family and the officer parents. David John was the sixth child, having been born in 1908. The family moved from corps to corps using a horse and cart, and also took along a cow to provide milk and other dairy products. The children learned how to look after these important animals as well as being involved in Salvation Army activities. In David John's case, he quickly learned to play a brass cornet. He had made his decision for Christ as a 13-year-old when his parents were stationed at Wangaratta.

Not long after, having completed some high school studies at Year 11 level, David left home and went to work for the Victorian Railways in their Ballarat office. Marvellously, he was preserved when a disgruntled employee fired a shot at a manager. The shot ricocheted from a wire and grazed David John's arm. The wound could have been much more serious. Later David was transferred to the Melbourne office of the Railways and still later to the company workshop in Yarraville. He boarded during those years with William, his older brother, in Kew. David was thoroughly involved at the Salvation Army corps in Kew. His musicianship was recognised and he became the corps bandmaster at about age 16. God called David John Southwell to follow him as an officer (minister).

With Will, David John entered the Victory Session of Salvation Army officer cadets in March 1927. He was dux of the College that year. In January 1928, David was appointed as cadet-sergeant—a prestigious junior position on the training college staff—to help and guide incoming cadets.

At the end of that year David was promoted to the rank of captain and took up his first corps appointment at Chudleigh Corps in Tasmania in January 1929. His previous experiences with horses was helpful because he needed one to help him collect the corps' target of 125 pounds for the Self Denial Appeal that year from scattered rural areas of Northern Tasmania. Twelve months later, David was appointed to the Queenstown Corps on the west coast of Tasmania. He suffered quite significant lung problems from breathing sulphur dioxide produced from copper-smelting undertaken without the environmental protection safeguards of the 21st century.

In 1931, David John was appointed to the Ulverstone Corps in northern Tasmania. Fifty-one years later his life and ministry was still remembered. In 1982 at the corps anniversary celebrations, a Mrs Perton recounted how her father carried the flag in the open-air meetings and marches. He would stand in the heavy rain although he had no overcoat. When the captain (David Southwell) asked him why he did not have a coat he said he could not afford one. A few days later, the captain brought around a good overcoat and said he read that, if a man had two coats, the Bible said he should give one to someone who had none. Mrs Perton concluded, 'He did not give his old one, but he gave the best one he had.'[10]

Perhaps because of the damage to his health at Queenstown and his clerical skills, David was appointed to the Finance Department at the Army's territorial headquarters in Melbourne from January 1932. His musical capabilities were also recognised with a concurrent appointment to the Melbourne Staff Band which continued for at least eight years including service as the band's secretary and treasurer.

In contrast, Ian's mother, Florence Lonnie, had been born in New Zealand in 1905, a couple of years earlier than David. Her parents, George and Jennie Lonnie (nee Hammer), were Australian officers who were serving

[10] From correspondence to Ian from the late Commissioner Donald Campbell.

on transfer in that country in corps and divisional work. Florence was born in Christchurch and made her decision as a four-year-old guided by the then Lieut. Mary Anderson. (Mary Anderson later became well known as a Salvation Army police court officer in Melbourne, eventually receiving The Salvation Army Order of the Founder[11] for her work.) Florence (often known as Florrie), with her sister Ivy and parents, subsequently moved from New Zealand to New South Wales and Queensland where the Lonnies were divisional leaders before returning to the Australia Southern Territory for more divisional leadership and territorial headquarters responsibilities.

During the influenza epidemic of 1919, Florrie became ill and, in praying for recovery, promised to serve God as a Salvation Army officer. She became a soldier[12] of the Army at Hawthorn Corps in Victoria. On moving with her parents to Western Australia, she became the primary Sunday school leader, life-saving guard chaplain, songster[13], corps cadet, and corps orchestra member—in which she played the mandolin—at the Highgate Corps.[14] Florrie entered officer training from the Thornbury Corps in 1926. Believing that God could be calling her to serve as a missionary in China, she expressed this to the leaders. On commissioning, she was appointed to Bethesda Hospital to train as an officer nurse.

In 1932, David almost lost his life when his appendix ruptured and he contracted peritonitis. Aside from a very slow and painful recovery, something else significant happened during his stay in The Salvation Army's Bethesda Hospital in Richmond. This enthusiastic 25-year-old saw some officer nurses in action and a special friendship developed with Captain Florence Lonnie who had, by that time, qualified as a general, midwifery and diet nurse. Eventually recovered from his illness, David resumed his service in the Finance Department, this time as cashier. His friendship with Florrie developed. Florence and David married on 29 December 1934.

---

[11] The highest Salvation Army honour for distinguished service.

[12] A soldier is a full member of The Salvation Army, over 14 years of age, who has signed the Soldier's Covenant (formerly called 'Articles of War'), been approved by the Senior Pastoral Care Council (formerly the Census Board) and publicly enrolled.

[13] Choir member.

[14] *The Young Soldier*, April 12, 1924, p. 6.

For a number of years they had to live in the retirement home of Lieut-Colonels George and Jennie Lonnie in Woolton Avenue, Thornbury. Not enough Salvation Army accommodation was available for them to live separately during those depression years. They were delighted when Florrie conceived, but equally devastated when the full-term baby they named John was stillborn. The umbilical cord around his neck in a fairly slow labour meant that he strangled. No scans were available in those days to warn midwives or gynaecologists of possible dangers before a baby was due to be born.

As it eventuated, Ian may not have been born safely either; the same situation applied to him. Being a second child, he was born more quickly and no damage took place.

Another factor may have meant that Ian might not have even been conceived in the first place. By 1940, the clouds of war were building up over Australia, as they were over the Netherlands East Indies. A potential Japanese invasion was imminent. Men of military age were called up or encouraged to volunteer to serve to protect the country and to extend the war efforts of the British Empire. David, having undertaken national service military training as a younger man, was asked by his Salvation Army leaders to become a chaplain in the forces. Because of his particular interest and expertise in musicianship, he thought he might have been involved with the Second 22nd Battalion as their chaplain. Many musicians in the battalion band came from the Brunswick and other Salvation Army corps from around Melbourne. They had enlisted to serve as a stretcher bearers and musicians. Their leader was Bandmaster Arthur Gullidge, a skilled musician and published composer of brass band compositions. Little did David and Florence know that early in 1942 the battalion and the band would be taken prisoners of war by the Japanese in Rabaul, New Britain. Most of them would perish when the unmarked prison ship transporting them back to Japan was torpedoed by a United States submarine.

As it was, David never spent more than three months as an active military chaplain. Having been appointed to Darnley Training Camp, he contracted scarlet fever. His condition was so serious that he needed 12 months leave to recover. During that time of sick leave, Ian was conceived.

When David was fit enough to be able to do some work, he was appointed to The Salvation Army Chief Secretary's office to compile records of Salvation Army military work. David Ian was born on 19 June 1942, and has always been known as Ian to avoid confusion with his father. Soon after Ian's birth, David and Florence were appointed to Western Australia. David was to be the Divisional Young People's Secretary and Florence to assist. Although Ian can remember little of those days, photographs in the family album remind him of some events. One black and white photo shows him wearing a knitted woollen pullover. He recalls it was brown with various animals embroidered on it. The photo (on page 80) shows him at about age three, standing in the backyard of their home in Smith Street, Highgate. He was mimicking his father. Having seen his father conduct open-air meetings with The Salvation Army, he was standing there with his father's concertina and a song book as though he was leading an open-air meeting himself.

He does remember the journey back to Melbourne in 1945 to the extent that by this stage his grandmother, Mrs Lieut-Colonel Jennie Lonnie, journeyed with them. She had joined the family after her husband, George, died just a year after Ian was born. The key event that remains in Ian's mind was tying his own little wooden train to the back of the Trans-Australia train somewhere the middle of the Nullarbor Plain during a refuelling or watering stop for the engine—and then worrying that he left it there when he could not find it later.

His father's new position was that of Divisional Young People's Secretary in the Melbourne Metropolitan division and the family lived at Separation Street, Northcote, for a time. Shortly after that, in 1946, the family moved to Ballarat when David became the Divisional Commander[15] for the Western Victoria Division.

By this time, Bible stories were becoming very precious to Ian. His grandmother as well as his parents were obviously encouraging him to follow Jesus. He commenced to attend primary Sunday school at the Ballarat West Corps in South Street on Sunday afternoons. On Sunday mornings he would journey with his parents as they conducted meetings for The Salvation Army around the Ballarat area. If David was away in a rural area, Florrie would attend the Ballarat West Corps with Ian, and participate in the primary Sunday school in the afternoon.

---

[15] The officer in charge of a number of Salvation Army corps (or churches) in an area.

David was definitely one of Ian's heroes. He purchased the first family car, a second-hand Hupmobile, in an attempt to make it easier to travel around the division than travelling by train. Ian remembered the car had two spare tyres—both of which were needed on a journey from Melbourne to Ballarat. Later, The Salvation Army provided his father with a Willys all-steel station wagon which looked something like a military jeep except it was designed for passengers. Painted red, with Salvation Army insignia on the side, the station wagon was fitted out with an amplifier unit and facilities for two loudspeakers on the roof so that it could act as a public address system for open-air witnessing or special events in the division. Appropriately, it was described as a 'field unit'.

Ian was challenged about the importance of loving Jesus and accepting him as his friend. Scripture readings and prayers at meal time occurred daily. So did prayers before he went to bed for the night. The necessity for young and old alike to be ready for the day of facing God's judgment after death was also regularly communicated in meetings he attended. Such readiness was only made possible by receiving Christ as Saviour. All these influences combined to encourage Ian, after a Sunday morning meeting on 25 January 1948 that his parents conducted at Creswick, just north of Ballarat, to make his decision to follow Jesus. As lunch was being prepared, he went to the room his father used as an office at home. 'Dad,' he said, 'I want to give my heart to Jesus.' Very lovingly, David guided Ian in a simple prayer of repentance and faith and Ian was assured that he belonged to Jesus. The prayers of his parents and grandmother were answered. While already familiar with praying simple prayers before he went to bed at night, those prayers now seemed to have much more meaning and reality because Jesus lived within him.

A few days later, Ian commenced his formal education at the Ballarat West State Primary School in Urquhart Street. He had already experienced much informal education with building blocks and storybooks, listening to educational programmes and music on the radio, and using construction sets in wood and Meccano pieces. He knew the alphabet and could count up to 20. Now he relished the opportunity of being at school and learning other basic things that he would need for the days ahead.

He remembers the ration cards that were still necessary in those days to buy food, clothes and petrol following the Second World War. A needed tonsil operation of Ballarat Base Hospital to help alleviate some of his ongoing tonsillitis remains a vivid memory—especially the chloroform used as the anaesthetic. Not having attended kindergarten and without the inoculations available in these days, he contracted mumps, measles and whooping cough that marred the early days of his schooling. In parallel to his formal studies at school, he was learning about cricket and football in the backyard of the home with his enthusiastic father and the then Captain Ray Beasy who, with his wife and daughter, Elizabeth, shared the 120 Errard Street house for a time. Ian is very grateful for parents who played sports with him as well as praying with him. They encouraged him in a wide range of activities and experiences.

His parents had an old Brownie camera which used fairly wide black and white film. Ian was fascinated by it. Having seen a camera in a shop in Ballarat, he saved up his pocket money to obtain one. At one shilling a week, it took 36 weeks to save the one pound sixteen shillings needed at that time to buy his own smaller Box Brownie Six-20 camera. It served him well for at least 20 years until he graduated to more sophisticated devices to produce coloured prints or transparencies. He learned a valuable lesson about the importance of saving money in his lion-shaped money box for a purpose.

He was also encouraged to collect and personally give money to help less fortunate people. The Army's annual Self Denial Appeal was then the main fundraising effort to assist needy people in Australia as well as overseas. (Since the mid-1960s the Red Shield Appeal[16] has focused on helping needy people in Australia and the proceeds of the Self Denial Appeal directed to support the international ministry of The Salvation Army.) Young people in Army Sunday schools were encouraged to collect from friends, relatives and neighbours. Each donation was 'receipted' by pricking the amounts received from each person—from one penny to two shillings—on a collecting card designed to achieve a target about one pound (20 shillings). As well as seeking donations from visitors to their home, Ian's parents encouraged him to write simple appeal letters to his aunts and uncles asking for support for the appeal and he recalls they gave quite generously. His parents then taught him the courtesy of writing to thank the donors, too.

---

[16] A financial appeal to the general public; also known as the Annual Appeal in some countries.

Ian also journeyed to Melbourne each year to share in Salvation Army congress meetings. The family stayed at the Army's People's Palace in Kings Street. Eight-millimetre movie film of those days taken by his officer-uncle, Allen Sharp, shows him waving a flag during General George Carpenter's visit in 1946 and being present when General Albert Orsborn visited in 1951. When the women's rallies were conducted during congress which his mother needed to attend, his father would take Ian to the Melbourne Museum, then in Swanson Street, to enjoy the wonderful range of exhibits—especially the working models of all manner of machines.

The Sea Rover was a popular programme on local radio that was illustrated by a comic strip in one of the newspapers at that time. The programme recounted stories about a heroic, but probably fictional, sea captain who fought against the wicked pirate, Blackbeard. So the Sea Rover became one of Ian's early heroes. Hopalong Cassidy was another fictional hero about that time. Cassidy was a cowboy who fought for justice against cattle rustlers and other criminals in the south-west United States.

Meanwhile, at school Ian was already seen as something of a leader, being given opportunities to propose votes of thanks when his class went on various excursions to such places as a farm or a factory. On a factory visit, he recalls that one of the workers suggested that the spokesperson for the class might one day become the prime minister of Australia!

How blessed Ian was in being born into a family with a love for good books. One that he treasured greatly was *Great Deeds that Helped to Build the British Empire*. The book contained stories of heroes who gave exemplary service to the Empire such as David Livingstone, Lawrence of Arabia, Grace Darling, James Watt and also William Booth. Ian was also fascinated by the adventures of people like William Tell who stood up against evil officials in Switzerland, or Robin Hood and his merry men who defied Guy of Gisborne at Nottingham. He took the part of William Tell in a class play at his school. For his sixth birthday, his parents gave him a copy of the King James Version of the Bible containing black and white photographs of Palestine and a concordance. They also provided him with a comic book version of the life of Christ that was easier to read and served to make the Gospel story more vivid for him. The groundwork was being laid for his ongoing Bible studies.

His grandmother, Mrs Lieut-Colonel Jennie Lonnie, often shared with Ian the story of how her husband George, as a single officer, was involved in pioneering Salvation Army work in Southern Cross, Western Australia. Having been born and brought up on the goldfields of northern Victoria near Yackandandah, George understood the challenges faced by gold miners and their families. George made his decision for Christ at The Salvation Army in Beechworth and trained as a carpenter. He moved to Melbourne in the hope of finding more work. Entering officer training from Brunswick in 1893 at the relatively mature age of 27, he was commissioned as an officer six months later. His appointment to the goldfields in Western Australia meant travelling by sea to Perth because no Trans-Australian train line existed in those days.

With Captain Charles Bensley, who brought his cornet, George travelled with his carpenter's tools as far as the rail line went east from Perth. From the rail head at Doodlakine, they carried their 'swags' the remaining 121 km to Southern Cross. George built a hall, Bensley played his cornet, crowds were attracted, the Gospel proclaimed, souls were saved, and the ill and dying experienced Christian care. Barely eight months later, George was appointed to Coolgardie where he built another hall and helped commence a school for children of gold miners. Following a rain storm which caused gold specks to become visible, he and Bensley collected enough specks at a spot near Fly Creek to make into wedding rings. Grandma Lonnie would show her ring to Ian as she told these stories of adventure in God's service. She recounted that Grandpa Lonnie placed great emphasis on loyalty to God. He would frequently write in autograph books: 'The world crowns success; God crowns faithfulness.' What she did not relate in such detail were her own faithful ministries as a single officer among prostitutes in Adelaide, South Australia, and near the opium dens in Little Bourke Street, Melbourne, as she attempted to encourage them to allow God to change their lives.

Ian's awareness of the need for some Christians to serve God *outside* of their home country was highlighted with the radio programme, *The Adventures of the Jungle Doctor*. Dr Paul White was no fictional character. As a missionary doctor, this Australian had worked in the then Tanganyika with the Church Missionary Society. Paul White told his stories in regular Sunday morning instalments and many of these were published in books which Ian's parents obtained for him in later years. Other inspiration came from to visits of furloughing missionaries. For instance, Major and Mrs Ernest Schmidtke, for a time the officers at Ballarat West, had served for many years in China. The Divisional Youth Leader, Captain Gladys Calliss, left Australia for the Netherlands East Indies (Indonesia) during the years the Southwells were in Western Victoria. Stories recounted by missionaries returning to Australia on homeland furlough in the following years also inspired Ian. They told of their adventures for Christ in working to bring the Gospel to people in such diverse areas as India and Indonesia, Africa and China.

When his parents were appointed as divisional leaders for the Melbourne Metropolitan division in late 1950, the family came to live at 38 Normanby Avenue, Thornbury. Ian moved into grade two at Thornbury Primary School in Hutton Street. Whenever possible, he attended directory (catechism) classes on Sunday mornings before the holiness meeting and Sunday school on Sunday afternoons at The Salvation Army Thornbury Corps. In the former, the children learned the basic principles of the Christian faith and, in the latter, many of the main Bible stories. Often on Sunday mornings, however, Ian would accompany his parents as they conducted meetings in corps around the Melbourne area and he participated in the activities at those corps such as open-air meetings or children's programmes.

Having given his heart to Jesus in Ballarat, Ian indicated his desire to become a junior soldier and was enrolled on Mother's Day 1951 together with Valma Ray, another officers' child, who attended the corps. A few years earlier, his father managed to secure a brass cornet in the hope that Ian might be able to emulate his own proficiency as a brass instrumentalist. Unfortunately, the cornet mouthpiece did not suit the configurations of Ian's thicker lips. When a young people's band commenced at the Thornbury Corps in about 1953, Ian found that a tenor horn was a much easier instrument to play. His father borrowed a tenor horn from the Yarraville Corps, which no longer needed it. Because the instrument was on loan, David, as the divisional commander, ensured that the arrangement was processed officially with the serial number of the instrument correctly recorded by both the corps and divisional headquarters. Ian well remembers the accountant-like detail his father used on occasions such as this. David's experience in the finance departments of the Railways and The Salvation Army, coupled with his high level of integrity, were obviously important to his approach to business matters and life in general.

If Ian learnt about business integrity and preaching from his father, he also learnt much about pastoral care from his mother. From time to time, Ian accompanied Florrie on hospital visitation and imbibed something of the ways in which she worked. As he was already praying publicly in young people's and senior meetings, his mother sometimes asked him to offer prayer for the person who was unwell or to read the Scriptures. Ian also accompanied his parents on Christmas Days when they visited retired officers in Western Victoria and Melbourne Central divisions, bringing Christmas cheer and perhaps a carol or two. David always accompanied the singing with his concertina.

Ian enjoyed listening to music—especially brass music. As a result, his parents secured an old record player, powered by a spring-winder mechanism that could play 78 rpm records. One of Ian's favourites was the Regal Zonophone disk of the International Staff Band with the marches 'The Conqueror' on one side—with a great cornet solo; and on the other side 'The Maple Leaf'—incorporating a tune fitting the words, 'We're marching on, We're marching on, We're marching on together. God bless our Army round the world, And keep us true for ever.' His other favourite contained the songster piece sung by Harlesden Songsters (UK) and organ accompaniment, 'Shepherd, Hear My Prayer'. The disk had a spoken introduction before verses one and two on the first side; and more extended comment by the writer of the words, General Albert Orsborn, before verse three on the reverse of the disk. Still today Ian can recite most of Orsborn's words, with its finale: 'And then, like the coming of the morning star, we see the Saviour Shepherd looking for us. He is God in man, taking a shepherd's crook, going out into the rough in all weathers. "For Son of Man is come to seek and to save that which was lost" ' (Luke 19:10 *KJV*).

By now Ian's reading skills were developing and he was always grateful for Sunday school anniversary prizes in the form of books. His parents also bought the various volumes of the 'Biggles' books by W.E. Johns as they became available—Biggles being a fictional First and Second World War fighter pilot and another hero. The Biggles stories were also dramatised on commercial radio and Ian listened avidly. He was also impressed by the true story of Douglas Bader, who lost both his legs in a flying accident but courageously went back to fly with artificial legs. Bader eventually became a fighter pilot during the Second World War, but was shot down and became a prisoner of war. His determination to survive and fight for his country was exemplary for Ian. So was the story of Sir Galahad among King Arthur and the Knights of the Round Table—another radio dramatisation to which he listened regularly. The Salvation Army's *Victory* magazine once had a depiction of Sir Galahad on its front cover with the words: 'My strength is as the strength of ten because my heart is pure.' Ian kept that magazine and its message for many years.

Ian had some ability to recite poetry. At a divisional talent quest in 1954, he won first prize in the under-12 non-humorous section for reciting 'The Song of the Wind' by Will Lawson. The poem appeared in his sixth grade school reader. A relieving schoolteacher for his class had presented the poem in a most dramatic way and Ian managed to emulate that approach to win the prize. Always keen to learn, Ian carried a pocket English dictionary in his schoolbag or pocket to discover the meaning of new words.

His personal prayer times were becoming more meaningful as well. In addition to Scripture readings and prayers at meal times, his parents always prayed with him before he left for school in the morning and at night before going to bed. By now he was starting to pray by himself. He knew his father read through the Bible every 12 months using a scheme outlined by The Salvation Army. Because that would have been too burdensome for a young person to follow, his parents provided him with a little pamphlet called *The Sword and Shield* which listed a Bible reading for every day of the year. A new pamphlet was issued each year so that over the course of several years most of the Bible stories were covered. Following this outline enabled Ian to fulfil his junior soldier's pledge in which he promised to 'pray, to read my Bible and abstain from all intoxicating liquor'. Since about 1988, those equivalent promises read: 'I promise to pray, to read my Bible and, by his help, to lead a life that is clean in thought, word and deed. I will not use anything that can injure my body or my mind including harmful drugs, alcohol or tobacco.' *The Sword and Shield* was eventually replaced by a helpful daily devotional commentary called *The Soldier's Armoury* which proved even more informative and inspirational. The equivalent at the time of writing is *Words of Life* published by Hodder and Stoughton.

With his public speaking ability and obvious seriousness about spiritual things, a number of people suggested that Ian should become a Salvation Army officer. He was more inclined to think he could be a missionary doctor like Paul White or even a flying padre in the Northern Territory such as the then Captain Vic Pedersen. Like so many of Ian's heroes, flying and travelling were things to which he aspired.

From time to time, David, Florence and Ian would visit the Southwell family home in Campsie, New South Wales. These visits gave him the opportunity of meeting his elderly paternal grandmother, Mrs Field-Major Sarah Southwell, and some of his other aunts and uncles. While the family usually travelled by train from Melbourne to Sydney, changing trains in Albury, on one occasion they flew and Ian was thrilled to be invited into the cockpit of the Douglas DC4. He had already spent several days watching planes come and go from Essendon Airport. As the Essendon Football team were known as 'The Bombers' he wanted to barrack for them. The team had won a couple of premierships and at that time had a brilliant full forward named John Coleman. He was another hero—until Ian learned that this amateur footballer earned his living selling alcohol!

On his mother's side, Grandma Jennie Lonnie lived with Florence, David and Ian for 11 years until 1954 when she was promoted to Glory[17] from their home at the age of 84. The reality of the finiteness of life had come to Ian a year earlier when his 19-year-old cousin, Isabel Sharp, contracted polio in the days before the Salk vaccine. Isabel died in an iron lung within about two weeks at the then Fairfield Infectious Diseases Hospital.

That niggling call to be a Salvation Army officer persisted. Ian was given opportunities to supervise lower classes at school, and speak and participate publicly at Salvation Army meetings. He voluntarily gave his testimony in meetings and offered public prayer.

Having seen and heard his parents in action, he knew how to speak well. He was invited by Mr Matthew J. Corcoran, the headmaster of Thornbury Primary School, to conduct the Anzac Day service at the school in 1954. In cooperation with his Grade 6 teacher, Mr David Armstrong, the

[17] The Army's description of the death of Salvationists.

headmaster and his parents, Ian put together a programme that contained all the elements of a good Anzac commemoration service. Ian even asked his corps officer at Thornbury Corps, the then Senior-Captain John Macintyre, to provide the Last Post and the Reveille for the service. At the end of that year, together with a senior girl from the girls' grade six, Ian received a citizenship award given by the Northcote City Council. During 1954, Ian also played cricket and football for the school. He was the vice-captain of the cricket team, scoring the winning runs in a 22-run partnership to defeat Penders Grove School team. That win helped Thornbury Primary School to be the champions for the Northcote district. Sadly, they lost to a Preston school team in the next stage of the competition.

Academically, Ian was the dux of grade six in 1954 and accepted to be a student of Northcote High School the following year.

The Australian tennis team won the Davis Cup in January 1954 and Ian's interest in playing tennis was stimulated. He was given a tennis racquet as a birthday present in June that year. His father received a similar racquet on Father's Day in September. When the family took some holidays at the Salvation Army's Cranbrook Lodge in Healesville late in 1954, most of Ian's time was spent on the tennis court either practising serving on his own or enlisting playing partners such as Nancy King, Major Ray Beasy or Ian's father. Sonja van Kralingen's parents were also holidaying at the same venue. Being a little older than Ian and more interested in playing with girls such as Rhonda Berry, the manager's daughter, rather than boys, Ian and Sonja only occasionally saw each other. How little they both knew what the future might hold! God knew, however.

In January, Ian's parents received notification of a change of appointment. They would be the divisional leaders in Western Australia—an appointment Florrie's father and mother had held in the 1920s. This would mean a change of school for Ian just at the transition between primary and secondary schooling. He already had his uniform for Northcote High School. As his parents always talked of changes appointment as adventures, Ian was not unduly disturbed. Many of his primary school friends were scattering to other schools—most to the then Preston Technical School. Only about six were going on to Northcote High School. He knew he had been in Western Australia before—and his grandparents before that as well. Major and Mrs Spencer Clark were also transferring from Brunswick,

Victoria, to the Leederville Corps in Western Australia, and Ian had become a good friend of their son Bernard. So he would know someone his age in WA.

As his parent's appointment would not commence until 6 March, Ian attended the annual Aquatic Night for the Melbourne Metropolitan Division in February. His father had to make the presentations to the winning swimmers. While Ian had learnt to swim some months previously, he was certainly not fast enough to be able to compete. In fact, his mind was elsewhere. The Holy Spirit was still challenging him about the matter of officership. That night, after returning from the Melbourne Baths where the event was held, Ian could not sleep. He knew the reason. God wanted him to be a Salvation Army officer. Eventually, he knelt by his bed and committed his life to the Lord to serve him in that way. And peace descended. Ian climbed back into bed, curled up and went to sleep.

Chapter 3

Ian's move to Western Australia—and back, 1955–57

Securing any high school place in Australia in the 1950s was always challenging. Ian's parents were hoping that he would be able to move straight into a high school in Western Australia, having already enrolled at a high school in Victoria. So he spent February 1955 at Northcote High School. He even commenced some lessons in French.

In the event, the Southwells moved in early March to 71 Lincoln Street, Highgate, in Perth, just around the corner from 17 Smith Street where Ian had lived from 1942 to 1945. His parents sought enrolment for him at Perth Boys High School in James Street, Northbridge. He attended the enrolment interview in his Northcote High School uniform to make the point that he was already a high school student. Ian undertook the entrance examinations and was quite surprised when he was graded into streamed Form 1E, having been top student in his primary school in Victoria. At least his friend, Bernie Clark, was a fellow student in the same form. Only much later did Ian and his parents discover that Form One in Western Australia was equivalent to Form Two in Victoria! Western Australia offered seven years in primary school and five years in high school before university entry, whereas Victoria had six in each plus a preparation grade before grade one primary school. While he could have travelled to school by bus, most of the time he rode his bicycle once it was registered and received its official bicycle number plate.

Although Ian secured good marks in histories and English, he struggled in mathematics. Something of the sequence in mathematical learning had been broken and he lacked the background of much foundational work in arithmetic, algebra and geometry. Nevertheless, after one term he was regraded to Form 1B and by the end of the year he did well enough to be promoted to the top class at Form Two specialising in studying chemistry, physics (with an inspiring science teacher, Mr William Borman) and German as well as the usual subjects of English, history and mathematics. He found German easier than French—it seemed more logical and phonetic. As most of the cricket teams were filled, he found tennis was a good elective sport. The grass courts and stable weather in Perth provided helpful conditions under which to develop his skills in tennis all year round. In 1957, his concern about his lack of some foundational arithmetic knowledge led him to ask his mathematics teacher, Mr Bradshaw, to provide personal tuition for him between 8.15 am and 8.45 am on some mornings. This tuition helped build his confidence and by the end of that year he finished as equal second top student of the school at the Junior Certificate level in 1957. The personal interest of Mr Bradshaw also demonstrated how a good teacher should operate with a student who needed extra help. God was obviously preparing Ian for something!

Following his conviction that God wanted him to be a Salvation Army officer, Ian set about learning all that would be needed to become an officer. His parents encouraged him to become a corps cadet in July 1955 at age 13 at the Highgate Corps. This corps was within walking distance of the quarters he and his parents occupied. Corps cadets, in those days, were junior or senior soldiers of The Salvation Army aged between about 13 and 22 who worked through the Bible twice in six years. They were also introduced to other Salvation Army publications such as the *Handbook of Doctrine, The Salvation Army: Its Origins and Development* and some of the Challenge Series books containing biographies of significant Salvation Army personalities—often missionaries. The corps cadet system encouraged members to attend and participate regularly in Salvation Army meetings through prayer, testimony and as much service as possible. Scripture memorisation was also encouraged. Ian enjoyed the studies, participating in Army activities and writing monthly papers for submissions to divisional headquarters. As he did so, he achieved excellent marks and 'honours' course certificates.

Other books he studied included the *Orders and Regulations for Officers* and the *Orders and Regulations for Corps Officers*. In the former, Ian read how holiness was important for anyone who wanted to be involved in officership ministry. His parents also possessed books on the topic of holiness by Commissioner Samuel Logan Brengle. Ian started to read those books and was challenged by their contents. As he often travelled with his parents to their Sunday appointments, he heard both of them encourage the congregations to live holy lives. So the conviction grew within him that he needed the blessing of holiness if he was to be an effective Salvation Army officer. As a result, on the evening of 1 January 1956, before his evening prayer time, Ian asked his mother to guide him in seeking the 'clean heart experience' of which Brengle had written and of which she and Ian's father had testified. A great sense of peace flooded him, convincing him that God was indeed guiding and directing him in his spiritual pilgrimage. From that time forward he included the words of Psalm 51:10 in his daily prayers: 'Create in me a clean heart, O Lord, and renew a right spirit within me.'

This desire to equip himself for service also led to him to have some piano lessons. He realised that as an officer he might need to be able to provide his own accompaniment for singing. Florrie was quite an effective piano player both from music and by ear, and his father could improvise on the instrument as well as playing the concertina and brass instruments. A former Salvation Army officer, Mrs Marsden, was prepared to offer piano lessons. On Saturday mornings from late 1955 to 1957, Ian would cycle across to her house to have these. Although he enjoyed listening to brass band and orchestral music, he was not too interested in playing classical music or passing formal grade examinations. Ian's focus was on developing his skills in handling four-part harmony because that was the way most Salvation Army accompaniments for songs (hymns) were written back in the 1950s.

As mentioned previously, while a junior soldier at Thornbury Corps, Ian learnt to play a tenor horn and so he became a junior band member at Highgate Corps. As he approached his 14th birthday he asked what he needed to do to become a Salvation Army soldier (full member). His parents supplied him with the *Orders and Regulations for Soldiers of The Salvation Army* and a copy of *The Articles of War* (these days called *The Soldier's Covenant*). The latter contains the declaration of faith and the promises that soldiers make. The *Orders and Regulations for Soldiers* expounded on those promises. All these he read and understood. Although no formal classes for soldiership had been offered by the corps, in the month of his 14th birthday he signed the file copy of *The Articles of War* and took it to Captain Cecil Ewan, the corps officer at Highgate. Ian asked if the census board (the group of leaders in the corps who determined who could or could not be a soldier) would permit him to be accepted as a Salvation Army soldier. If so, could he be publicly sworn-in (enrolled) when Ian's parents conducted the Sunday morning meeting at Highgate Corps on 24 June 1956 just after his 14th birthday? Captain Ewan was surprised, but was willing to accept the initiative of this bold young man who was enthused about becoming a Salvation Army soldier. So Ian's father enrolled him as a soldier of The Salvation Army on that date. His first uniform, secured some months later, was a second-hand bandsman's uniform handed down from an officer's son who had outgrown it.

Because his parents were the divisional leaders in Western Australia, and he was deemed too young to be left at home alone, Ian travelled with them to many appointments on Sunday mornings and evenings around Perth and closer rural areas such as Northam, York, Bunbury and Busselton. His father would always drive home after the conclusion of the 7.30 pm Sunday meetings so Ian would not miss any schooling and he himself would be at the office by 9.00 am on Monday. Sometimes Ian would attend the Highgate Corps with his mother when his father travelled to the more outlying corps and could not return on the Sunday night. During May school holidays, he journeyed with them by car to Geraldton and Carnarvon in the north; during the September holidays to Katanning and Albany in the south; and in January to Kalgoorlie and Boulder in the east—a very hot time of the year to do so.

Often the family would sing Army songs and especially choruses in the car as they travelled—sometimes choosing them alphabetically. 'A never failing friend' might cover 'A'. Because no choruses commenced with 'Z', they often finished with '[Z]ing on in sunny days, [z]ing on in darkened ways; Sing, O sing …' The family even had a 'kneedrill' (prayer meeting) in the car as they travelled to country appointments on Sundays—they all sat rather than knelt. David, as the driver, prayed with his eyes open! Of course, Ian participated. These indeed were 'sunny days' and Ian thoroughly enjoyed them.

Ian learned much about the state and navigating the roads of Western Australia that would eventually stand him in good stead some 35 years later when he and Sonja became the divisional leaders. He also learnt about driving during daytime and night as he observed how carefully David did so.

While his father was away at a country visit in 1957, a private and confidential telegram arrived for him. David and Florence had already been asked about their availability for overseas service with the Army. Their only concern was Ian's schooling. Florence thought the telegram might notify such an international appointment. When she opened it she found that it contained notification of David's promotion to the rank of lieut-colonel. What a surprise he received when Florrie and Ian greeted him on his return with the words, 'Welcome home Lieut-Colonel Southwell!' Florrie quickly re-trimmed one of his uniforms so he could be properly attired for a forthcoming engagement.

But 'darkened ways were coming'. In September 1957, David fell ill. He had conducted meetings at Rivervale and North Fremantle on Sunday 8th and on Monday complained of very severe headaches. Florence, having been a nurse, called the local doctor. He diagnosed clinical influenza. Ian did not know what the doctor prescribed for his father, but it was pink in colour. In retrospect, and having talked to medical professionals, he thinks it may have been a morphine-based painkiller. If it was, that might also explain why early on Thursday morning David complained of more pains in his chest and left arm. He took another dose of the medicine. In these days, we would have rung 000 (the emergency telephone number in Australia) and called for an ambulance to take him to hospital with a suspected heart attack—but this did not happen. The medicine may have reduced the pain. While Ian and his mother ate breakfast about 8.00 am on Thursday, 12 September, David was promoted to Glory[18].

As the realisation of what had happened dawned on them—and the many implications—Ian recalls quoting the second verse of a song by Albert Orsborn the family had often sung during their Sunday morning prayer meetings:

[18] The Army's description of the death of Salvationists.

[Our] all is in the Master's hands
For him to bless and break;
Beyond the brook his winepress stands
And thence my way I take,
Resolved, the whole of love's demands
To give for his dear sake.[19]

Obviously, David's passing was a huge shock to Ian and his mother—and the rest of The Salvation Army in Australia. The Territorial Commander, Commissioner George Sandells and Mrs Commissioner Flora Sandells, and the Territorial Youth Secretary, Brigadier Frank Saunders, were on their way across to Perth to conduct youth councils that coming weekend. They heard about David's passing on news broadcasts on the Trans-Australian train en route to Perth. When they arrived, they gave what comfort they could to Florence and Ian. Then they prepared for a funeral service on the Saturday and a memorial service on the Sunday. The funeral services took place in Perth Fortress and Karrakatta Crematorium. Because the weekend was designated for youth councils with youth and their leaders attending from across the state, it was decided that the Sunday morning and afternoon sessions would go ahead as planned. The evening meeting would become a memorial service for 49-year-old Lieut-Colonel David John Southwell. Thirty-five seekers were recorded that night, just 35 years after David made his own commitment to Christ as a 14-year-old.

Commissioner Sandells was most helpful in ensuring that Ian's schooling would be uninterrupted. Ian was only two months away from sitting for his Form Three Junior School Certificate examination (the equivalent of the Form Four [Year 10] Intermediate Certificate in Victoria at that time). Florence and Ian were permitted to remain in Western Australia and in their current quarters until Ian had completed his last examination early in December. After that examination, they travelled back to Melbourne by train. Lieut-Colonel Leonard Stranks, who had served in China and had been a divisional commander since his return to Australia, was living in retirement in Western Australia. He was given interim command of the division during the intervening three months until the general change in January 1958.

19 Albert Orsborn, *SASB* (2015), Song 610.

In going through David's personal papers after his promotion to Glory, Florrie found one of a number of sets of objectives that David had drawn up for himself at various times. She showed the list to Ian. He was so inspired that he set about preparing similar lists for himself—a habit that has continued over the years. A recent set of these goals and objectives is contained in Appendix 1 on page 239 of this volume.

Ian and his mother arrived back in Melbourne and were allocated quarters at 102 Mansfield Street, Thornbury, within walking distance of Florrie's sister Ivy and her husband Lieut-Colonel Allen Sharp in West Preston. Having entered the Training College from Thornbury and being part of Thornbury Corps when David was divisional commander, Florrie thought it might be better to attend the Thornbury East Corps which was also within walking distance of their quarters. This small corps in Wilmoth Street was delighted to have an enthusiastic corps cadet and bandsman in Ian and an officer-soldier in Florrie, who were willingly involved in open-air ministry and active in corps meetings. As a result of seeing the style of writing Ian used for his corps cadet studies, the corps officer, Lieut. Len Gale, asked Ian to become the corps correspondent—writing reports for corps activities for Army publications. This proved to be a useful preparation for some of Ian's later appointments as an officer.

As mentioned, the Mansfield Street quarters were relatively close to Allen and Ivy Sharp. Ian and Florrie walked there most Friday evenings for some company, to watch their black and white television set, and for Allen to provide some male role modelling for Ian. Having lost their only daughter, Isabel, they were delighted to provide such support.

Chapter 4

Ian's studies and corps service, 1958–64

Returning to Melbourne produced fresh challenges for Ian's schooling. Having been enrolled in Form One (Year Seven) for one month at Northcote High School in 1955, the same headmaster, Mr Alex Sutherland, logically believed Ian should be in Form Four (Year 10) in 1958. Because Ian had studied neither French nor Latin in Western Australia, he was placed in the Form Four class specialising in the less academic subjects of art and woodwork. He very quickly found other subjects such as history, science and mathematics were repeating much of which he had studied before in Western Australia—and at a lower level. In frustration, he produced a piece of artwork symbolising the conflicts between the education systems in the different states of Australia.

This tension and dilemma went on for almost a month before Ian persuaded his mother to come to the school with the examination papers of the subjects he had written at the Junior School Certificate and place them before the headmaster and senior staff. Suddenly, the headmaster realised that Ian had gained a year on his peers during the three years on the other side of Australia. Mr Sutherland's next question was 'What subjects would you want to do at Form Five level?'—perhaps thinking that Ian would not have any idea, and might choose 'soft options' that could not be accommodated. The Lord had already gone ahead in preparing the way. During that first month back at Northcote High School, Ian had volunteered to help the Form Five coordinator confirm the allocation of subjects that students would be studying. As a result, he had already considered possible subject combinations he could take at that level. He had previously studied physics and chemistry as specialist subjects, and also took two mathematics subjects, English and economics, giving him the groups he needed in those days for the Leaving Certificate. God was leading him safely.

The promotion to Form Five was more socially than academically challenging. He was not easily accepted by the Form Five students one month after term had begun. Some of his peers in Form Four who had studied with him at Thornbury Primary School, or were his opponents in cricket and football from other schools, wondered why he was able to make that change. By gaining top marks in chemistry and strong marks in physics in the first term examinations, he convinced most that he was at the right level. In retrospect, it may have been easier if he had transferred to University High School where he could have continued his German studies and been away from his former classmates. However, cycling from his home in Thornbury in 1958 (and from Dennis near Fairfield in 1959) was faster and less expensive than taking trains, buses and trams. At that stage he actually planned to leave school at the end of Form Five and work in a bank or some other form of accountancy before entering The Salvation Army Training College, much as his father did before he became an officer. His Uncle Allen Sharp and Colonel Colin Begley, a former missionary in India and China, encouraged Ian to study as much as possible before becoming a cadet.

Ian's strong Christian and Salvation Army convictions soon became well known in his Form Five class. During the weekly form assembly, Mr Dean, the English teacher, encouraged students to present a brief talk. One of Ian's classmates, John Gowans, suggested that the 'newcomer' to 5A bring his talk immediately. At that time, the Australia Southern Territory Youth Department had produced a special youth charter. This charter encouraged high moral and social values amongst adolescents and young adults and was being carried around southern Australia much like an Olympic torch. Ian spoke about the charter and its contents, providing small copies of the document for his classmates. He thinks that John, who suggested he speak, may have felt a little shocked by the ease with which he presented his talk. However, the whole class came to appreciate what he had said when, on 13 May, Senior-Major Ron Smith, the new Territorial Youth Secretary, brought the charter to Northcote High School and spoke about it to all the boys at the main school assembly.

Ian particularly enjoyed his economics studies, doing some extra research during the May school holidays at the office of the Bureau of Statistics in Melbourne. Mr Slater, his economics teacher, suggested that his top student might want to go on to Form Six Matriculation with economics as a subject, study commerce at university through a scholarship with the Victorian Education Department, and take up economics teaching at least for three years. This certainly stimulated some ideas in Ian's mind—if he had been convinced that economics was the field for him. His chemistry teacher, Mr Alan Smith, also saw potential in Ian and gave him an opportunity to demonstrate how nylon is produced at an Education Week display. Ian was in his element. He thoroughly enjoyed the opportunity of explaining the chemistry to parents and friends who came to see the work of Northcote High School. Mr Smith also arranged for him to attend a special evening at the Chemistry Department of the University of Melbourne to sharpen his appetite for science. Although remaining convinced that he should become a Salvation Army officer, Ian had not envisaged entry to the officer training college at the minimum age of 18. In order to raise sufficient money for books, uniforms and fees plus gaining some work experience, he would need to find employment. Would secondary teaching provide such an opportunity? Could this be a skill that he might be able to use as an officer—perhaps even as a missionary? The Lord was prompting him through so many avenues at that time.

At the end of 1958, Ian and his mother needed a change of accommodation. The 102 Mansfield Street house was going to be demolished and two maisonette apartments built in its place. After some discussion with the Army's Property Department, including a suggestion that they might move on the top floor of the Training College building then situated at 68 Victoria Parade, East Melbourne, they were eventually transferred to a single-fronted house at 6 William Street, Dennis. Ian could continue to cycle to Northcote High School and they would be able to attend the Fairfield Corps which was within easy walking distance.

At Fairfield, Ian became thoroughly involved with the corps cadets, brass band and, most particularly, as junior soldiers sergeant at the suggestion of the corps officer, Major Arthur Watson. Clarence (Clarrie) Percy was both the corps sergeant-major (the chief local officer of the corps) and acting corps cadet guardian. Mr Percy strongly encouraged the study of the Bible and Ian continually enjoyed writing extensive answers to the questions posed by the programme each month. Tools such as commentaries and a concordance proved useful. He kept on gaining honours certificates as he had in Western Australia and at Thornbury East.

Envoy[20] Vic Barker was another fine role model at the Fairfield Corps. He managed the public address systems for the evangelical open-air meetings held each Sunday morning at 10.00 am and evening at 6.00 pm from the trailer he could attach to his car. Having recorded the Army's 15-minute 'Kneedrill of the Air' produced by Envoy Claude Bloxham each week for a number of years for broadcast on a commercial radio station at 8.00 am on Sundays, Vic knew how to encourage efficiency in presentation. 'No dead air' was his catchcry. Everyone participating had to be ready to move quickly to the microphone when it was their turn. The open-air meeting programme should run as smoothly as a good radio broadcast.

Bandmaster Ed Cooper was in charge of the band. He was very patient—especially when Ian could not attend band practices because of his studies. Having been an officer and a Salvation Army welfare representative during the Second World War, Bandmaster Cooper understood Ian needed to concentrate on passing his matriculation examinations and whatever other studies he needed to undertake. During school holidays, Ian always attended band practice and, during term-time, practised at home to ensure he embarrassed neither the band nor himself when playing tenor horn. He always attended the full Sunday programme: kneedrill (prayer meeting), the morning open-air meeting, the holiness meeting, corps cadets in the afternoon, the evening open-air—except when he was leading the junior soldiers meeting—and the salvation meeting at night. Vic Barker's son, Graham, was the young people's sergeant-major. He also had very high standards for Sunday school work, encouraging dynamic presentations of Bible stories to the boys and girls who attended.

From teaching in Sunday school, with the junior soldiers and from his own Bible studies, Ian gained inspiration from the stories of Daniel standing alone for God and St Paul risking all on his missionary journeys.

---

[20] Envoy is a rank given to a Salvationist whose duty is to visit corps and similar centres to conduct meetings. An envoy may also be appointed in charge of such a centre.

They served as some of Ian's biblical heroes. Visiting missionaries came to the Fairfield Corps in those days, such as Lieut-Colonel Gladys Calliss, Majors Milford and Olive McPherson, Captains Walter and Jean Smart, Brigadier Cath Stevens, Captain Gwenda Watkinson, Captain Dorothy Baird, Captains Margaret and Keith Earl, and Brigadier Ruth Wilkins. They all encouraged Ian and the other young people in the corps to be thoroughly committed to God and The Salvation Army. All of them emphasised that missionaries needed some special skills aside from being good and godly Salvation Army officers. Medical doctors were needed overseas. Ian's matriculation year studies, especially in chemistry, could open the door to gaining entry to medicine. His cousin, Bram Southwell, had recently graduated as a doctor. Ian was hesitant, however. What if he made a mistake in surgery and somebody died…? What roles could he fulfil as an officer-doctor back in Australia if he and other missionaries were forced out of a post-colonial country in Africa or South Asia in which some of these missionaries were working? On the other hand, the excitement of teaching and communicating to others seem to be a special gifting from God that Ian could not ignore. And if he made a mistake in the facts he was teaching, he could always re-teach the material correctly the next day.

These same missionaries indicated that it would be best for male missionaries to be married before moving to the mission field. During the years at Fairfield and contacts with other youth during the East Melbourne Division youth councils, Ian had opportunities of meeting a wide range of Salvationists. The attraction of the opposite sex was increasing—as it does for any teenager. Sadly, although there were some very lovely and talented women he met who were also looking for marriage partners, few indicated any calling to officership—and certainly not to missionary service. God must have somebody else in mind—but sometimes Ian found the waiting frustrating.

As his matriculation year progressed, Ian eventually applied for a studentship with the Education Department. Such a studentship would allow him to study at university for four years to obtain a bachelor degree in science and a postgraduate diploma in education as a teaching qualification. He would then be required to spend three years in teaching in government schools to repay the fees that the Department had covered for him. That would obviously make his age of entry to Training College 24 rather than 21 which he had in mind. After much prayer and consideration, Ian believed this was the way he should go. When they learned what he was planning, some well-meaning people suggested that he could break his studentship to go to the Training College earlier. However, Ian believed that if he made a contract he should fulfil it to the letter. So he made application fully understanding the implications.

When he came to write his matriculation examination at the end 1959, he passed well with first class honours in chemistry and passes in his other four subjects. His overall results were so good that he won both a Commonwealth Scholarship for university study and also the Education Department studentship. As he could not hold both, and he wanted to teach at secondary school level, he took up the studentship. So in March 1960 he entered the University of Melbourne to study science. About the same time he signed an agreement with the Education Department, candidates' papers for officership also arrived. Obviously, the divisional candidates' secretary did not want to lose track of someone who had already indicated that he felt called to be a Salvation Army officer.

Having now indicated 1967 as a possible year of entry to the Training College, he was encouraged to learn more of what it meant to be a Salvation Army officer. In 1961, Ian gained his Corps Cadet Badge of Merit, having secured 12 honours-level certificates over the preceding six years. CSM Clarrie Percy was happy for Ian to become the assistant corps cadet guardian, especially to help some of the younger members with their studies. Ian appreciated this opportunity more than teaching Sunday school with younger, primary school-aged children. High school students would be those he would eventually teach in schools so it was a good preparation. He also enjoyed playing cricket with The Salvation Army Northcote team in the Northcote Preston Churches Association on Saturday afternoons during summer from 1960 till 1966.

During those years, his mother was appointed in charge of the Advanced Training Department within the Field Department at THQ with responsibility for officers' post-commissioning studies. Ian undertook some work experience in her office during 1958-59 and was impressed with the distance education programme to up-skill officers after what was then an intense 10-month residential officer training programme. In 1960 Florrie became the Territorial Home League Secretary[21], being promoted to the rank of Lieut-Colonel in

[21] A Salvation Army leader responsible for resourcing women's ministries in the territory.

her own right soon afterward. She was an excellent role model, supporting the Fairfield Corps in their full range of meetings and also as pianist for the junior soldiers meetings that Ian led every second Sunday night from 6.00 pm. With some help from his Uncle Allen (before more formal driving lessons) and some finance from his mother to supplement what he was now earning on his studentship, Ian gained his driver's licence and bought his first car in 1960—a second-hand 1956 Morris Minor. The car gave him and his mother more mobility than at any time since David's passing. Florence gained her own licence the following year. Ian generally enjoyed his chemistry, physics, biology, and mathematics studies at university—and also successfully completed a translation course in science German.

While attending high school, Ian had worked through the matter of the relationship of science to Christian faith. He was most impressed by the then Mrs Commissioner Bessie Coutts, also a science graduate, who made the point at a Congress meeting that, 'There is no contradiction between true science and true religion.' Ian was convinced that, whereas science explains the 'how'—the method of creation—the Bible explains the 'why'—the purpose. He could understand how the two approaches are like the opposite sides of the same coin—apparently contradictory but really complementary to each other. God was in control of the universe no matter what methods he used to fulfil his purposes.

Although usually well prepared for examinations, Ian experienced a panic attack during his final organic chemistry examination in 1962. Or was it a Holy Spirit blockage? As result, he was called in for supplementary oral examination which he passed. While he secured the Bachelor of Science degree, the borderline score in this major subject meant that the doors closed on him taking the honours year he had contemplated—even if it had meant further delaying entry to officer training. So in 1963 he commenced the first year of the postgraduate Bachelor of Education course for which he would eventually earn a Diploma in Education and his high school teaching qualifications. He thoroughly enjoyed the year as he learnt about the history and principles of education, educational psychology, comparative education, and educational methods, as well as undertaking practical teaching in schools. The schools at which he taught seemed to be impressed with him and head teachers of at least two of them said he would be most welcome to apply to come to teach at their school the following year.

During 1963 something else significant happened which Ian has already recorded in the preface of his book *Holiness: A Radiant Relationship*. Graham Barker organised a special weekend at the Army's Cranbrook Lodge holiday house in Healesville with Bruce Dench as the leader. Bruce had recently come into a very significant experience of the Holy Spirit in his life. Most of the young men and women from the Fairfield Corps gathered from Friday night till Sunday. Various bush hikes and Bible studies took place. On the Saturday evening, Ian and his friends watched a black and white movie film entitled *The Power of the Resurrection*, emphasising the working of the Holy Spirit in the lives of the early believers. As those present discussed what they had seen, they commenced to pray together. The Holy Spirit broke through to the group in a way almost as dramatic as the day of Pentecost although without the obvious 'tongues of flame' and the sound of a violent wind. The Holy Spirit's presence was very real. For Ian, it was reconfirmation of what happened on 1 January 1956. Some of his friends who had questioned what Ian had said about his experience of the Holy Spirit realised the Spirit did indeed exist and wanted to reside within them, too. The time of prayer continued until at least 2 am on Sunday morning and many testified to a radical change within them.

The group followed through with its plan to go to the 11 am Sunday morning meeting at the local Healesville Corps. During the meeting, group members testified about what happened the night before. As they did so, the Holy Spirit broke through to the congregation. No sermon was needed during that meeting. Numerous people lined the mercy seat seeking God's power. The group members were elated. Their original plan was to stay at Cranbrook Lodge and have further fellowship in the afternoon and evening, but a consensus following the Healesville meeting was that they should return to Melbourne in time for the 7 pm meeting at Fairfield and testify to that congregation about what had happened. They were permitted to do so—even though it was the final meeting of a weekend visit by the Morwell Corps Band. Again the Holy Spirit broke through and a number of very significant commitments being made in that night.

As happens after periods of such high emotion and spiritual ecstasy, the feelings of the weekend faded. People had to be busy about their work, studies and family matters. Naturally, the question arose as to whether the experience was real. Had they missed out on something? Should they have been speaking in tongues, for instance? Fortunately the corps officers, Major and Mrs Harry Chapman, and Ian's mother were of great help in assisting all concerned understand that a *relationship* with the Lord was more than a matter of *feelings*. Relationships need time and effort to grow. Ongoing prayer and Bible study coupled with God's grace were essential.

Relationships also grow through times of challenge. Ian also discovered this during 1963. With all his studies in philosophy and psychology undertaken during the Diploma in Education studies, he had to face the question: 'Is my Christian experience real or have I been brainwashed into this because my parents were committed Christians?' This was a serious period of doubt for him. In retrospect, he was grateful to God for it. The doubts forced him to go back and analyse the intellectual basis of the Christian faith. Were the Gospels reasonable historical records of the life of Christ? What about the claims Jesus made about himself as recorded in the Gospels—especially those recounted in John's Gospel? How did all this align with the experience of the early Christians together with his own experience—including the spiritual breakthrough for his friends earlier that year? His careful supplementary studies that year provided the assurance that the Christian faith had a sound intellectual basis. Books such as Frank Morrison's, *Who Moved the Stone*? and John W. Stott's *Basic Christianity* were helpful to him in thinking through these matters. As a result, he came out of the period of doubt and challenge with a stronger, more settled faith.

He successfully completed that year, gaining the Diploma in Education with some very good results and was appointed to the Watsonia High School in the north-eastern part of Melbourne near Greensborough—an easy drive from Fairfield.

Chapter 5

Guided together—engagement and marriage, 1964–67

Watsonia High School was situated in a new housing area on the southern edge of Greensborough and had only been in operation for three years when Ian became a staff member. That year, 1964, saw the commencement of the fourth year of teaching at the school with students in Form Four (Year 10) preparing for the Intermediate Certificate examination in November. Ian had hoped to be teaching Form Five chemistry but, in the event, he became the senior science teacher for the first four years of general science and also taught some mathematics. The assignments provided good experience as only one other partly qualified teacher for science was on staff at that stage. Between them, they had to cover all the general science studies. Teaching general science certainly meant learning much more about geology and astronomy than he knew at the end of his degree in order to help students with those aspects of the course. In company with the geography teacher, Mrs Judith Weston, a daughter of CSM Clarrie Percy, Ian took the senior students to the Yarra Bend National Park to view some of its significant geological formations.

Having experienced some good science teaching as a student himself from Mr William Borman in Perth Boys High School and Mr Alan Smith at Northcote High School, Ian believed that science teaching should be exciting and interesting. He was a great believer in using experimentation, working models, 16 mm movie films, and plenty of diagrams to help his students understand what he was teaching. This applied at school and also for the junior soldiers and corps cadets he taught at the corps. He was convinced that there were some unifying concepts in science that could help students better grasp the integration of science. One of these was the concept of energy. So he commenced his first science class by setting up a tin can of freshly generated hydrogen gas in such a way that it would burn gently until the mixture of air and hydrogen in the can reached a certain point at which the lid would blow off. He insisted that his students watch and listen carefully—at a safe distance. They probably never forgot what happened that morning as the explosion echoed around the room and the lid hit the roof. He encouraged them to come forward quickly to feel the warmth around the tin and come to understand how chemical energy could be transformed into heat, light, sound and movement. As Ian had not pre-warned the school administration of his plans, the headmaster rushed to the science room in case there had been an accident. Ian certainly started his official teaching career with a 'bang'!

Meanwhile, Bandmaster Cooper had tried Ian on first tenor horn, solo horn and then flugel horn. Ian struggled with the higher registers on each of these instruments. Eventually, he was moved to playing trombone—an instrument which suited his lips and which he thoroughly enjoyed playing. He felt he could more easily adjust the pitch of notes, rather having a fixed length of tubing to vibrate. Ian used the instrument to demonstrate to his science classes how sound varied with the lengths of a vibrating column of air.

Students in the school were divided into a number of groups called 'houses'. The term 'houses' came from its use in boarding schools where those who resided in different accommodation houses competed against each other in all manner of academic or sporting areas. At Perth Boys High School, the equivalent groups were called 'factions'. Ian also served as a house master and, as such, encouraged his house to prepare a drama item for the inter-house drama competition. The house members decided to perform the play, 'The Man in the Bowler Hat'. Sadly, they had very little opportunity to memorise their lines and the actors were feeling despondent. So Ian struck on the idea of turning it into a play-reading so that the actors could actually refer to their notes as though it was a first rehearsal. He adapted the script to that end. His house won! Some other house leaders were upset about the approach, but he had some excellent actors and actresses in the group and they performed well.

Also during 1964, Ian had the opportunity of attending in-service training around the Physical Sciences Study Committee (PSSC) version of the new physics curriculum for Years 11 and 12 that would commence in Victoria in 1965. This approach to physics teaching grew out of concern in the United States of America that their physics curriculum was not up to standard—especially when the Russians were able to launch the Sputnik satellite in 1957, well before the USA. Ian thought it would be wonderful to teach physics at this level with the new approach. However, late in 1964, the Education Department promotions for the following year were announced. As a result, a new deputy principal would be coming to the school. He was a specialist physics teacher and would teach that subject. Ian would have to be content with teaching chemistry at Year 11.

Ian had commenced attending some of the Saturday night rallies of Youth for Christ in the Melbourne Town Hall during the latter half of 1964. Some of his fellow young adults from Fairfield Corps were planning to attend the Youth for Christ Gold Coast Crusade in Queensland at the end of the year and so Ian applied to go as well. He enjoyed the adventure of travelling by train from Melbourne to Brisbane commencing on Boxing Day 1964. At Burleigh Heads, where the group was camped, a number of visiting preachers gave relevant and challenging Bible messages. Ian had been frustrated at the Youth for Christ rallies in Melbourne because he was not considered a 'qualified' counsellor to help seekers, despite his experience in The Salvation Army. At the camp, an elective was provided on this topic and Ian attended. The skills he learnt to use allowed him to counsel three or four people to come to faith in Christ during the course of the Crusade. The fact that he was a qualified science teacher and worked through some of the challenges of the relationship of science to Christianity was helpful in dealing with individual problems as well. He also gathered some ideas and skills he could use and develop to teach others to counsel seekers effectively over the next 45 years or so.

The 1965 school year commenced well with Ian teaching Form Five chemistry as well as general science and being involved in encouraging the school cricket team. Whilst he was umpiring an inter-house cricket match being played on the Greensborough Oval, a scrub fire started to threaten the ground and the match was abandoned. Ian returned to the school to discover a phone call had come from the Education Department. Because teachers in the first two years were seen as 'temporary', they could be moved to wherever the Department most needed them. The Department wanted to transfer him to Greythorn High School in North Balwyn. The matriculation level chemistry teacher at the school was not well qualified and the parents were afraid that their adolescent young people would suffer as a result. Ian was in the position that he could be moved because other teachers were now on staff that could cover his subjects at Watsonia. He had expressed a desire to be able to teach at that level and was willing to be moved. After saying goodbye to students at Watsonia, he transferred to Greythorn High School within a matter of days.

Before commencing this new and significant teaching assignment, he arranged a visit to his former chemistry teacher from Northcote High School, Mr Alan Smith. Alan was now in charge of the chemistry department at Carey Baptist Grammar School and was one of the examiners for chemistry at years 11 and 12. Ian obtained from Mr Smith as much information as he could about teaching at Year 12 level, together with some of the exercises and other additional materials that Alan Smith used to ensure that his students always achieved well in that subject.

A full year of intense teaching followed with Ian giving extra tutorial support to students after school hours as Mr Bradshaw had given him at Perth Boys High School. He was delighted with the good results his students achieved. His contributions to the school extended beyond teaching, however. When it came to a staff and student school concert, he presented the Brindley Boon trombone solo 'Count Your Blessings'. One of the music staff provided the piano accompaniment. His rendition was certainly not perfect, but was probably some of the best playing he had undertaken as a bandsman. The trombone really suited him.

About the same time, the Fairfield Corps Band from Victoria visited the Fairfield Corps in New South Wales. Ian enjoyed the opportunity of being involved with the pieces the band presented, including a trombone ensemble item. In 1965 Ian also accepted the full role of corps cadet guardian. Having this local officer position meant he gained firsthand experience of being a member of both the senior and young people's census boards in the corps and its administration.

School inspectors came to Greythorn High School in 1965. The one who inspected Ian's work was obviously impressed by what he saw and confirmed the promotable 'Very Good' rating Ian had received the year before at Watsonia. This made him eligible for promotion from Level IV to Level III in the current Education Department promotion system—in which Special and Level I were the highest—and permanency as a teacher. Ian hoped to be promoted at Greythorn High School, but indicated a willingness to serve at other schools where a Level III teacher might be needed. In the event he received promotion, but it meant moving to Northcote High School where he had previously been a student. He hoped to be able to teach Year 12 chemistry again, but another well-established teacher was in charge of chemistry and so Ian was allocated to teach Year 11 chemistry, some general science and one subject of Year 11 mathematics. Again, God's hand was in this. Not having the heaviest academic side to cover, Ian was able to be involved as a staff representative to the Inter-School Christian Fellowship (ISCF) at the school, coaching cricket, umpiring Australian Rules football and occasionally conducting the school's brass band during assemblies. While the school had a visiting brass band teacher who regularly came to the school, Ian was permitted to take the band to the Interschool Bands Competition for 1966. A number of the players were younger members of various Salvation Army bands in the district.

This final year of his bonded teaching also meant that he needed to complete his final application papers for acceptance to the Officer Training College. Acceptance came readily. The Salvation Army had been waiting many years for this. His photograph was published in *The War Cry* and some of his teaching colleagues saw it. So they knew that he had plans other than school teaching in 1967.

General-elect Frederick Coutts and his wife, Bessie, had passed through Melbourne from Sydney en route to London some years before in 1963. He knew of Ian's background because his aunt, Brigadier Elsie Southwell, had been his private secretary when he was Territorial Commander of Eastern Australia Territory. In fact, the then Commissioner Coutts broke the news to Elsie of Ian's father's promotion to Glory in 1957. Coutts told Ian that his son, Captain John Coutts, who was the principal of the Army's Akai Secondary School in Nigeria, would be glad to have another science teacher there. Brigadier Levinia Benson, a New Zealand officer serving in Rhodesia (now Zimbabwe), wrote encouraging him to consider service in Africa: 'Science teachers are more precious than gold.' Brigadier Cath Stephens, a nursing friend of Ian's mother, who had served at Chikankata Hospital in Northern Rhodesia (now Zambia) described the work of the secondary school there, as well as the hospital. In 1966 Colonel Edward John, then Territorial Commander of Nigeria, visited Australia on homeland furlough and told Ian of the needs in Africa for science teachers. He also suggested that Ian use any delay in getting to Africa to study the anthropology and sociology of the African people. (Of course, studying anthropology and sociology is good advice in preparing to move to any area not one's own.) All this helped reinforce for Ian the prompting of the Spirit that missionary teaching was in God's plan for him—most likely in Africa. The need for officer-teachers in India and the Far East did not seem as great at that time.

One of Ian's objectives during those three years from 1964–67 was to find a suitable wife to share the missionary officer work with him. As mentioned in the previous chapter, furloughing or returned missionaries who visited Fairfield, or spoke personally to him, continued to reinforce the benefits of going on missionary service married. The frustration experienced earlier continued to point that he had almost reconciled to the fact that he would have to enter Training College single—and then be delayed from missionary service. Yet visitors to the Inter-School Christian Fellowship at Northcote High School and Army leaders continually reiterated the importance of trusting God's timing. In preparing to teach his corps cadet class in March 1966, Ian came across these words that he included in the 'Answers to Prayer' section of his prayer list: 'God, who chooses his man [or woman], also chooses his hour. Never too soon, he is never too late.' In addition, Brigadier Iris Walters, then the Assistant Territorial Women's Social Services Secretary, gave a Bible address Ian heard on one occasion that year entitled 'God's clocks keep good time'. Could he trust that this would be the case?

Ian's interest in music was developing and he tried to compose a short tune for the competition held in conjunction with the 1966 Musicians' Councils to be held in August or September. The words had been penned by the then Brigadiers Arthur and Merle Linnett.

Vast are the treasures of his boundless grace,
Mirrored completely in our Master's face;
Rich the resources by which I may live,
Blessings unnumbered he loveth to give.

In the event, Ian was awarded equal third in the competition for his tune. The piano theory and practical lessons had not been wasted.

Sonja van Kralingen had commenced attending the Fairfield Corps some months before. As mentioned in Chapter 1, her sister, Joan Stolk with her husband George, who had been attending the corps for some time, suggested that Sonja come and perhaps get to know the band's second trombone player. Sonja also attended the musicians' councils at which Ian was recognised, and seemed most appreciative of his success.

Ian certainly had become aware of Sonja and commenced to pay attention to this attractive, blue-eyed blonde. He discovered that she was a daughter of Dutch missionaries, Brigadier Ryer and Mrs Brigadier Johanna van Kralingen. He learned that Sonja had been born in Indonesia. She was a medical nursing sister with certificates in general, midwifery and infant welfare nursing. Sonja had recently completed a postgraduate course specialising in eye, ear, nose, and throat (EENT) medical and post-surgical care. On completion of this qualification she remained in the Eye and Ear Hospital and worked in the eye theatre. She had already served in the Northern Territory as a nurse. As a child she had been interned as a prisoner of war with her parents. Sadly, however, like so many of the fine and talented young women that Ian had considered as possible marriage partners, she was not a candidate to become a Salvation Army officer. Sonja certainly had a heart for cross-cultural ministry as demonstrated by her willingness to work in the Northern Territory for a year—but apparently not for officership.

How little Ian knew! Sonja was battling God's calling to officership that went back many years to her time in Indonesia, as outlined earlier. Part of the reason she had gone to the Northern Territory was to try to avoid the officership calling by serving as a nurse! The reason she recently studied EENT surgery was to be equipped to serve in Third World situations.

Some more of that story outlined in Chapter 1 became clear to him as they went for a drive around the Dandenong Ranges on Saturday

15 October 1966 for the purpose of getting to know each other. Sonja, however, was not yet ready to become an officer. Obviously this became a matter of intense prayer for them both. They prayed together at the end of every 'date' which occurred frequently in the days following. On Sunday afternoon 23 October, Ian received a phone call from Sonja to say that she had said 'yes' to God's call to officership during the morning meeting at Box Hill Corps. Her corps officer, Mrs Major Gwen Collins, had immediately given her a preliminary application form for training as an officer. Ian drove to the Eye and Ear Hospital where Sonja was going back on duty and asked her to marry him. She said 'yes' to another 'calling' and we had our first kiss before further prayer together. We agreed to be unofficially engaged with official engagement confirmed once she was officially accepted as a candidate.

According to Salvation Army rules within the Territory at that time—when the minimum age for College entry was 18—couples had to be married for at least six months before entering training together as cadets. Furthermore, couples engaged before or during session had to wait one year after commissioning before marrying. However, Sonja had just turned 27 and Ian was in his 25th year. We both had professional qualifications that the Army could use. Another obvious complication in our case was that Ian was an accepted candidate for the next session and Sonja was not yet—although she quickly submitted her full set of application forms. Ian had already resigned his position at Northcote High School in preparation for entering the Training College in March 1967. He also believed that God had called him to serve as a missionary teacher in Africa as soon as possible. Then we discovered that Ian's friend, Accepted Candidate Ian Smith B.Com., a 26-year-old banker from Malvern Corps, and Accepted Candidate Nancy John, a trained medical laboratory technician also 26, and daughter of missionaries Colonel Edward and Mrs Colonel Joyce John, had been given permission to marry in January 1967 and enter College in March. So exceptions could be made. However, the Candidates Secretary and Training Principal, Brigadier Howard Orsborn, stated quite categorically that no rooms would be available the following March for married couples without children in the Training College then housed at 68 Victoria Parade, East Melbourne.

At the prompting of Major Milford McPherson, a former missionary in India and the current Education Officer at the Training College who visited Fairfield, we wrote a joint letter to the Territorial Commander, Commissioner Hubert Scotney, outlining the situation. We asked for some special consideration so our entry to the Training College was not delayed for a year. Sonja delivered the letter personally to the commissioner's secretary. Having received the letter, he instructed Brigadier Orsborn to contact us and let us know that as soon as possible he would look into the matter. Commissioner Scotney knew us both and had seen us in action separately earlier: Sonja at a Salvation Army Student Fellowship weekend; and Ian at a conference about the future of the Army in Australia. The commissioner's message indicated he had a high regard for us both. We believe he instructed Brigadier Orsborn to 'knock out another wall if needed' between two single rooms to create one suitable for a couple.

Meanwhile Cadets Peter and Sandra Callander, who were almost completing their first year of training in the 'Witnesses to the Faith' session, told their leaders they were expecting a baby. As a result, they would need to move to the accommodation for married cadet-couples with children in nearby Nicholson Street. Their present room on the main college building would be available—without needing to knock out a wall between two single rooms. God's clocks were certainly keeping good time!

Because Sonja had completed the full six years of the Corps Cadet programme with good results, and achieved the Corps Cadet Badge of Merit, she was granted exemption from the usual candidates' lessons. Sonja was accepted by the Candidates' Board on 15 December with permission to marry in February and enter College in March. Ian learned about the news while participating in an end of year staff versus student cricket match at Northcote High School. As soon as we had this confirmation, we announced our engagement and made plans firm for the wedding. Our rapid courtship had transitioned into a rapid engagement. We married in high collar style, navy blue Salvation Army uniform, on the very hot Saturday, 4 February 1967. Ian's uncle, Lieut-Colonel Allen Sharp, conducted our wedding at Box Hill Corps, then situated in Station Street, Box Hill. Sonja's fellow songsters, Roslyn Sheppard and Jenny Wright, were her bridesmaids. Colin Keast and David Percy, fellow trombonists in Fairfield Corps Band, were Ian's best man and groomsman. Sonja's niece,

Ingrid, was flower girl. At the wedding breakfast Sonja's father and Ian's mother both rejoiced at the ways in which the Lord had led their families, and we did also. Ian's Uncle Allen, who chaired the reception, aptly quoted from Psalm 37:25, 'I was young and now I am old, yet I have never seen the righteous forsaken or their children begging bread.' God is so good to his faithful people.

After a wonderful honeymoon at Lakes Entrance in eastern Victoria, we returned to temporary accommodation at Sonja's sister and brother-in-law's house in West Heidelberg. The house was being put on the market, but the 'granny flat' attached to it was just sufficient to tide us over until we entered the Training College on 7 March as members of the 'Messengers of the Faith' session. God's timing was immaculate.

Even before we entered the Training College we always had prayer together after each 'date' while courting and before we slept at night after we married. We also ensured that we read from the Bible and prayed at the conclusion of every meal—practices modelled by our parents that we have continued ever since.

God had led us safely individually in the past. Now he was leading us safely—together.

Chapter 6

Officer training and first appointments, 1967–70

Entry to the Training College in March 1967 was almost a relief after the hectic five months before. We had one room which was both our bedroom and study. Although not large, it was double the size of the rooms occupied by the unmarried cadets. At least it was a base for our life together. We shared bathrooms and toilets with four other married couples on the same floor.

Rooms for married cadets without children were on the upper of two floors in the middle of the rectangular building with two internal quadrangles. The quadrangle on the east near the Eastern Hill Fire Station was reserved for men, and the western quadrangle was for women. Sonja had to go to the women's side for work duties, recreation and similar activities. Ian was with the men. The sexes were very much segregated in those days. The college's dining room and common room were in the section of the building between the two quadrangles—almost directly beneath our bedroom. They served as areas of common ground in which we shared meals together with our fellow 'Messengers of the Faith' and those from the concurrent session 'The Witnesses to the Faith' when they returned from five months of 'out-training' in May. Many lasting friendships were made with members of both sessions. Communal living was certainly an experience! We were blessed to have Brigadier Howard

Orsborn and his wife Olive as our training leaders during our first year—although, sadly, Olive was promoted to Glory due to cancer, toward the end of 1967.

Brigadier Orsborn was a thoroughly international Salvationist, the son of General Albert Orsborn (Rtd) who had only recently been promoted to Glory. Brigadier Orsborn was an excellent Bible teacher in his own right. Some of his lectures were based around the 'Servant Songs' from Isaiah 40 to 55 and gave us a new insights into biblical scholarship and some of the challenges of that particular part of the Bible. Above all, he directed our thinking to Jesus and his servant leadership as the model for our leadership as officers.

Brigadier Arthur Rothwell was the Men's Chief Side Officer and Major Jean Healy the Women's Chief Side Officer. They were fine Salvationists and teachers, setting excellent examples for us all. Major Milford McPherson was the Education Officer and he endeavoured to maintain the highest academic standards within the college. Major McPherson certainly had encouraged us in the weeks leading up to our engagement to make representation to enter the Training College in 1967. For this we were very grateful. Milford and his wife were passionate about missionary work, having served in several territories in South Asia. Major Jean Bloxham, one of the field training officers and an experienced corps officer, provided us with excellent insights into Salvation Army procedures and practice.

Classes in Bible, doctrine (theology), homiletics (sermon preparation), Salvation Army procedures, church history, Salvation Army history and a variety of lectures were held on Mondays to Thursdays. At least 30 minutes were allocated on the timetable for daily prayer and devotional Bible reading, thus emphasising their importance for spiritual development and leadership. One Wednesday a month was also devoted specifically to such development through 'Spiritual Day' meetings led by the Territorial Commander, the Chief Secretary or the Training Principal in rotation. Thursday nights were spent marching or walking to the Melbourne City Temple in Bourke Street for a united holiness meeting for the corps in Melbourne, usually led by the principal and staff with cadet participation. We spent Fridays preparing for practical work as well as house-to-house visitation, distributing *The War Cry* at hotels, often participating in an evening open-air meeting, and always in an evening meeting at a local corps led by the cadets. In Sonja's case the venue was Williamstown; in Ian's case, Richmond. On Sundays cadets led open-air Sunday schools and shared in Sunday meetings at Kensington and Brunswick respectively. One Sunday a month was an 'In-Sunday' with devotional meetings conducted by college staff and personal interviews about one's spiritual, social and academic development. Saturday morning was given over to house cleaning with the afternoon and evening as free time. Because we anticipated being appointed overseas fairly soon after training, we often used the afternoon to visit Sonja's parents in Croydon and Ian's mother who had been living with her sister and brother-in-law in Preston since she retired from active service in 1965.

Finances for Salvation Army work have always been limited—even for officer training. As a result, the home officer at the college tried to economise on food as much as possible. One Friday, just before the cadets left for visitation and other evangelistic activities, the lunch-time food supply ran particularly low. This was not the first time. Several cadets, including Ian, only received one sausage and a very small amount of potato—not really enough to provide the needed energy for the afternoon. Ian felt that something should be done. He went to the servery window and politely asked to speak to the principal who was eating in the staff dining room. Brigadier Orsborn was appalled at the situation and acted to rectify it. Meals improved significantly in the following months and certainly in 1968.

As well as the classes and special events outlined above, Sonja and Ian were among a group of cadets who travelled to Morwell for a campaign in the latter half of 1967. At least we could do that together. We were also involved in the annual Training College open day where we participated in the play written by a fellow cadet, Brian Mundy, entitled 'The Eternal Sword'. This drama was based around the history of how the Bible came to us in the 20th century. Ian was given the part of a Salvation Army missionary, Captain Dr Frank Mortimer, in India. Captain Mortimer had been instrumental in discovering the script of the Tibeto-Kanauri language during his medical work so the Bible could be translated into that Himalayan/Tibetan language. Quite inspiring!

Major McPherson was keen to encourage us to consider serving in India. He allocated Ian to undertake research and give a talk at a college assembly about Army work in India Western Territory. Ian's cousins, Dr Bram and Mrs Margaret Emma Southwell, had worked there recently at a Salvation Army hospital. Yet we felt no positive conviction about service in south Asia. Particularly growing out of Sonja's experiences of separation and uncertainty during World War II, we were not at ease with the expectation that any school-age children of missionaries in India would need to be separated from their parents and attend the Hebron School at Ooty (Ootacamundi) in the cooler, mountainous regions of Tamil Nadu for much of each year. Bram and Margaret Emma's older children, Judy and Jane, had attended Hebron. Their pre-school age son, Peter, had died while they were in India. Of course, conditions were probably healthier and safer at Hebron than where we might be working, but were such separations (and potential losses) what God required of us if we had a family while serving in India?

Residential officer training had only been extended in most territories from 10 months to 22 months in 1961–62. January to May of the second year was reserved for 'out-training' and cadets were appointed to lead small corps that might otherwise be without officers. We were appointed to lead the then Maidstone Corps situated between Footscray and Sunshine in the inner western suburbs of Melbourne. This proved to be a good experience. We could work together in leading Sunday meetings, Sunday school, and a corps cadet class, as well as '*War Cry* evangelism' in the local hotels. Organising a money-raising fete on a service station forecourt was a feature. Maidstone was close enough to the University of Melbourne for Ian to undertake—with the blessing and financial support of the Army—concurrent full-time studies toward a postgraduate Bachelor of Education degree. While at Maidstone, we attended the annual officers' fellowship for the Melbourne Central Division at Cranbrook Lodge in Healesville. Ian was given the task of speaking about the victory of Elijah over the prophets of Baal on the 'mount of victorious faith.' He thoroughly enjoyed doing so.

Returning to the college in May, many of our session-mates were deeply concerned. The corps to which they had been appointed had, by and large, been left without officers once they had left. Newly-married Envoys Ken and Barbara Wilson, who were candidates for a forthcoming training session, took over from us at Maidstone Corps—but this was an exception. We felt that some other scheme for training might have been better—perhaps cadets being appointed to a large corps where they could understudy experienced officers and know that the people belonging to that corps would be cared for when they returned to the next residential period of training at the college. (In the case of Maidstone, our leaders suggested that we might stay on run the corps, but we felt that returning to the training college would at least give us an opportunity for undertaking similar activities together and the greatest amount of the regular training concurrently with Ian's university studies.)

However, a bigger picture of training cadets came together after the out-training. Under Ian's chairmanship, the session formulated a proposal that fellow cadet, Roslyn Pengilly, typed up and we presented to the Training Principal about how we believed the overall training programme could be modified in the future. In addition to recommending appointments to larger corps mentioned above, the proposal also suggested greater integration between the men's and women's sides in the college—so that training would be much more natural than it had been in the past. How little Ian knew that he would be involved recommending and encouraging implementation of those ideas regarding officer training around the world within six years. Again, God was leading us faithfully and safely.

Ian gained the Bachelor of Education degree in 1968. With the completion of second year residential training, Sonja and Ian were commissioned as officers in January 1969 and appointed to the Little Bourke Street Corps. This corps building was on the corner of Greville Place and Punch Lane, west of Little Bourke Street itself and barely 300 metres from the Melbourne City Temple Corps. Those attending the corps, however, were dramatically different to the attendees at the Temple. Alcoholic and homeless persons who wanted to hear the Gospel felt at home at Little Bourke Street Corps. Years before, Doctor John Singleton had owned this mission hall. When he became too old to look after it, he passed it to The Salvation Army on the understanding that the Army would continue running such a ministry. We were delighted to do so, although we had been hoping to be appointed to teaching and nursing roles in Africa immediately after training.

In an interview with the new Territorial Commander, Commissioner Frederick Harvey, in the latter half of 1968 while we were still cadets, he made it clear that he believed we should serve for at least 12 months in a corps appointment in Australia. We were disappointed and Ian expressed his feelings quite strongly at the time and also in a follow-up letter. How little we knew of God's big picture! He was faithfully guiding. By November 1968, we were expecting our first child. Our baby would be born in Australia. As it was, we were the first married couple appointed to Little Bourke Street Corps. Previously a couple of single women officers had been appointed there for fear that men officers might be attacked. Also, it was believed that women officers could provide helpful links for prostitutes and drug addicts who frequented the area and wanted to commence new lives. The few stories Ian's maternal grandmother had told of her service in that area came to life. At end of the 19th century as a single officer, she had worked from a Salvation Army centre in Exhibition Street trying to assist drug addicts from the opium dens in 'China Town' situated further down Little Bourke Street than Singleton's Hall as well as prostitutes.

In 1969, Little Bourke Street Corps provided a tremendous example of cross-cultural ministry in every sense of the word. It was so much like the early-day Salvation Army of which we had read in Army history books. Homeless, alcoholic and drug-dependent persons wandered the area. Little in the way of social security benefits was available in comparison to 30 years later. Amongst many others in our congregation, we had a defrocked lawyer and a deregistered medical doctor. Both had been undone because of alcohol. If ever we had any doubts about why the early-day Army took such a strong total abstinence stand, they were completely dispelled during our appointment there.

We were responsible to lead three meetings on Sunday at 11 am, 3 pm and 7 pm. On Tuesday nights we held a meeting at 8 pm. On Friday nights, after taking copies of *The War Cry* to hotels in the area, we led another meeting commencing at 8 pm, and another on Saturday nights at a similar time. Before each of the evening meetings—except on Fridays because we were involved in hotel ministry—a small group of dedicated soldiers conducted an open-air witness on Exhibition or Russell Streets between Bourke and Lonsdale Streets. Among them was Sister Etta Graham who brought the drum, and a more recent convert, John Rogerson (not his real name), who our predecessors had enrolled as a soldier and encouraged to wear uniform. He always brought the flag.

The work was tiring, but we had a small and very faithful team of people who helped us. In addition to the two mentioned, the most significant of these helpers was Harry Kelly, an adherent of the corps. On most nights, he would make a pot of heavily sugared tea and milk for those attending. We collected, and he heated, doughnuts or other unused food items from Myer department store to supplement the cups of tea for those attending. Many of the attendees were homeless or moving from one place of temporary accommodation to another. The most common locations for their accommodation were the Army's Gill Memorial Home in A'Beckett Street, Gordon House in Little Bourke Street or Oznam House in Flemington Road.

Knowing that there were refreshments at the end of our weeknight meetings, a number of the homeless persons who frequented the area tended to arrive around the time we usually concluded our meeting—about 9 pm. One night we decided to close the front door of our hall at 8.30 pm. That evening, Ian was expounding on Jesus' parable of the young women who had been invited to a wedding feast (Matthew 25:1-13). As he came to the part where the five foolish and ill-prepared young women who had to go to buy oil for their lamps arrived at the wedding feast, there was loud knocking on the hall door. Ian could not have had a better living illustration of the dangers of missing out on receiving Christ and being excluded from the feast in heaven. We think everyone present understood the message that night.

Generally we held some our open-air meetings near Her Majesty's Theatre and a nearby restaurant in Exhibition Street until such time as the owners complained to our Salvation Army headquarters about the 'noise' we were making. Ian would have liked to try to change the owners' minds or fought for the Army's freedom on the streets, but our leaders felt that we should step away from those particular venues to slightly less obvious sites outside some closed shops.

The most wonderful thing about serving at Little Bourke Street Corps was the number of both men and women who came to the mercy seat making decisions to follow Jesus Christ. Most significantly, across the speaking rail above the mercy seat were the words 'To The Uttermost He Saves'. Following-up the 39 who responded in those first six months was so difficult, however. Ian faithfully recorded all seekers, including what these seekers gave as their current addresses. Sadly, by the next morning when he tried to visit, they had moved on to another accommodation house—or the next tree in Flagstaff Gardens.

By March, Sonja was obviously pregnant and the men and women who came to Little Bourke Street were so polite, caring and protective. Having a married couple in charge was a new experience for them—especially one with a wife who was expecting a child in the next few months.

For the Sunday afternoon meetings, Ian felt that it would be helpful to organise the gathering as a Bible study. We had a set of transparency slides of the filmstrip series called *Survey of the Scriptures* from Moody Bible Institute for which we recorded our own soundtrack. Together with his own growing biblical knowledge, Ian presented these studies as a way of enriching the spiritual lives of the people who attended. They appreciated the content.

We were so glad we had arranged for Harry Kelly to receive a certificate of recognition in May 1969 for his outstanding service making 'the Army cup of tea' and undertaking so much other good work at Little Bourke Street. The Field Secretary, Colonel Raymond Beasy, attended to present this on behalf of the Territory. A reporter and a photographer from *The War Cry* attended to record the event. Seeing the camera, a few of the attendees quickly left, unwilling to be photographed even accidentally in case the police or other authorities recognised them.

At that time, Lanes Motors owned much of the property from Exhibition Street to Punch Lane. For some years, the company had been offering a large sum of money to buy Dr Singleton's Hall from the Army to expand their business. During the first half of 1969, Major John Macintyre, the Divisional Youth Secretary, and Ian proposed to territorial leaders developing a mission style of outreach at Little Bourke Street similar in scope to the current (2016) Melbourne 614 Outreach—with even accommodation for people who were homeless. Sadly, the proposal was not accepted. Although we had a vision of what could be done, we were going to be moving overseas at the end of the year.

About May of that year, we were called in to the office of the Chief Secretary, Colonel Frank Saunders, with the question raised from International Headquarters (IHQ) as to whether we were prepared to go to the Hong Kong Command with Ian in charge of the schooling system. The Salvation Army had a number of primary schools, kindergartens and nurseries in the Command. No secondary school existed at that time. An officer with a degree plus a bachelor of education was needed for this work—the very qualification Ian possessed. However, our strong conviction was that Africa was the place to which we had been called. Howard Institute in Rhodesia (later renamed Zimbabwe) or Chikankata in Zambia had both hospitals and secondary schools. In such centres, Sonja could serve as a nurse with her qualifications as well as Ian as a teacher. So the proposal lapsed and we knew that we would be in Australia until at least until the end of 1969.

Then unexpectedly, a breakdown occurred at the nearby Melbourne City Temple Corps. The current male officer needed to be dismissed and, as required by the Army regulations in those days, his wife lost her officer status and appointment, too. We were stunned when appointed pro tem as the officers in charge. In the midst of our sorrow over the loss of two very capable officers, we read the words that God conveyed to Jeremiah when he was called to be a prophet. 'But the Lord said to me, "Do not say, 'I am only a child.' You must go to everyone I send you to and say whatever I command you. Do not be afraid of them, for I am with you and will rescue you," declares the Lord' (Jeremiah 1:7–8). What an assurance!

The week before we moved, our daughter Sharon Joy was born at the Army's Bethesda Hospital in Richmond. The Sunday after we were installed, the corps was involved in the annual Red Shield Appeal. What a contrast Melbourne City Temple was to Little Bourke Street Corps. From a corps with limited personnel and resources reflecting the early days of Salvation Army mission we moved to a fully-fledged 1960s corps with brass band, songster brigade, male voice party, excellent home league, young people's sections, sporting teams and a full complement of local officers. Three indoor meetings on Sundays, at least two Sunday open-air meetings, Sunday school activities, weeknight practices for musical sections, and Friday night '*War Cry* evangelism' visits to hotels became the revised pattern of our activities. Melbourne City Temple was used for divisional events such as the Central Holiness Meeting each Thursday night, plus some territorial ones such as visits by international officers and some meetings held in connection with Commissioning. Obviously, we needed to be on duty for all of these. Ian also was rostered to conduct chapel services at the Army's People's Palace in King Street and at the Spring House Young Women's Hostel in Spring Street.

Lieut-Colonel Allen Sharp, Ian's uncle, conducted the dedication[22] of Sharon on one special Sunday morning—and we all thanked God for his goodness as Sonja's parents and Ian's mother joined with us.

Ian converted the Sunday afternoon praise meeting into a Bible study to continue to build up Bible knowledge amongst the corps members—many of whom travelled from the outer suburbs to be part of the corps. Few lived in the immediate corps vicinity. While at the Little Bourke Street Corps, our quarters was in Kerr Street, Fitzroy. Now our residence was in Thornbury—on the western half of the block of land which held the house Florence and Ian moved to after returning to Melbourne from Western Australia in 1957. Ian reintroduced himself to the neighbours whose window he had broken with a misguided football kick from the backyard during a school correction day in 1958. Having been well taught by his father about taking responsibility, he had measured the frame of the broken window, walked to the nearest hardware store, bought a suitable window pane plus putty, walked back and reinstalled the window. He knew what to do because he had helped his father repair windows broken by similar accidents in Normanby Avenue in 1951–54. Eleven years later (1969), the neighbours still remembered the incident and were most complimentary about Ian's repair work.

Candidate and Mrs Derek Atkin were appointed to lead Little Bourke Street Corps for the remainder of 1969 before Captain Glenda Thomas and Lieutenant Shirley Zoutendijk took over in 1970. Little Bourke Street was eventually attached to Melbourne City Temple from 1973 to 1974 before its closure in 1976 while we were serving overseas—and a significant era for ministry in the centre of Melbourne had passed.

---

[22] A public presentation of infants to the Lord. This differs from christening or infant baptism in that the main emphasis is upon specific vows made by the parents concerning the child's upbringing.

About November 1969, however, we received a message from International Headquarters that we would be appointed to Zambia. Unfortunately, with dependence on airmail, we were confused about the actual destination. We had no specific letter of appointment. Would we be going to Chikankata Secondary School or an ecumenical teacher training facility at Livingstone which a New Zealand Salvationist couple had just left? For this reason we did not feel we were able to label our cabin trunks clearly to a specific address—just to 'The Salvation Army, Zambia'.

Colonel Bramwell Lucas, the new Chief Secretary of the Territory, conducted our farewell meeting at the Melbourne City Temple early in January 1970. In our comments, we emphasised that we had been called to carry the Gospel to others. And as the meeting concluded, John Rogerson from Little Bourke Street Corps came to the mercy seat as a seeker.

We set sail from Melbourne to Adelaide on 18 January 1970, en route to Perth and then on to Cape Town on the liner MS *Achille Lauro* on its return journey to Italy. When Sonja had taken journeys by sea from Indonesia to Australia, to Holland, back to Indonesia and years later to Australia, the waters were fairly calm in the tropics. The furthest Ian had travelled by boat was on calm waters in a ferry across Sydney Harbour to Manly and back. By contrast, in January 1970 severe storms occurred in the Southern Ocean. Even exiting Port Phillip Bay distressed Ian and little Sharon. Both suffered seasickness then and later while sailing through the Great Australian Bight. We were pleased to have a few hours in Perth with our session-mates, Lieutenants Ian and Nancy Smith, who were corps officers at South Perth.

Even worse was to come weather-wise when a cyclone bore down on the ship in the Indian Ocean. The ship's captain had asked Ian to conduct an 'other Protestant denomination service' a few days out of Perth. Ian remembers choosing 'peace' as his topic! How glad we were when we arrived at Cape Town on Sunday 30 January, 14 days after leaving Melbourne. By that time, Sharon was showing signs of an upper respiratory infection. We were so glad a South African officer was at the wharf to meet us and take us to recuperate for a few days at a Salvation Army holiday home in Fish Hoek, Cape Province. On Wednesday 4 February—our third wedding anniversary—we were taken to catch a steam train north to Salisbury (now Harare), Rhodesia (now Zimbabwe). Arriving on Saturday, we were greeted by Captain Valma Ray, an Australian officer who was serving at territorial headquarters in Salisbury. Enrolled as a junior soldier with Ian at Thornbury in 1951, she had been on the staff at the training college in Melbourne when we were cadets in 1967 and it was good to meet her again.

We had arrived in central Africa safely to serve.

Chapter 7

Zambia: Chikankata, 1970–73

Captain Allan Tong from Chikankata Hospital was in Salisbury to meet us. He had come to collect the three of us plus our immediate luggage—including a fold-up pram-cum-cot—in a Peugeot 404 station wagon. Unfortunately, one of the staff members from Zambia Command Headquarters had taken a ride in the same station wagon to visit family members in Salisbury. She was transporting some luggage back from Rhodesia as well. As result there was no room for the trunk containing our cream-coloured Zambian uniforms. So we had to travel in our grey winter-weight uniforms and trust that the trunk would be picked up from Rhodesia on a later trip. That day we travelled through the border post of Chirundu and on to Chikankata arriving on Saturday night—12 hours after our departure from Salisbury. By that stage Sharon was most unwell and Captain Dr Paul du Plessis, Assistant Chief Medical Officer at The Salvation Army Chikankata Hospital, quickly diagnosed that she had pneumonia. He prescribed and supplied antibiotics so she suffered no major side-effects.

We were welcomed at the school's Sunday morning meeting the next day and given a few days to recover and orient ourselves before Ian commenced teaching later that same week. A trip to Lusaka with other staff members in an attempt to register as official foreign workers in Zambia the following Saturday ended in frustration. Someone at the mission station had failed to replace the radiator cap in the engine of the four-wheel-drive vehicle. The radiator boiled dry and another vehicle had to be sent from Chikankata to rescue us all. In addition, the registration office was closed on Saturdays. We had to return another day.

As head of the science department of only three teachers, Ian had many classes to teach, as well as striving to lift the standards of the science room and its equipment. The wooden laboratory benches in the older of the two science rooms were badly damaged by termites. An early project was to kill the termites and repair the benches.

Zambia was a financially impoverished country—aside from the proceeds of copper ore mined in the north. Subsistence farming was common among the village people, consisting largely of growing maize or raising a few cattle mainly used for ploughing. Rains in December to March sometimes failed because most parts of Zambia were at least 800 km away from either the Indian Ocean or the Pacific Ocean. The Army had pioneered primary school education in the area, but this had more recently been taken over by the government. The village chief, Charlie Chikankata, had provided land to The Salvation Army some years before on condition that the Army would build a school and a hospital. By the time we arrived, the mission station was well established, with a 450-student secondary boarding school, 200-bed hospital, leprosarium, and tuberculosis unit.

Secondary education for adolescents was rare and relatively expensive at that time. Only one or two children in a family could attend high school. Many students had to leave after the Form Two (Year Eight) Junior School Certificate examinations because insufficient places existed at higher levels of schooling and few appropriately qualified national teachers were available. Six hundred primary students from all over Zambia applied for the 180 Form One places at Chikankata annually. Because of a backlog in secondary education from the days when Zambia was still Northern Rhodesia, many of our Form Five students were in their mid-20s. The University of Zambia in Lusaka had only opened in about 1966 and the first medical doctors graduated in 1973. Secondary education was only for five years, leading to the Cambridge School Certificate qualification, with examinations set and marked overseas to ensure fairness. University bachelor degrees were extended from three years study to four, the first year being the equivalent of Form Six (Year 12) in Australia. In a country of at least five tribal vernacular languages—none of which were particularly strong in scientific, legal, or commercial vocabulary—English was the medium of instruction and assessment. When we arrived at the school, almost all staff members were qualified expatriate teachers from the United Kingdom, Canada, USA, Australia, New Zealand or the Netherlands. We all worked under the leadership of Brigadier Laura Dutton, a fine New Zealand officer. By both their work and lifestyle examples, these staff members made significant contributions to the development of future leaders for Zambia.

Ian quickly immersed himself in the teaching and Sonja's nursing skills were speedily put to use by the hospital staff. Until that time students from the school who were unwell would make their way to the hospital's outpatients department at all hours. As the time drew near for examinations, headaches and virus colds seemed to occur frequently. Together with Mrs Jacqueline Bates, wife of the business manager at the school who also was a nurse, Sonja provided a hospital triage unit at the school. So, one room of our quarters became an outpatients' clinic each morning at 7.30 am and on Saturdays at 10.30 am. Sonja saw the boys who were unwell and Jacqui saw the girls to determine whether a student needed to see a doctor or could be treated with some other medications they were authorised to distribute. Sonja was also involved in lecturing the nurses-in-training, teaching a Girl Guide troop about first aid, and also helping the tutor sister at the hospital as an examiner for hospital examinations for the nurses. In cooperation with the hospital, Sonja organised an immunisation programme against tetanus and poliomyelitis for the students. These activities also provided a good link with the girls in our discussion groups.

Bilharzia (schistosomiasis) and malaria were two common diseases that our students faced. After school holidays the prevalence of these increased due to problems in the villages from which they came. For instance, few villages had supplies of mosquito nets or insecticide to stop malarial mosquitoes. Antimalarial medications were rare, although we ensured that we always took preventative tablets daily throughout our overseas service. Almost all the rivers and lakes south of the Sahara were infected by bilharzia. This waterborne disease, bred in a certain type of snail, was released into the water and could pass through the skin of anyone entering the stream or lake. From there the parasites would travel to the kidney and bladder. The first indication of the disease was usually blood in the person's urine. In village areas where there were no toilets, infected urine sometimes returned to the waterways and the cycle continued. Unless treated, bilharzia could be fatal. The life cycle of the parasites involved in both these diseases made excellent topics for some of our general science classes. As result, we found that students in higher forms who had this background took a more educated approach to disease prevention and the incidents dropped significantly. Hopefully, they were sharing these insights with the village elders as they visited their homes.

Chikankata mission had its own radio recording studio called Salvation Studio that produced recordings of Bible readings, prayers for the day, and longer services for transmission over Zambian Broadcasting Service. We took the opportunity to train for such productions—training that proved useful in later years. Very few television sets were available or useable in Zambia at that time. Radio was a key form of securing reliable information about the local and wider world. We were grateful to have purchased a portable shortwave radio so we could listen to the BBC news broadcasts, for instance, for objective views of world events.

At that time, the hospital ran an ambulance service. If a villager was sick, they could send someone to the hospital and a four-wheel-drive Landrover would travel to the village to pick up the patient. Male staff members from the hospital served as ambulance drivers during the day and male teachers from school were usually enlisted to do this work at night on a roster basis. Ian was involved in several night-time ambulance trips. A most memorable one was the occasion he was woken about 4 am with a request to pick up a female patient who was suffering malaria. A female nurse went with him. When they eventually arrived at the village, in pitch darkness, they were told: 'It is all right—the baby has arrived!' Some malaria case!

The other memorable ambulance trip occurred when Ian was called with a nurse to village where a man had fallen off a roof. When Ian and the nurse arrived at the village all the man's vital signs had ceased. They could find no indications of breathing or of a pulse. Not knowing the procedure that only the Chief Medical Officer of the hospital could certify a death, they decided to leave him for burial at the village. In fact, they should have transported his body back to the hospital just to confirm that in fact he was dead and not in a very deep coma. Was he really dead? Ian thinks so, but he has always had a lingering doubt.

It was a delight to share in activities outside of Chikankata. In July 1970, together with two other fine British officer staff members, Majors Ruth Chinchen and Ethel Carmody, we travelled 450 km south to conduct the denominational weekend at the David Livingstone Teacher Training College. The college was run by the Christian Council of Zambia, of which The Salvation Army was a member, and employed staff recruited from all the affiliated denominations. Our task was to conduct a typical Salvation Army meeting on a Sunday afternoon. The local corps band of about eight players provided the music as we marched down the assembly hall aisle. The band also played some music for the meeting from a fairly limited repertoire. It was also a joy to meet Salvation Army students at the college in an informal gathering that same day. These student teachers organised their own weeknight activities and several were very active in the Livingstone Corps. Those who were able and willing had to walk about 6 km from the college to the corps and a similar distance back again afterwards. Earlier, on the Sunday morning, we were pleased to be involved in an open-air meeting and the regular Sunday meeting at the Livingstone Corps during which Ian joined their band. We also took the opportunity to see something of the area.

Viewing the magnificent Victoria Falls during that trip also made us very aware, however, of the political tensions between Zambia, Rhodesia, and South Africa. Armed and camouflaged troops were stationed along the borders to deter any potential terrorist activities. The bridge carrying the rail line that had eventually brought the bulk of our luggage to Zambia from South Africa via Rhodesia was officially closed. No locomotive engine from Rhodesia could cross the bridge. To overcome the restrictions, an engine in Rhodesia would push the trucks with sufficient momentum so they would roll to the Zambian side of the bridge. There they could be connected to a Zambian engine. Then the Zambian engine would pull the trucks north via Choma to Mazabuka—the closest town to Chikankata—before going on to Lusaka or beyond to the Copperbelt area cities of Kabwe, Ndola and Kitwe near the border with Zaire (now the Democratic Republic of the Congo). That was the way our luggage had eventually moved into Zambia from South Africa and Rhodesia some months after we arrived. Mail, groceries and, occasionally, luggage for reinforcement personnel were picked up by truck from Mazabuka on Tuesdays and Fridays. We always tried to have air-letters to our respective parents ready for posting on Monday nights for the Tuesday trip.

Six months into our appointment at Chikankata, Ian found he was battling to stay on his feet. The dizziness and middle-ear imbalance may have been due to the stresses and disturbed sleep resulting from driving at night for the ambulance pick-ups. Also, Chikankata was on a plateau almost 5,000 feet (1,500 metres) above sea level, making air pressure less than normal and the atmosphere somewhat rarefied. He really wondered if he was in the right place. In the midst of his concerns, he came across the words of a song by Anna Laetitia Waring in a senior staff devotional meeting one Sunday night:

Green pastures are before me which yet I have not seen,
Bright skies will soon be o'er me where the dark clouds have been;
My hope I cannot measure, my path to life is free,
My Saviour has my treasure, and he will walk with me.[23]

Reassured he was in the right place and could make a contribution, he recommenced his work after a period of rest with new confidence and determination.

Ian also learned the value of a midday siesta to regain his energy. Perhaps Noel Coward's song reflected truly that only 'Mad dogs and Englishmen (in Ian's case, Australians) go out in the midday sun!' Everyone else wisely takes a rest—or suffers the consequences.

Perhaps we also needed time away from Chikankata occasionally. Almost none of the staff owned private cars. Use of official vehicles was severely limited to about one or two shopping trips per term to Lusaka (132 km away) on a Saturday. Early in 1971 we used some of our savings and the proceeds from the sale of Sonja's Volkswagen sedan in Australia to buy another second-hand Volkswagen plus a roof-rack in Zambia from a departing non-officer staff couple. At least the vehicle allowed us to travel on holiday to neighbouring Rhodesia (now Zimbabwe) a couple of times over the succeeding years.

While our teaching and clinical work at Chikankata was satisfying, some of our greatest thrills came when the students felt free to approach us not only about their studies but also about their spiritual needs. On many occasions, Ian's office and Sonja's home-clinic became places of quiet counsel and prayer with students.

---

[23] Anna Laetitia Waring, *SASB* (2015), Song 711.

A number of the students at the school came from non-Salvation Army backgrounds or had no Christian understanding at all. Of course, their spiritual development had to be catered for. In our first year, Ian was much involved in supporting them on Wednesday nights in a Bible study and together in a fortnightly Sunday evening discussion group in our quarters. Later he was also able to be involved with Salvationist students on Wednesday night in their corps cadet classes. Captain Gwenda Watkinson, a fellow Australian, provided excellent leadership for the corps cadet programme and involved some other staff members in the process. Often on a Sunday afternoon she would take groups of corps cadets out into the surrounding villages to witness for the Lord and conduct open-air village meetings. Ian did so occasionally with non-Salvationist young people who were similarly enthusiastic for their Lord.

Easter was always a special occasion at Chikankata. In our first year there, the celebrations fell during term-time and many students were involved in Good Friday and Easter Day meetings led by Major David and Mrs Dora Ramsey. Very early on Easter Day, Salvationists from village corps in the area and our students marched to a hill on the outskirts of the Institute—near our hospital, leprosarium and graveyard—appropriately named 'Easter Hill' for a sunrise service. As they marched, they sang, in the local ciTonga language, 'He lives, He lives, I know that my Redeemer lives' accompanied by much traditional African drumming. After the sunrise celebration of the resurrection, staff from the school and hospital would gather for an Easter breakfast at one of the larger staff quarters.

With a rearrangement of staff toward the end of 1970, Brigadier Dutton suggested that Ian might take charge of the 'corps' (worship) activities in the school. She sensed how enthusiastic we were to communicate the Gospel and develop the spiritual lives of students and staff. The role involved organising the Sunday meetings, the Self Denial Appeal, Easter meetings and special events that are typically 'corps' (church). Our desire was to keep the focus on Jesus and also make the atmosphere as 'Salvation Army' as possible. The former emphasis was helped by the ethos of the school, the Christian commitment of the staff members and the fact that Biblical Studies was a subject taught from Form One (Year Seven) to Form Five (Year 11). Our deepest desire was that all our students would come to faith in Christ. The complementary emphasis on the Army was designed in order to increase understanding of our denomination and its mission amongst the Zambian students who were not associated with any other church. Perhaps they would want to make the Army their church when they left Chikankata.

Ian planned a teaching series for the Sunday meetings with suggested topics rather than individual teachers or visiting preachers potentially bringing the same message again and again. During 1970, the story of the would-be disciples of Jesus who found excuses not to follow him had been the topic three or four times. Ian vowed to reduce the likelihood of the same thing happening again. Boredom needed to be avoided with our intelligent and receptive students. So he prepared a ministry plan such as he had at Little Bourke Street and Melbourne City Temple, providing consistent and systematic teaching and preaching. For a number of weeks in term one, Ian preached himself to demonstrate the idea.

Our deep desire was to train the next generation of Salvation Army soldiers (members), local officers and officers. In Zambia, the needs were great. Almost no officers had been trained since Zambia had ceased to be Northern Rhodesia. Border restrictions made it difficult for Zambians to go to Rhodesia to attend the nearest Salvation Army Training College that used English as the medium of communication. So we were delighted when plans were announced to open an Officer Training College in Lusaka in 1971.

We were blessed to have mature Zambian non-teaching staff members such as Mr Simeon Mhende as corps sergeant-major and Mr Ken Maguswi as young people's sergeant-major[24]—not that we had a large children's ministry other than young children of staff members who attended Sunday school. Mr Mhende and Mr Maguswi were deeply committed Christians and Salvationists, providing good examples to the students and excellent cultural awareness for expatriate staff. Ken Maguswi offered ciTonga language classes to expatriate staff in which we participated.

Zambian Salvationists in the local area had formed their own corps named Chitumbi, about a kilometre outside the gates of the Institute. All singing, testimonies and preaching were in the local ciTonga language. Following a midweek meeting at which Ian preached, we were invited to

[24] A local officer responsible for young people's work in a corps, under the commanding officer.

conduct the third anniversary celebrations of the corps. Before the main meeting, the comrades marched to an open-air meeting singing the ciTonga version of 'Marching along... The Salvation Army is marching along' over and over again. How thrilling it was to hear Envoy Hachitapika, who was in charge of the corps, tell how it had grown from eight soldiers to 18 with six more to be enrolled shortly. The soldiery was being well trained, singing groups and the young people's work were flourishing, and much volunteer labour given to complete building the hall.

We were also involved in the Zambia Command Corps Cadet Congress at Chikankata in 1970. Ninety-four corps cadets came from the hospital and school and another four joined the group from Lusaka. Quite a number expressed a desire to become officers—and the Command certainly needed them. Not enough trained and commissioned officers were available for all the corps and outposts[25] in the Command.

With financial gifts from family and friends, we were able to support projects such as buying song books for the meeting place at the school, chairs for the recreational hall, some science and agricultural science equipment, and a variety of science reference books. In November 1970, the school presented some 60 Form Five students for the Cambridge Overseas School Certificate Examination. At least 45 of the students obtained the Certificate and 10 were accepted for first year university studies. Ian was particularly pleased that the results in Physical Science—the subject he taught—were better than in previous years.

December 1970 school holidays also allowed us to journey again to Livingstone Teachers' College, which we had visited earlier in the year, this time spending some weeks journeying around the area in a borrowed car, viewing the scenery and feeling refreshed. This experience probably encouraged us to buy our own vehicle the following year as mentioned on page 68.

Our second daughter, Jennifer (Jenni) Ann, was born on 1 February 1971. In the absence of a personal car at that time, we thought Ian may have needed to use the hospital's four-wheel-drive ambulance to transport her to hospital, but Sonja managed to walk a couple of hundred metres from our house. Not having either grandmother or other relatives available,

[25] Churches and localities in which Army work is carried out and where it is hoped a society or corps will develop.

Ian had to take Sharon to school while he taught later on that day until he managed to sort out what we needed to do. Shortly after sending messages to Australia regarding Jenni's birth, we received the news that Sonja's father, Brigadier Ryer van Kralingen, had been promoted to Glory. The telegrams must have crossed. It was a time we felt deeply the distance from Australia. Travelling home to Australia to be with Sonja's mother, sister and brother-in-law at the funeral was impossible. Plane travel was not the usual form of transportation then. At that stage we certainly could not have afforded the journey personally. Skype and the Internet were non-existent.

Nevertheless, we felt greatly supported by our fellow Salvationists and staff members of Chikankata, and by our Command leaders in Lusaka in those days. Many of them knew what it was like facing challenging situations during their overseas service. The then Chief Medical Officer, Captain Dr Paul du Plessis, who had delivered Jenni, conducted her dedication at a Sunday morning meeting at the school. Barely a month later, Paul and his wife, Margaret, lost their newborn child to a disease that even he as a doctor could neither prevent nor cure. You can imagine the united grief at Chikankata.

During the 10 months of observation before Ian was appointed as the corps officer of the school corps, he had become convinced the corps should have specified local officers to help develop leadership. So in the months after he became the corps officer, he set about appointing senior students and some staff members into positions of leadership. As a result, they were encouraged to attend corps council and census board meetings, learn about Salvation Army procedures and feel that they had a stake in the organisation of the corps.

Despite the emphasis on Salvation Army activities at Chikankata, Christian students from other churches were also given opportunities to lead group activities and even open-air meetings in surrounding villages. Ian arranged for them to have 'letters of authority' for this latter activity in recognition of their efforts and have a representative on the corps council as well.

Easter in 1971 was quieter than Easter in 1970 because it fell during the scheduled school holidays and our students were not with us. However, school and hospital staff still walked to Easter Hill, and then came back to our quarters for breakfast. For the first time in many years, rain fell this Easter. Eighty staff members from the hospital and school crowded onto our verandas, into our sitting room, living room and kitchen. Trying to sing a few Easter songs in English provided a challenge with scattered groups around the house. The clean-up afterwards was huge—but so was the fellowship we had enjoyed.

Life was relatively safe at Chikankata, but did have its more challenging moments where we sensed God's protection. Having had a pet dog in Indonesia as a girl, Sonja was keen to have one for our family. We obtained a dog from a departing school staff reinforcement couple. Born in one of the nearby villages, the dog's ciTonga name was 'Muluma', meaning 'You bite!'—not a bad name for a dog that might guard our family! Mostly, we called him 'Luma'. One day Sharon and Jeremy Hay, toddler son of our neighbours, Captains Laurence and Margaret Hay, were playing in a sandpit we had in our quarters yard. Sonja was indoors preparing a meal and Ian was teaching. Luma started barking furiously. Attracted by the noise, Sonja went outside to see a snake slithering toward the children. Luma had placed himself between the snake and the children and was barking for assistance. Sonja gave the help needed. With a few swift blows applied to its back from the long-bladed double-edged 'slasher' used for cutting the long African grasses, Sonja killed the snake. 'Well done, Luma!' 'Thank you, God.'

In April a set of officers councils was held—the first in the Command for about four years. These were led by the newly arrived officers commanding, Brigadier and Mrs Keith Anderson. Ian was asked to speak on 'The role of the young Salvationist in Zambia today', particularly from the viewpoint of being the corps officer of the school corps. The preparation needed helped him to crystallise in his mind a number of matters that he raised in the African Survey organised by the General and carried out by his special representative, Colonel Thomas H. Lewis, a little later. The middle of the year was particularly busy with examinations, school inspections, a corps cadet weekend and many sporting fixtures.

In August the term break became an opportunity for still more activities. Ian left for a long-awaited course in the ciTonga language at Choma. He found the course to be of great benefit. As a result, he had enough confidence to give a simple testimony without a translator at Congress the next month. For the Congress, he had the privilege of organising some of the Saturday activities. The Congress delegates included Salvationists from the Gwembe Valley (part of Zambezi Valley region) as well as from around Chikankata and the Lusaka area. Activities included follow-up classes for recent converts; and counsellor training for mature counsellors which Ian conducted personally with the help of a translator. In these classes he emphasised the importance of listening to the seeker and asking appropriate questions in order to help them most effectively. What a thrill it was to see some of these newly trained counsellors helping seekers at the Sunday morning meeting!

The next weekend, we led a corps cadet weekend at Matero Corps in Lusaka—at that time a predominantly Shona language corps commenced by Salvationists from Rhodesia. However, as all the corps cadets spoke English, this was the medium of communication. Some delegations travelled overnight to attend. As we hoped, some non-corps cadet teenagers expressed a desire to become corps cadets. Other decisions and consecrations were made over the weekend also.

Sonja continued to be busy with the clinic. Her patients now included both girls and boys because Jacqui and Rodney Bates had returned to the United Kingdom to train as Salvation Army officers. She helped out with some nursing duties at the hospital during an emergency and provided training for the home league leaders at Chitumbi Corps.

Food was often in short supply at Chikankata—especially when the rains had failed or been minimal. How delighted we were that, before he was promoted to Glory, Sonja's father had sent us a supply of red papaya seeds from Australia. We planted them in the yard of our quarters and the trees bore abundant fruit. (Thirty-five years later they were still doing so.) We were also pleased when we heard of an unattended orange orchard some kilometres away from Chikankata where fruit was available if we would go and pick it. Many staff members jumped at the opportunity. Another unexpected blessing, at a time when yellow vegetables were in short supply, was finding several large pumpkins, including one huge one that was almost the weight of our daughter Sharon. They were growing from seeds we had disposed of on the vacant land over the back fence of our quarters. We shared these blessing with our neighbours.

During the middle of that same year, 1971, the Command's Officer Training College was opened and the first cadets accepted. Our neighbours at Chikankata, Captains Laurence and Margaret Hay from the Chikankata staff were appointed as the Training Officers, leaving a gap in the English teaching staff that took a while to fill. Two cadet couples were accepted with the hope that there would be some others coming later—and certainly more cadets in mid–1972. Developing national leadership for the Army in Zambia was absolutely vital. At that stage there were only 23 national officers in the Command, several with only just a few years to serve until they retired. Between them they needed to provide leadership for 55 corps, four districts, one social service institution, and provide chaplaincy at the Chikankata Hospital. Training soldiers who could potentially act as corps leaders was also vitally important. Hopefully the Training College would play a significant role in fulfilling those objectives.

During one of her clinic sessions Sonja noticed a rather irregular heartbeat in Josie Moyo, one of the students. Sonja referred him to the hospital and the chief medical officer agreed that Josie had more serious heart problems than could be treated at Chikankata. He was referred to the University Teaching Hospital in Lusaka. Josie was very underweight and that situation needed to be addressed before he could enter the hospital for surgery. In order to protect him from infection and also make sure he had enough nourishment, he lived in our quarters for some time.

Eventually Josie was moved to Lusaka and the operation was performed at the University Teaching Hospital. How distressed we all were when his elder brother, Nelson, who was also a student at our school, came to tell us that Josie had died. The operation had been successful, but his heart went into fibrillation and the medical staff were not able to overcome this complication. Nelson asked Ian to try to arrange to secure Josie's body from the hospital. Ian gained permission from the Principal, Brigadier Laura Dutton, and took a four-wheel-drive vehicle into Lusaka. It was quite an effort for Nelson and Ian to find Josie's body in the mortuary and carefully place it in the back of the vehicle to return him to his village. The fact that Ian was travelling in Salvation Army uniform certainly helped in working with the hospital authorities. He was also able to participate in the funeral service for Josie, who was a Salvation Army soldier.

Ian had also been able to assist after Captain Saul Hangoma's father passed away about the same time. Saul was a chaplain at the hospital, and his home village was quite close to the Chikankata complex.

Around 1970, the Zambian Government decided to accept a project to construct an earthen wall water-storage dam near the Chikankata complex. This would ensure a more secure water supply for the hospital, school, and some of the surrounding villages. Fortunately, one of the local creeks flowed between two hills near the school and hospital toward the Gwembe Valley and Zambezi River. By building a dam wall between those two hills it was hoped to capture the water in the creek, especially during the rainy season from November to March. The engineers thought it would take two or three years to fill. In fact, the dam filled in the first rainy season and some water even passed over the newly constructed concrete spillway.

Unfortunately, the engineers had ignored an important geological fact: one of the hills had a layer of mica in it—making that section somewhat porous. Some of the same soil was in the dam wall itself. Within a year of the dam filling, water started to trickle through the wall at the level of the mica layer and near the point where the wall connected to the hill. The erosion increased. Urgent action was needed. That Friday night, teams from the school and hospital walked down the valleys to warn the nearby villages that a flood could take place if the dam wall broke. On that occasion, Ian did not go as he did not know the area and could not have communicated well enough to explain the situation in ciTonga.

Before the warning teams left Chikankata, one member had suggested that if a pipe could be inserted near the main point of weakness, it might carry the leaking water to the valley floor. Then the barely compacted lower part of the dam could be preserved from further erosion and prevent a possible collapse. Early on Saturday morning, Ian climbed out onto the dam face. The eroded soil from the dam was quite muddy and difficult to walk through. He could have been in serious danger if the mud had gotten into his almost knee-length Wellington boots and he had been trapped in the bog-like conditions. He carried a piece of heavy PVC piping and inserted it where he sensed the water was seeping through. In retrospect, it may have been a foolhardy thing to do because the dam wall could have broken while he was there. But he believed it was the right thing to do and no-one else was around to do it.

Inserting the piping fulfilled the purpose. By channelling the water down through the pipe to the valley floor rather than across the newly constructed dam wall, further erosion was minimised. In the weeks following, that tubing was improved and rocks encased in wire mesh inserted in the eroded part of the dam so that it would be stronger from that point on. (A photograph of the early stages of that repair is included on page 84.) We thanked God for his protecting mercies.

With the departure of Laurence Hay to lead the Training College in Lusaka, Ian took on some career counselling work with the boys in 1972 as well as his physical science, general science and mathematics teaching work spanning 33 40-minute teaching periods per week. Sonja continued her clinic work.

What a delight to have a congregation of 480 students and staff on a Sunday morning, 131 of those being Salvation Army soldiers! For the second year Ian was able to arrange a teaching programme in the Sunday meetings with the help of the staff. In 1971 the programme focused on the person and work of Jesus. This second year (1972) focused on 'The Kingdom and Kingship of Christ', 'Living in the Kingdom', and 'The Christian in the World'. Ian was able to arrange the commissioning of a full census board and corps council. We were delighted that over 100 of the students made commitments to Christ during the course of the year and between 20 and 30 of those were enrolled as soldiers. A Sunday school was firmly established for staff children and Sonja was involved in teaching. Four members of staff became recruiting sergeants, and three were appointed as corps cadet leaders, another as a Scripture Union counsellor, a young people's sergeant-major, two corps finance local officers and 40 Bible study group leaders. Our aim was to ensure that students from the school acted as understudies to any of the local officers who were expatriates so that they would learn what it meant to be a local officer in the event that they joined a corps that needed leadership in the future. United Sunday night meetings were conducted every second week. On the alternate weeks, the school and staff population was divided into 24 discussion and Bible study groups in the staff homes, or in classrooms. After that, senior staff would move to the hospital chapel for a senior staff and worship meeting. These meetings included songs, Bible readings and prayer, together with a message from God's Word in English without the usual pauses for translation into ciTonga.

One of the thrills during the year was an excellent effort to raise funds for the Self Denial Appeal—an annual feature of Salvation Army activity around the world. Everyone was encouraged to participate. Having taught about the parable of the talents (Matthew 25:14–30), Major Gwenda Watkinson decided to make this practical for as many of the students as would like to participate. She gave them each 10 ngwee—a small amount in the Zambian currency. They were then encouraged to use this money in such a way as to multiply it. Some were able to increase this initial amount five times, 10 times or even 20 times. One student invested to buy bread and jam. Another bought some soft drink. Yet another purchased shoe polish. One of the girls purchased a length of material. These items were profitably sold again as sandwiches, cool drinks, shoe cleaning services and dresses respectively. The students' inventiveness was amazing. At the Altar Service that concluded the appeal, they brought the proceeds and placed them in individual envelopes on the holiness table at the front of the assembly hall which served as our church. Best of all, some of them also came forward to 'give themselves'. In one envelope we found the words, 'I haven't any money, but I give myself.' No-one knows where such consecrations might lead.

With the help of the now Brigadier John Macintyre, the Territorial Youth Secretary, Australia Southern Territory, we were able to start an experimental postal Sunday school system in Zambia. We used material prepared for children of farmers and cattle station owners in remote regions of Australia. Our attention had been focused on children of European farmers and those of better educated Zambian public servants who understood English quite well. Because of their parents' locations or appointments, these children had been unable to attend Sunday school or even church. The programme was well received among those for whom it was intended.

On a long weekend in July, staff from the hospital and school combined to set up an exhibition of Salvation Army work at an agricultural show in Mazabuka, about 65 km away. Three stalls displayed Chikankata's efforts in medical, educational and evangelical work. Ian was responsible for the last of these. Much interest was aroused and many worthwhile contacts were made.

Various donations from Australia again helped us buy teachers reference books, books for counselling seekers and for follow-up work at Chikankata. We were able to make a special contribution toward the new Officer Training College in Lusaka which now had three couples in their first year of training to augment the two married couples in their second year.

Photos 1 1939–75

(Top left) Sonja [right] with sister Joan at Malang, Java, before Ryer's departure to Tarakan

(Top right) Junior Soldier Sonja [left] with sister Joan and mother Johanna in Jakarta c. 1953

(Centre right) Sonja with parents Johanna and Ryer, and Joan as soldiers of Clayton Corps, Vic. c. 1957

(Bottom left) Sonja as nurse and midwife c. 1963

(Bottom right) Sonja as songster of Box Hill Corps, Vic. c. 1964

(Top left) Ian with his parents at Nedlands, WA, 1943
(Top centre) Ian's maternal grandparents, Lieut-Colonel George and Mrs Lieut-Colonel Jennie Lonnie
(Top right) 'Leading an open-air like his father,' at home in Smith Street, Highgate WA, c. 1945

(Centre left) With Uncle George Southwell, father, Major Sarah Southwell [grandmother] and Uncle Alan Southwell, at Campsie, NSW, c. 1949
(Bottom left) Ian's first day at school, Ballarat Vic. 1948
(Bottom centre) With Grandma Jennie Lonnie on possibly her 83rd birthday at Thornbury Vic. in 1953.
(Bottom right) At home after leading the Anzac Remembrance at Thornbury Primary School, 1954

With his father in Perth, 19 June 1955 (13th birthday)

Ready to participate in a Congress march during General Wilfred Kitching's visit to Perth, 1956

Ian as a soldier of Fairfield Corps, Vic., 1959–67

On Bachelor of Science graduation day with uncles Brigadier William Southwell (left) and Lieut-Colonel Allen Sharp (right)

(Left) Ian as occasional conductor of the Northcote High School Brass Band, 1966
(Middle row left) Wedding at Box Hill Corps, 4 February 1967
(Middle row right) Wedding party outside Box Hill Corps building, from left: Ian and Sonja, Colin Keast and Roslyn Sheppard, David Percy and Jenny Wright, with flower girl Ingrid Stolk, 4 February 1967

'Messengers of the Faith' Session 1967–69. Back row: Robin Callander, Neville Tyson, Brian Mundy, Ian Southwell, David Perry, Victor Poke, Robert McDonald, Ian Smith, Howard Smith, Brian Robertson. Front Row: Margaret Newdick, Valis Slater, June Tyson, Heather Mundy, Sonja Southwell, Janet Perry, Brigadier Howard Orsborn (Principal), Roslyn Pengilly, Barbara Munro, Nancy Smith, Kathy Smith, Irene Robertson, Mavis Grinter.

(Left) Ian received his postgraduate Bachelor of Education degree in 1969, with his mother and Sonja in attendance
(Above) Last family gathering before departure for Zambia in 1970 with Ian's mother Florence [left]; Sonja's parents Ryer and Johanna; her sister Joan, brother-in-law George, and their children: Ingrid, Bill and Patricia; and our daughter Sharon
(Below left) Sonja inoculating students at Chikankata against tetanus
(Below right) Testifying via translation at an open-air meeting at Livingstone, Zambia

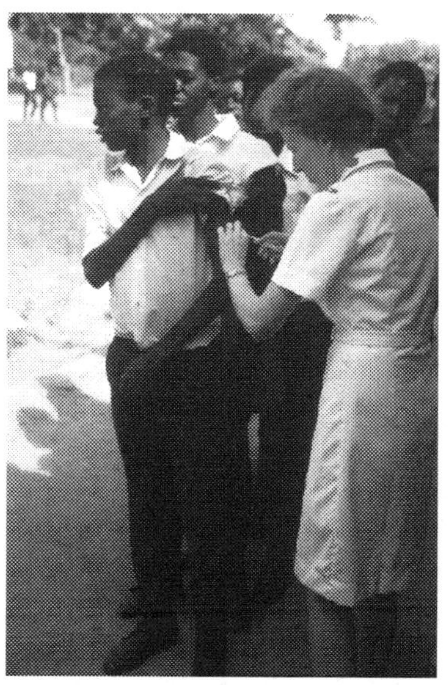

(Above) Ian teaching via translation at a Zambian Congress meeting c. 1971–72
(Right) Early stages of more permanent repairs to leaking dam wall at Chikankata, still using a run-off pipe similar to the one Ian inserted
(Middle row) With the cadets commissioned in Zambia in 1973, together with the Assistant Training Officers, Captains Saul and Jenny Hangoma [on right].

(Bottom row) Delegates to the 1974 Training Principals' Conference with General Erik Wickberg, Chief of the Staff Commissioner Arnold Brown and Colonel Eva Burrows, Principal of the International College for Officers, who coordinated the event. Ian is in the middle row, fourth from the left.

Chapter 8

On to Lusaka, and back to Australia, 1973–75

The year 1973 proved to be an eventful one in many ways. Just before Christmas 1972, we made our second journey to Rhodesia (now Zimbabwe) with Sharon and Jenni using our own car. We booked to stay, as we had during the previous long school holiday, at the Braeside Senior Citizens Hostel in Salisbury. The visit gave us opportunities to visit the Salisbury Corps (English-speaking) and the Harare Corps (Shona-speaking). Of great interest to us was a visit to the relatively nearby Mazoe (now Mazowe) High School in East Mashonaland where we met a few of the staff not holidaying elsewhere. We also visited a few tourist spots around the city. On 9 January 1973, a few days after we returned to Zambia, the Rhodesian Government fully closed the border with Zambia to stop incursions by groups opposed to President Ian Smith's regime. Trips to and from Rhodesia through Chirundu near Kariba Dam in the east, or Livingstone in the south near Victoria Falls, would be a thing of the past for many years. The restrictions included even foreign nationals and other missionaries such as us.

Toward the end of 1972, negotiations commenced to change the status of the Institute Corps of which we were the corps officers. The school administration took over the running of the Sunday morning meeting, making it a compulsory school worship service on more ecumenical lines in order to suit the increasing population of non-Salvationist staff and students. Every second Sunday evening the corps would run a voluntary meeting in typical Salvation Army style with every opportunity for free participation. Because only those students and staff who *wanted* to attend did so, these evening meetings were much more effective than when an element attended that resented the event being compulsory. As it was, between 150 and 200 people came to each of these Sunday evening gatherings—and up to 300 on special occasions. Salvationist students became enthusiastic to invite their friends. They had something to work towards. Even the Salvationist staff were more focused and determined. God honoured those efforts by a number of students making significant commitments to Christ. That stimulus was even reflected in the result of the Self-Denial effort for that year that saw an increase of 20 per cent.

From February to July 1973, Ian accepted an invitation from the new Officer Commanding, Lieut-Colonel William Evans, to write a series of meditations in a religious monthly in Zambia called the *Mirror.* Ian based these articles around the fruits of the stimulating in-depth studies he was taking by distance education toward the London University Certificate of Proficiency in Religious Knowledge on the book of Romans. He entitled the series 'Looking at a Letter'.

During the first term holidays in May 1973, we received farewell orders to go to the Officer Training College in Lusaka to fill the positions of Training Officers in charge. Very wonderfully, another science teacher had been recruited to cover Ian's teaching role. The college had been without training officers for two months since our predecessors, Captains Laurence and Margaret Hay and their children, had left for homeland furlough in New Zealand, not intending to return. The five cadet couples (two second-year couples and three first-year couples) had been sent for out-training while new training officers were sought. As it was, the 'Blood and Fire' session was due to be commissioned in June. We effectively had two weeks to shift house, prepare a Commissioning programme for the events and learn all we could about the college before the cadets returned.

The following four weeks were spent in helping both sessions settle back into the college routine after their weeks away, and prepare them for Covenant Day and Commissioning. Other preparations included preparing Commissioning uniforms and helping the cadets complete any outstanding assignments. Captains Saul and Jenny Hangoma became

Assistant Training Officers in succession to Major and Mrs Ben Musambila who were appointed to Command Headquarters as General Secretary[26] and Command Home League Secretary respectively.

Commissioning was a very special event. The Zambia Command had been waiting for this for many years. The two couples commissioned by Lieut-Colonel William Evans were almost the first to be trained since Zambia became a separate command in 1966. The only other one was Mrs Captain Jenny Hangoma who received some basic officer training at Chikankata.

At the same time, Ian was finalising his own preparations for the Certificate of Proficiency in Religious Knowledge final examinations which were due in the week after the commissioning. In the event, he managed to gain the certificate with marks of 'credit' in both Old Testament and New Testament. The hours of study in Bible and theology during the last three years provided a good preparation for the change from teaching chemistry, physics and mathematics to Bible, doctrine, church history, Salvation Army history, pastoral counselling, and homiletics—as well as lecturing on the vocation of Salvation Army officership. Similarly, Sonja changed from school clinic duties to the medical care of the cadets and their children, including antenatal and postnatal care, home craft and home league teacher, chief designer and producer of uniforms for women cadets, and typist of lecture notes. We had many opportunities to lead meetings both inside and outside of the college. Great help both with classroom teaching and sound advice was provided by the Command leaders, Lieut-Colonel and Mrs Evans, who were originally from the Australian Eastern Territory.

The new Assistant General Secretary, Major May Sylvester, from the United Kingdom taught Ian the techniques of using a special institutional style cashbook, with manual ledgers, journals and trial balances. We experienced the tribulations of trying to run the college on a very tight budget financed by the international Self Denial Appeal proceeds plus donations from kind friends around the world. If it had not been for donation money sent to us personally, we would have been struggling to keep the college financially afloat. We appreciated every donation and each effort made to raise money in the annual Appeal. Being closer to the administrative receiving end of this appeal money than we were previously

[26] The officer second in charge of the Army in a Command.

made us thoroughly aware of how much a command such as Zambia relies on money so generously given from overseas.

The College was situated on the Command Headquarters compound. Originally an old church property, purchased from the Dutch Reformed Church some years earlier, it featured a large church building now used for the Lusaka Central Corps. The back room of the church building became our main college classroom. Sonja installed some plush blue curtains to cover a blackboard at one end, as needed to convert the room into a chapel for spiritual days and similar meetings. A church fellowship hall some distance away on the property was partly used for storage, and the rest of the building had been subdivided into CHQ offices. Seven small apartment rooms with bathrooms and toilets had been built on the property to accommodate the cadets and other course attendees if cadets were on out-training. Another small building contained college supplies and served as a library. The rest of the compound held quarters for the General Secretary, Assistant General Secretary, Training Officers and Assistant Training Officers.

We wrote to Commissioner Frederick Harvey, now living in the United Kingdom, to thank him for insisting we experienced a year of corps leadership in Australia Southern before being appointed overseas and apologised for the strength with which we made our case to be appointed overseas immediately after Commissioning. We could never have fulfilled our roles as corps officers in Chikankata or have had credibility as training leaders without those experiences at Little Bourke Street and Melbourne City Temple Corps. God was guiding safely for service through our leaders and their decisions.

The security situation in Lusaka was poor by comparison with Chikankata. Thefts occurred from the Command Headquarters compound, from our house and from the Training College. The college minibus lost its starter motor in one audacious theft.

Our new responsibilities gave opportunities to conduct one or two experiments in Lusaka. With the cadets, we organised a sponsored walk that raised about $60 largely from within Zambia. We also organised a vacation Bible school in one of the shanty towns with average attendance of 115 over the five days. Another feature was a prison visitation ministry. About 100 inmates would attend meetings held on Saturday mornings. This gathering was conducted in an open prison courtyard.

We hoped to commence a social services project in Lusaka the following year because much need existed in these areas. The living conditions in the 19 shanty towns around the city were appalling. At least three to four hundred people slept out each night in the Central Railway Station or main bus terminal for lack of adequate accommodation. For some of these rough sleepers, the places mentioned had become their home. At that stage, we found great challenge and fulfilment in this work amongst the cadets and delighted in the opportunity of serving God in The Salvation Army in Zambia. We looked forward to introducing the cadets to social services work similar to that undertaken by William Booth's helpers in the East End of London back in the 1860s to the 1890s and inspiring them to replicate it where they would be appointed.

However, all was not well at the college. The next year and a half were most difficult. As our predecessors had found, not all the cadets were open to correction and teaching—especially from expatriates. The Christian lifestyle challenged them. One couple, now in their second year of training, returned home. Two other married male cadets reacted by accusing Ian of being racist—a very sensitive matter in a newly independent African country bordering on the then white-ruled Rhodesia and the apartheid-organised South Africa. When Ian was appointed to attend the second International Training Principals Conference in London at the International College for Officers in March 1974 their anger grew. Why should a white man represent Zambia? Why not the Assistant Training Officer, Captain Saul Hangoma? Or Major Ben Musambila, the General Secretary? So the cadets went on strike. They walked to the offices of the main newspaper and also to the District Governor of the United National Independence Party (UNIP) in Lusaka, hoping that the decision would be changed and we would be deported. Newspaper headlines in the *Times of Zambia* were most dramatic and featured a photograph of cadets in uniform demanding our deportation. This was a particularly sensitive time about Christmas 1973. Sonja had given birth to our third child, Catherine Ruth, by caesarean section at a private hospital in Lusaka on 26 December.

Lieut-Colonel Evans was in a difficult position. He was also an Australian and fair skinned, although he and his wife had served in Africa for a number of years before and had much credibility. He came to a hearing convened at the office of the District Governor on New Year's Eve.

Ian felt a wonderful sense of peace as he went to the hearing that afternoon. As we calculated later, the time difference between Zambia and Australia meant that family and friends were praying for us at about that time during the Watchnight services being held that night—not that they knew about the situation because airmail letters had not gotten through to them. As mentioned earlier, there were no such things as Skype, Facebook or email. We just knew they would be praying for us.

In preparation for that afternoon, Lieut-Colonel Evans had made some investigations at Chikankata. During the hearing, he related how we had looked after Josie Moyo as a guest in our house and then cared for his body after he had died at the University Teaching Hospital. 'Would these actions suggest that the Southwells were racists?' asked Colonel Evans. The African District Governor was a very wise man. The case was thrown out. He recommended that the cadets be given an opportunity to continue their training, and they did so albeit reluctantly.

Just before Ian left for the Training Principals Conference early in March, Sonja's mother and stepfather came to join her. Mrs Brigadier van Kralingen had married Colonel Garnet Palmer who had lost his wife a little earlier than she had lost Ryer. Colonel Palmer was an excellent Bible teacher who had served in corps, war services, on training college staff and in many senior positions before retiring from the position of Chief Secretary in the Australian Eastern Territory. It was hoped his presence, particularly, would also settle down the cadets. Colonel Palmer conducted the dedication of Catherine on the Sunday before Ian left for London.

Ian found the conference inspirational as it provided great insights into officer training worldwide. The then Colonel Eva Burrows, as Principal of the College, was the director of the conference programme. General Erik Wickberg brought the keynote address about the purpose of the conference and the profile of a training principal—today and tomorrow. The Chief of the Staff (second in command of the Army), Commissioner Arnold Brown, showed great interest in the conference, visiting frequently and bringing stimulating messages such as his lecture on the aims and philosophy of Salvation Army training and a vision of what the officers of tomorrow would need to face around the world. Other principals such as Major Bramwell Tillsley (Newfoundland) spoke about Salvationism; Colonel Charles Talmadge (USA Eastern) spoke about the training officer and

Major Paul Rader (Korea), spoke of the challenges facing smaller colleges. Colonel Burrows emphasised the theology of officership. The fact that three of these four last named officers subsequently became generals of The Salvation Army emphasised the quality of the conference discussions and the interactions that took place. Many of the other delegates subsequently held senior territorial or command positions around the world.

Most of the lectures led on to discussion groups. Ian was part of one group considering the administrative structure of training colleges. He had already commented about the topic in a pre-conference submission requested from all training colleges around the world. This discussion was needed because for many years the international regulations for officer training were based on the situation at the International Training College (ITC). Officer training commenced in England in the 1880s with separate colleges for men and women. These were combined some years later into ITC. The administration and structure of the ITC reflected this, with leadership by men's side officers and women's side officers and supporting staff under a principal appointed by the General. From Ian's point of view, the college in Zambia was so small and with such a limited number of training staff, a total college concept was needed. Many small training colleges were in similar positions. He helped draw up staffing structure diagrams showing that staff needed to be divided into *functional roles* such as teaching (academic), domestic arrangements, spiritual care of cadets, practical training, and business and administration. He then drew up specific diagrams to reflect the situations of a small college with six to 15 cadets with about three available staff; medium to small colleges with 15 to 30 cadets and six available staff; medium to large colleges of 30 to 60 cadets and 10 available staff; and finally a college such as the ITC with very large numbers of cadets and staff. In most cases, the position of a senior training officer became very significant—something akin to that of a chief secretary in a territory or the general secretary in a command. He was particularly gratified when the 'total college concept' became the accepted norm for the structure of training colleges within a few years.

Ian also valued the opportunity to visit the birthplace of William Booth in Nottingham and the areas where the Founder commenced the East London Christian Mission. He also had an interview with Commissioner Stanley Cottrill, then International Secretary for Africa and the Far East. The commissioner was aware of the problems in Zambia and had copies of the newspaper reports as well as some material from the Officer Commanding. Commissioner Cottrill had served for many years in Rhodesia and was able to give some helpful advice. Sadly, Ian felt the commissioner did not really understand the situation in Zambia at that time.

After the conference concluded, Ian spent a couple of days exploring London and surroundings in southern England before flying across to the Netherlands. There he met the more immediate relatives of Sonja's who mainly lived in the vicinity of The Hague. Sonja would have wished to share in this occasion, but Ian's visit helped prepare the way for one a few weeks later by Sonja's mother and Colonel Garnet Palmer. The last time Sonja and her parents were in the Netherlands had been in 1947 after the Second World War, before they returned to the Netherlands East Indies. At least Sonja's surviving aunts, uncles and cousins had an opportunity to meet Ian and he was able to share Good Friday and Easter with them around 12–14 April that year.

As Zambia Airways had a direct flight from Amsterdam to Lusaka, it was an easy return journey and the time difference between the Netherlands and Zambia was only one hour. Ian barely had time to complete a report on his visit and the conference before Johanna and Garnet Palmer left for Europe.

The next Sunday, 21 April, was scheduled as an in-Sunday, a Sunday during which the cadets would attend a meeting led by training staff rather than them going to conduct meetings at a neighbouring corps. Problems resurfaced. The cadets refused to attend the meeting that we were to lead, opting to go instead to the Sunday morning meeting at Lusaka City Corps conducted by Captain Saul Hangoma. Lieut-Colonel William Evans and his wife were actually present in the Lusaka City Corps meeting that day and became thoroughly aware that the cadets were present there and not at the in-Sunday. Their behaviour was a challenge to us and to The Salvation Army administration.

Despite being confronted about their lack of obedience, the cadets persisted in their behaviour. A cadet review board decided that they would be suspended from the college. The men cadets then forced their way into Lieut-Colonel Evans' office on Thursday 25 April, and basically held him hostage there in the hope that he would change his mind. He refused. Their suspension was confirmed despite them going back to the Lusaka District Governor of the United National Independence Party (UNIP). The District Governor called all the parties to his office once more, astounded that so soon after Ian's return the cadets would take such action. Lieut-Colonel Evans' decisions were endorsed and the cadets told that only those who were subsequently invited back could return to college. The intention was that the first year cadets would return and the second year cadets be dismissed because it was the two men in the latter group who were causing most of the problems.

Eventually six cadets—all from the first-year session—were re-accepted for training. The atmosphere in the college improved greatly during the latter months of the year and some very constructive training work was undertaken. Despite the turmoil in the college, candidates were still coming forward and others were accepted to enter training in February 1975.

The period during which the college was without cadets provided opportunities to prepare additional training college materials and, at the request of the Officer Commanding, conduct meetings at a teachers college and colleges of advanced education. During those meetings some attendees made decisions for Christ. We were also able to assist Command Headquarters with various matters ranging from customs and immigration to public relations and special efforts. One of the greatest joys was the extension of the Army's prison ministry from Lusaka Central Prison to prisoners in the remand and women's sections, and to their relatives. Approaching Christmas, and with the aid of money raised by sponsored walks, the Army was able to distribute 700 presents to those we had brought the Gospel message to during the year. With the assurance of continued interest in and support from prison authorities, the future of the work seemed assured.

During those months we were asked by International Headquarters if we were prepared to be reassigned to South Africa after our scheduled homeland furlough in 1975. We thought and prayed about this very carefully. In our response we stated that, provided Salvation Army leaders did not mind about us standing firmly against the apartheid programme in South Africa and identifying as closely as we could with the black South African population, we would be happy to take the appointment. The response from International Headquarters was that in those circumstances we would be reassigned elsewhere. We had already indicated that we would be prepared to serve in Rhodesia with the same provisos. Sadly, those provisos did not seem to be viable options for The Salvation Army at that time.

The International Secretary for Africa and the Far East, Commissioner Stan Cottrill, visited the Command during those months and it was good to be able to chat with him again. I think he came to appreciate that we were definitely not racists and were very enthusiastic to support African people wherever and whenever possible.

Toward the end of 1974, Ian was asked to coordinate a corps cadet weekend. In collaboration with Major Gwenda Watkinson from Chikankata they put together a very effective weekend on the topic 'Jesus power!' Many seekers were recorded amongst the corps cadets who attended.

Earlier in the same year, Sharon commenced correspondence lessons under Sonja's guidance toward completing the equivalent of Victorian Preparation Class—a type of kindergarten level in schools. This would stand her in good stead when we were on homeland furlough as anticipated in early 1975.

Just before we were due to leave Zambia, Ian caught chickenpox from visiting the shanty towns around Lusaka with the cadets. He then managed to infect Sharon, Jenni and Cathy. While this meant a delay in our departure, it was not outside God's will. It provided an opportunity for Ian to assist in providing transport for the general change of officers in the command during late December. When headquarters gave farewell orders to officers, it also needed to provide the means of moving them because public transport to areas where the corps were generally situated was either non-existent or very expensive. Every vehicle and driver was needed when the move took place—especially during the rainy season. Much skill was required to negotiate slippery roads, submerged bridges and boggy side-tracks. The delay also gave us an opportunity to prepare a comprehensive information brief of information for Major Jonah Kaumba, a senior Zambian officer who had been appointed to take our place. As he arrived in Lusaka before we left, we were able to personally give him some details.

Whilst our new appointments were not announced officially before our departure, we received indications that we would be reassigned to the

Philippines where we would have responsibility for youth work; literature, including editing the bimonthly *War Cry*; and post-Commissioning studies. This certainly gave us objectives to prepare for on leave.

One chapter of our international service was closing and another beginning.

Leaving Zambia, we flew from Lusaka to Blantyre, Malawi, and on to Johannesburg where we slept overnight before travelling on to Mauritius, Perth and Melbourne, arriving in January 1975. Our three young children, including one-year-old Cathy, were exhausted. At least the trip was faster than spending two weeks on a ship. The Salvation Army in Australia was able to accommodate us in the vacant Mitcham Corps quarters during the five months that we were due for furlough. The prep (preparatory) grade studies Sharon had undertaken by correspondence in Lusaka with Sonja as teacher allowed her to fit into grade one at Mitcham Primary School in February. This term in a regular school environment did her much good in many ways—especially mingling with English-speaking peers.

Chapter 9

The Philippines, 1975–79

Homeland furlough in Australia gave time for Ian to have corrective surgery on a groin hernia—damage resulting from moving suitcases (without wheels), cabin trunks and 44 gallon drums whilst travelling overseas. At least our heaviest luggage was being shipped directly from Zambia to the Philippines and we did not have to handle it ourselves in Australia.

During those months, Ian was able to spend some days with the editorial department staff at Territorial Headquarters in preparation for one of his next roles. The staff members taught him about photographs for publication, a standard style-guide, and editing and layout of a publication. He was also encouraged to study the layout and design of tabloid newspapers such as *The Sun* (now *The Herald Sun*) to learn about attention-grabbing journalism.

Furlough also gave Ian time to write his first article for *The Officer*[27], namely 'What translation shall my people use?' Back in Australia we found that the King James Version (KJV) of the Bible was still commonly used in meetings. From our experiences in Zambia working with people unfamiliar with Shakespearean English, and Ian's biblical studies, he concluded that the best translation at that time in English was the Revised Standard Version (RSV). Rather than needing to carry several different versions of the Bible to meetings, or use in evangelism, why not use that one? Many conservative Salvationists were shocked. After his article was published later in the year and we had left for the Philippines, we learned that the

[27] A monthly magazine specifically for officers around the world produced by International Headquarters of the Army in London.

current Territorial Commander sent out a directive encouraging officers to still use the KJV in meetings. Ian was gratified that about a decade later, however, General Eva Burrows specified the even more recently published New International Version (NIV) as the definitive English translation for use in the Army.

All our expectations were that we would be moving into the Philippines in June. In fact, difficulties securing visas meant that our entry was delayed until mid-July. This delay was also beneficial in giving Ian an opportunity to be assigned to the Public Relations Department at Territorial Headquarters in Melbourne on a temporary basis. The preparation for the Red Shield Appeal was taking place and he saw the workings of the department at that stage led by the then Major Frank Linsell. The knowledge gained from those experiences Ian was able to use to good effect in later years.

Winter in Australia contrasted sharply to the wet and humid monsoon summer in the Philippines when we arrived in July. The temperature was rarely below 25°C day or night and humidity almost always above 70%.

The rented quarters provided for us in Project Seven, Quezon City, was quite close to a good Filipino school called the Jose Abed Santos Memorial School, or JASMS for short. Sharon and Jenni were able to settle into that school quite well. Fortunately, at that stage, the language of instruction at JASMS was English and they were able to pick up a little of the national language called Filipino which was based on Tagalog, the major dialect in Luzon Island around Manila. We were permitted to employ a live-in Filipina helper, Lucy, to assist with our housework. Her presence at home allowed Sonja time to mark corps cadet lessons for teenage Salvationists and advanced training lessons for officers. Sonja could also prepare for some Sunday school class materials.

Ian's appointment as Command Youth Officer was rather like being a combined version of divisional and territorial secretary for youth and young people's work in the island chain. The Army had 29 corps, 35 outposts, seven social service centres and one institution at that time. Ideas, inspiration, training, visual and programme tools, inspection reports and assistance to all other departments were supposed to emanate from his office. Lieut-Colonel Nancy Hulett, the Officer Commanding, wanted to ensure that junior soldiers and corps cadets were key features of the Christian education programme for Salvationist young people in the

Command. Having benefited from both programmes ourselves as young people, we were delighted to encourage these. In addition, Ian accepted a role in teaching Doctrine and Public Ministry subjects at the School for Officer Training (SFOT). Traffic to Command Headquarters, SFOT or the airport was always heavy so we needed to be up early each morning to have our times of personal prayer and Bible study, plus breakfast before leaving for our first appointments each day.

Initially Ian shared in compiling and editing the bimonthly *War Cry* with Lieut-Colonel Hulett, before taking over the work fully himself in 1976. We both learned a great deal about design, layout, proofreading, paste-ups, photography and editing—to say nothing of the art of writing. Occasionally Ian would send his feature articles to *The War Cry* or *All the World* in London and see how an experienced team of editors would modify and use them. He was also abundantly grateful for the time he had spent with Major Rowland Hill and others at the Editorial Department in Melbourne while on furlough for the insights that they gave into Salvation Army editorial work.

Ian was also involved in preparing counselling materials for seekers, processing candidates' papers for prospective officers and travelling around the Command meeting officers, local officers and youth. Within the first six months these journeys took him as far as Laoag City in northern Luzon by road; and as far south as Iloilo on Panay Island by plane. Our first impressions were that the people in the Philippines seemed most responsive to the message of Christ, although much teaching was needed about the implications of Christianity in daily life.

We attended classes to learn Filipino and these certainly helped us in our ministry around the Manila area. Unfortunately, this provided little help in many other parts of the Philippines where Cebuano, Ilocano, Hiligaynon, Bicolano and Pangasinan were used in Salvation Army meetings. The government was certainly trying to make Filipino the national language together with English, but in rural areas the message was still being communicated in their preferred dialects.

We needed wisdom and good information about where and when we should travel. President Ferdinand Marcos had placed the country under martial law in 1972. In addition to opposition action against the President himself, the Moro National Liberation Movement (Islamist) in Mindanao Island was seeking independence for that island and was prepared to use violence and hostage-taking to achieve this goal. Similarly, the New People's Army (Communist) was seeking to exert influence and gain power in Northern Luzon—Luzon being the island on which Manila and many of our corps were situated. For much of our time in the country, President Ferdinand Marcos placed the country under an overnight curfew, meaning that everyone had to be indoors between 1 am and 4 am. This last restriction was challenging when Ian had to catch early morning inter-island planes to distant parts of the archipelago.

When we were not officially visiting the then five corps around Manila, we attended Quezon City 2 Corps based at Bethany Children's Home nearby in Project Eight, Quezon City. This gave our children an opportunity to mix with children of similar ages who were learning about the Christian life in a secure environment with English as a common medium of communication.

Poverty was common in the Philippines in those years. We were appalled to see small children on the streets begging or offering themselves for prostitution in order to raise money for their families. Any person with a white face, or wearing a uniform similar to the USA forces that helped to provide security to the Philippines, was approached. To counter the situation, The Salvation Army ran family-helper programmes to assist families become self-supporting. Our Bethany Children's Home provided secure accommodation for some abandoned or orphaned children and those whose families could not cope financially.

Very early in our appointment, Lieut-Colonel Nancy Hulett indicated that General and Mrs Clarence Wiseman would be visiting the Command to conduct congress meetings in May 1976. In connection with the congress, the youth department was asked to produce a musical for presentation on the Saturday night. The Gowans and Larsson musical 'Jesus Folk' seemed to be appropriate and within the capabilities of the Command. This would be the first full-scale musical ever produced by the Army in the Philippines. So before Christmas 1975 was over, preparations were well underway. Early in 1976, Ian commenced Saturday morning rehearsals at Manila Central Corps. The number of Salvationist youth in Manila was not large and there were more young women than young men. Further, to our disappointment, we discovered that some school and college classes took place on Saturdays. Compulsory military training was scheduled on Saturdays *and* Sundays for those in their final years of high school and at college level. All these factors created serious problems for integrated youth programmes of any description, let alone a musical.

We managed to assemble a cast of 35, including several corps officers and older Salvationists from around the Metro Manila area, with piano and brass sextet backing. Eventually we put on the production of a slightly shortened version on the Congress Saturday night. Mrs Captain Beulah Pacey (piano), Captain Robert Saunders (brass) and Grace Rodriguera (choreography and makeup) gave invaluable help to Ian, who acted as both producer and conductor. All the songs had to be taught by ear, as very few of the group were able to read music. Having vinyl LP (33 rpm) records of the Melbourne Australia, and the United Kingdom productions, helped when the musicians—many of whom were officers with busy appointments requiring travel outside of Manila—could not attend rehearsals. The participants' excellent abilities to hear a piece and then sing harmoniously, their enthusiasm, and desire to share their faith more than compensated for any lack of music-reading ability. The group had frequently prayed together that souls would be won for Jesus. After a brief appeal by General Wiseman at the conclusion of the performance, over 100 people joined the cast on the stage as an indication of their desire to be 'Jesus folk' in the truest sense of those words. Undoubtedly, all the efforts put in were worthwhile. This was confirmed on the following Saturday afternoon when, at the conclusion of a repeat performance, a further eight people made similar decisions.

Nurturing our Salvationist young people, youth, candidates, and officers were high priorities for us. We were involved in preparing more Sunday school lesson material and associated visual teaching tools. A live-in institute for candidates and the Future Officers Fellowship (FOF) members at the School for Officer Training (SFOT) was helpful in encouraging commitment toward officership. Each year we needed to distribute materials for the daily vacation Bible schools which were held in all corps during the school summer vacation in April and May. The youth department was also responsible for distributing corps cadet materials and marking lessons. Because we were responsible for advanced training, we also had the responsibility of handling correspondence courses for officers—both those marked in the Philippines and others tutored at the International Training College in London. As youth officer and candidates secretary, Ian needed to process candidates' cases for the group of cadets entering training in July 1976 as well as cases scheduled for 1977. Sonja continued to undertake most of the marking of corps cadet lessons, candidates lessons and advanced training assignments at that time.

Through until March 1976, Ian continued regularly teaching doctrine at SFOT as well as public ministry including public speaking and preaching. He found this to be a most stimulating experience. The cadets wanted to think through the implications of the faith which God called them to proclaim. With increasing pressures of other important commitments, teaching at SFOT had to be left to someone else. We were, however, delighted to conduct a spiritual day at the college later in the year.

Ian became the representative of The Salvation Army on several committees of the National Council of Churches of the Philippines. Such committee work was time-consuming, but useful in providing contacts with senior representatives of other churches. He used the opportunity to clarify for them the Army's positions on evangelism—unashamed and enthusiastic; on politics—strictly not aligned to any party; and on tobacco and alcohol—total abstinence.

As Command Youth Officer, Ian needed to travel to all corps for inspections of youth and children's work in Luzon, Mindoro, Panay, Cebu, and, in later years, to Negros and Mindanao islands. Where possible, he tried to conduct teacher-training seminars to help improve the quality of the teaching amongst the children and youth. He had to organise youth councils in a number of regional areas, too—fewer in 1976 than the normal expectation because of his commitment to 'Jesus Folk' and the regular rehearsals he needed to lead.

The Philippines featured very much in international news during 1976, with typhoons leading to floods in Luzon, and earthquakes in Mindanao. In both situations, The Salvation Army was involved in relief work, earning high praise from government officials. Our personal involvements were largely supportive and organisational. Ian needed to sleep overnight at CHQ on the airbed he normally used for his lunch-time siesta, because the road outside CHQ was flooded on one occasion. At least he could phone home to let Sonja know where he was. Much worse was when he was stranded overnight in his car on a flooded city ring-road just before the General's congress. No mobile phones existed in those days and so he could not contact Sonja to reassure her that he was safe.

We were privileged to be involved in a camp for underprivileged children coming from the social services programmes in the inner suburbs of Manila during August. Ian acted as a camp counsellor and Sonja as a nurse. The weekend camp was held in the Batangas Province in the south-west of Luzon, not far from Taal volcano—fortunately a week or so before it started to erupt once again! Over 300 children attended and really enjoyed the fresh air, sunshine, tent life, competitive games and social interaction. At the conclusion of the Sunday morning meeting more than 70 made decisions for Jesus.

Sonja became more involved in social services as an advisor to the Bethany Children's Home—especially when Mrs Major Josephine Blundell, the wife of the Officer for Social Affairs, was on homeland furlough. During that period Sonja visited one of the prisons with Christmas cheer. As the group was conducting a Christmas service, one of the prisoners offered to sing. She had been an opera singer who had somehow fallen foul of the law. Sonja recalls her rendition of 'O Holy Night' was particularly moving.

Because most of our Salvation Army properties in the Philippines were rented, the lease on the house in which we were living expired a year after we arrived. We were glad to leave the house as it was very compact, and electrical problems meant inordinately high electricity bills. Obviously, we needed to find an alternative. Eventually, we found a suitable house in West Triangle Homes, Quezon City, within walking distance of JASMS so that Sharon and Jenni could continue to attend. That decision came after much prayer and investigations of more than 25 properties. This new quarters had a garden in which the children could play quite securely. Generally their health improved as result. Sonja could teach religious instruction to two grades at JASMS for those children whose parents, like ourselves, did not wish their children to receive Catholic religious lessons. She continued to do so for about two years. This provided worthwhile links with the school, staff, and the children. At that stage, and probably still today, the Philippines is a predominantly Catholic country. The shift of house was completed just before a hectic month of October when three sets of officers councils were held in Pangasinan, North Central Luzon Island; Iloilo, Panay Island; and in Manila. At all of these Ian needed to participate.

As parents, we were obviously concerned about the health and well-being of our children. Sharon developed well and seemed to be adjusting to the school in which she was a student. To our sorrow, we found later that she had been bullied and this grieved us deeply. Nevertheless, she read widely and developed a great love for books. She attended the Quezon City 2 Corps as often as possible, although we found it helpful for her to do her junior soldiers' preparation classes at home with Sonja. Jenni struggled health-wise. Tonsil trouble from the time of our arrival and constant doses of penicillin provided a prelude to removing the offending glands in February at St Luke's Hospital in Quezon City. Having just started to pick up from that, she caught a fungal ear infection. However, with additional vitamin C, and the fresh air and sunshine at our new quarters, she commenced to thrive. Cathy, with two older sisters pioneering the way, seemed to be more adventurous than the other two at that time.

Maintaining good physical health in a tropical country is always challenging. Throughout, we ensured that our inoculations against smallpox, typhoid fever and cholera were up-to-date. We also took malaria prophylactics as we had in Africa. Unfortunately, none of these preventative measures stopped the dengue fever which Ian contracted that was initially diagnosed as typhoid fever—despite the records of our inoculations. That acute viral disease with resulting fever, body aches, and annoying body itch, was transmitted by a bite from a mosquito that was active in daylight rather than at night.

One of the great thrills that year was involvement in securing the Quirino Grandstand in Rizal Park near the Manila Town Hall for a community carols service on Christmas Sunday night. Between 1,500 and 2,000 people sat in the grandstand and many more listened as the music and song presented by the Army was piped throughout the park. Immediately after Christmas, 28 corps cadets joined us for a corps cadet institute at the School for Officer Training.

Ian was still busily involved in representing the Command in a number of areas including the President's Conference on Child Welfare and at various committees of the National Council of Churches. Additionally, he was appointed by the Army to several committees connected with the Billy Graham Crusade to be held late in November 1977. The Salvation Army had been given the responsibility of organising the ushering for the crusade with projected attendances of between 500,000 and one million. Ushers from many churches needed to be enlisted and trained. Some of Ian's time was also spent in being the special representative of the Army's General Secretary, Brigadier Rodolfo Rodriguera, in the matter of training and coordination between the various on-site committees for the Crusade. In addition, both of us trained as counsellors so that we were officially qualified to support those who were making decisions for Christ during the Crusade.

We were thrilled that during 1977 we saw some of our own counselling and follow-up materials for seekers coming into print in booklets in both English and Filipino languages. The ongoing work of translation is always a large one in countries using languages other than English. Lieutenant Fred Salegumba, a former language teacher, was enlisted to make a first draft translation of the newly published edition of *Orders and Regulations for Soldiers*: *Chosen to be a Soldier* into the national language. Based on this draft, Ian chaired a translation committee that tried to more adequately explain the English so that the Filipino would be understandable and would communicate the book's message effectively. We decided a dynamic equivalence translation would be better than a word-for-word approach.

During his time as editor, Ian was delighted to see the circulation of *The War Cry* increasing to 6,000 per edition. The Christmas edition in 1976, featuring earthquake relief in Mindanao, ran to 13,500 copies. In 1977 the equivalent edition with a Christmas Public Relations/Annual Appeal centrefold ran to 22,000 copies. Having to rely on outside printing houses meant that it often took more than a month to progress from manuscript to a final and relatively error-free production. Because Ian was involved in many distant trips out of Manila in connection with youth work, this meant that sometimes the whole process was slowed down. He often took material to edit and proofread while journeying.

Ian enjoyed the trips out of Manila as youth officer. These involved using foot, car, inter-island jet plane, provincial buses and open boat trips on fairly rough seas between islands. He even travelled in an overcrowded jeepney with luggage and people piled on the bonnet and roof as well as being squeezed inside. He was more than gratified that all the corps and officers in the Command were visited within a year and a half of our arrival.

Special events were always interest-builders, but demanded much preparation. For instance, in 1977 we organised the talent quest and a youth congress. The former was held in February in Manila. Dramatic, vocal, instrumental music and Scripture-reading skills were featured. Judges were enlisted from non-Salvation Army schools and colleges. Sharon was delighted when she won the under-nine declamation (elocution) section with the poem 'My Shadow'. At the time her grandmother, Lieut-Colonel Florence Southwell, was visiting the Philippines from Australia and was able to share in the excitement. An even greater thrill for us all was to witness Sharon's enrolment as a junior soldier at Quezon City 2 Corps around the same time.

A youth congress was combined with the 40th anniversary of the Command in 1977 and proved to be a marvellous occasion. We were all delighted to welcome Commissioner Gladys Calliss, an Australian officer, as the special guest. She had inspired both of us in different ways earlier in our lives. The commissioner's service in Indonesia, especially, put her quickly in sympathy with the situation of people in the Philippines. From Wednesday to Saturday the focus was on youth development, with discussions, Bible studies, open-air witnessing, plus sporting and other competitions. Best of all, in the final session on Saturday, 96 of the 350 delegates made special decisions. Anniversary meetings on the Saturday night and the commissioning of cadets on Sunday also provided opportunities for many in the congregation to make decisions to serve the Lord more faithfully in the future.

When we arrived in the Command we were most concerned that the only Filipino officers on the staff of Command Headquarters (CHQ) were Brigadiers Rodolfo and Mrs Vivian Rodriguera. From our experience in Africa, we realised how important it was for national leadership to be ready to take over the administrative leadership of departments in any territorial or command headquarters. So Ian drew up a scheme whereby promising couples who were corps officers could be assigned to CHQ for a six-month apprenticeship-style of training. This proposal was agreed by the new Officer Commanding, Lieut-Colonel Ingrid Lindberg, and International Headquarters. Captains Jose and Thelma Aguirre, then corps officers at Manila Central Corps, were the first couple appointed to this special course. They were assigned to work alongside each of the main heads of departments at CHQ for between two weeks and a month, sharing the work, and learning all they could about each department and how they operated. Academic courses at a nearby school of business, practical experiences and inspection tours, attending board meetings, preparing *The War Cry* for printing and organising special events were included in their training. Following that course, the Aguirres took charge of Cebu Central, the largest corps in the Command, to reflect on and put into practice what they had learned. Captains Remigio and Teodoro Lacambra took the Aguirres' place in the course. Within two years we hoped that four couples would have the experience, thus preparing them for possibility of wider responsibilities in the future.

Training in one form or another is always considered essential for the ongoing work of The Salvation Army. We were delighted to be involved again in teaching one or two classes at the SFOT during 1977 and conducting in-Sunday meetings.

Sonja's workload increased with the number of corps cadets rising from 95 to 140 and all the lieutenants doing their first post-commissioning study in the Philippines, rather than sending these to the International Training College in London for marking. She became the chief tutor for both courses. Recent growth in interest in the Nurses Fellowship, of which she was the secretary, widened her ministry in that field also. In addition, she continued her work of preparing activity sheets for Sunday schools and her teaching of Christian education at JASMS. Sonja served as secretary of the Future Officers Fellowship and wrote occasional articles for *The War Cry* including a regular column entitled 'Through my window'. Fortunately, most of her weekday work could be done at home so as to keep good control there, particularly when Ian was away on tour or at lengthy evening committee meetings.

Sadly, toward the end of 1977, changes started to occur in the curriculum of JASMS with more Filipino language subjects being introduced. We commenced to look around for alternative schools for Sharon and Jenni. Cathy could still survive in the kindergarten environment for a time.

Increasingly, we were grateful for the support given by Salvationists in other countries through the Self Denial Appeal, part of which was channelled to the Command as grant aid. Other individual donations made by kind family members, friends and our territory's Missionary Fellowship all helped to support our work.

The plans for the Billy Graham Crusade went through well, although the crowds were considerably less than expected—the maximum attendances ranging between 50,000 and about 200,000. The number of volunteer ushers was proportionately smaller, creating quite a few problems as well. However, it was a thrill to be involved in counselling and advising a few of the many seekers who responded to the invitation to accept Christ during the five meetings held in Rizal Park. As always, Billy Graham gave excellent messages pointing the way to the Lord Jesus Christ.

One new feature Ian undertook was organising the Command Music Camp. In contrast with previous music camps conducted by Captain Robert Saunders, which emphasised brass, this one was designed to encourage string, vocal and timbrel playing as well. Stringed instruments were very popular in the Philippines, reflected in the fact that 54 delegates enrolled for string instruction on guitar, ukulele and bandurria—the last named being a lute or guitar type of instrument with six pairs of double strings. Colonisation of these islands by the Spanish from 1521 till 1896 probably led to introducing this range of stringed instruments. Local Salvationists with skills in these instruments willingly gave support to the campers as instructors. As a result, more string bands developed within the Command in the following years.

During 1978, the activities outlined earlier continued at even a greater pace. Lieut-Colonel Lindberg invited Ian to present the subject 'Holiness in Church and Army traditions', plus a session on intercessory prayer at the Brengle Institute for officers early in 1978—the first such institute to be held since 1970. Preparing for this assignment was a wonderful stimulus to read about the life of holiness in depth and develop a model of a multifaceted approach to the doctrine of holiness. In his sessions, Ian pointed out that being holy, sanctified, having a clean heart, being filled with the Spirit, and anointed with the Spirit, were all different descriptions of the same experience of Christlikensss.

Following a well-earned and restful furlough in the coolness of Baguio, some 1,500 metres (5,000 feet) above sea level, we were given new appointments as the Training Officers in charge in succession to

Captains Robert and Carol Saunders who were returning to the USA with their children. Ian still maintained responsibility for literature and post-commissioning studies. The experiences of being the Training Officer in charge in Zambia in 1973–75 and teaching at SFOT during our time in the Philippines made the transition fairly easy. Attending the 1974 International Training Principals Conference in London also provided excellent preparation. How we enjoyed being involved in training 13 enthusiastic 'Proclaimers of Salvation' who commenced their session in July 1978, and the company of three 'Joyful Evangelists' who returned from summer field training assignments for their second year at SFOT! We were well supported by Mrs Captain Elizabeth Manano as Field Training Officer and Lieutenant Jaime Macayana as the Home Officer, cashier and brigade officer. They provided us with a mixture of enthusiasm, experience and expertise necessary for the work. Sonja taught Bible and Army procedure. Ian recommenced teaching doctrine, homiletics, pastoral counselling, Christian education, English, and united singing. Of course he also coordinated the total process and programme. Not long after we were appointed, Jaime married Lieutenant Lilia Agustin and she joined the team as a brigade officer.

We felt a great sense of satisfaction when, in the latter part of the year, recently promoted Major Remigio Lacambra was appointed as Assistant General Secretary. Captain Jose Aguirre had become the Command Youth Officer in Ian's place. This meant that at least two Filipino couples were now serving at CHQ, in addition to the General Secretary and his wife as a result of the course Ian designed.

An evangelism institute held at SFOT early in the session helped to focus the cadets' attention on the Army's major task—taking the Gospel to people everywhere. We led them through a number of experiments. One was to try to set up an evangelistic outreach, similar to a Billy Graham Crusade, at Cubao, Metro-Manila. We had plenty of empty seats, because no-one attended! So we went back and studied the Acts of the Apostles and how the early Church grew. In most cases, we discovered, planting and growth came about through house groups and house churches. So we asked the cadets if they knew of people who would host such a group with a room available where we could commence a house group as the focal point for a new outreach. Two cadets did. Following further prayerful consideration and enquiries, we moved to commence a society—a smaller type of outpost—at Guadalupe. Through their involvement in this outreach centre, the cadets learned first-hand how to develop the skills needed for planting new corps in the future as well as practising their preaching, teaching, pastoring and visitation skills. As a result, Guadalupe Society was established and local officers appointed. Finding a building other than the house in which the society started was a problem that took some time to overcome. However, eventually the Guadalupe Society became the Makati Corps—although not during the years that we were in the Philippines.

Provincial hospital conditions in the Philippines often fell far short of Australian standards. Patients sometimes shared beds, for instance. Before he left the local hospital, newborn baby Joel Macayana, the first child of Lieutenants Jaime and Lilia Macayana, contracted a serious infection—possibly golden staph. Rather than keeping him there and possibly infecting others, he was sent home to the SFOT. Lieutenant Lilia knew Sonja was a qualified nursing sister, so Sonja gave him his daily injections to clear the infection. The risks of returning Joel to the hospital for injections were deemed to be too great—especially when we had a nurse on staff. Joel survived and thrived.

The cadets had previously demonstrated their enthusiasm to share their faith by counselling seekers during The Salvation Army carols service at Rizal Park in December 1978 which Ian led, and also at an ecumenical Easter service in April 1979. Many seekers were also recorded during their campaigns in February.

Salvation Army officers need to be ready for anything. On 14 September 1978, Ian received a phone call from Lieut-Colonel Lindberg indicating that an aeroplane had crashed into a residential area near Manila International Airport. Would the cadets please investigate and provide whatever assistance they could? Regular classes at SFOT were abandoned for the next few days. The cadets and staff ministered with food, comfort and counselling to those in the barrio (district) in which the propeller-driven Fokker aircraft had crashed during a heavy rainstorm. Their efforts were deeply appreciated by the residents, many of whom had lost houses and loved ones. Those few days provided practical lessons in caring ministry that could not have been gained from a textbook.

Eventually the three 'Joyful Evangelist' cadets, Mario Apelo, Jessie Barayoga and Blesselda Corpuz (nicknamed the ABC cadets), were commissioned as lieutenants in April 1979. Twelve cadets of the 'Proclaimers of Salvation' session completed their first year of training and received practical out-training placements. We were able to develop an effective vocal group, a well-balanced string band and a pageant entitled 'The training of an evangelist' for the commissioning events. The pageant recalled the fact that Salvation Army officer training operations commenced 100 years before in England.

Whilst, in many ways, we would have liked to have remained in the Philippines for at least another two years, a visit from the new Zonal International Secretary for our region from IHQ, Commissioner George Nelting, indicated that the only options were for us to either serve for another four years or return home—even though we had already completed a five-year term in Zambia. We were concerned that another four years would make it more challenging for Sharon, especially, to settle into school in Australia. She was now approaching high school level. We felt blessed that after our appointment to SFOT she and Jenni had been able to transfer to Faith Academy, a school for missionary children, with a USA-based curriculum. However, this was not really ideal, in our opinion, for eventual transition back to Australia. We also felt some of the national officers may have resented the fact our children attended such a school. While we received financial support in paying the prescribed fees at Faith Academy, they were not. We were already finding some challenges in attending the nearby Filipino-speaking Pasig Corps when not sharing in the field work of the cadets. This corps used no English in its worship and had no translators. So we accepted the fact that it was probably best for us to return to Australia at the end of our term of four very fulfilling years in the Philippines in July 1979.

We learned our successors, Captains John and Pamela Hodge and their children, would not be able to come to the Philippines before the end of the year. When we realised that our scheduled departure in July would mean that either the officer commanding or the general secretary would have to live at SFOT to provide personal supervision, we prayerfully offered to stay on until November. Lieut-Colonel Lindberg gratefully accepted our offer. This four-month extension meant we would be able to prepare in a better way for the arrival of the new training principal and his wife who were coming from the Australia Eastern Territory. It also meant our arrival would fit in with the general change of officers in our territory and the commencement of the new school year for our children.

Ian was glad to be able to return to CHQ the files connected to *The War Cry* so that the wife of the general secretary, Mrs Major Barbara Johnson, was able to take over the editorial role until the end of 1979. All the other activities and representations in which we were involved on various councils and similar groups continued.

We rejoiced in the leadership given by Officer Commanding Lieut-Colonel Ingrid Lindberg, and new General Secretary Major Ronald Johnson and Command Home League Secretary Mrs Major Barbara Johnson. During those four months they convened a stewardship consultation of national officers to set visions and prepare strategies to achieve faith goals for future developments. Ian presented a paper on the Army's place/role in the Philippines.

Growing out of his observations and involvement over the last four years, Ian's paper emphasised soul-saving, outreach to the unchurched, and a positive witness to the life of holiness, including total abstinence from anything which would pollute our bodies—God's temple. He pointed out that Salvationists needed to witness that ritualism is not necessary for salvation or holiness, and that women and men equally have the right and responsibility to proclaim the Gospel. Ian emphasised that we need to care for the poor; and also demonstrate that the Christian life is one of joy now and in eternity because physical death is not the end. To do that, every soldier needs to be encouraged and trained to be a soul-winner. We need to take risks by doing new things. Officers need to plan joyful meetings, as well as preaching, teaching and living a holy life. He suggested that new corps only be registered as such when they are financially self-supporting so funds can be channelled to new openings.

What a delight it was to learn that in the next 10 years or so after that event enough corps were planted to allow the Command to be redesignated as a Territory.

Toward the end of those four months, Sonja was hospitalised with a severe attack of haemorrhagic fever—a syndrome due to dengue fever. Her white blood cell count was very low and grave fears were held for her survival. On top of that, Jenni shared the same hospital room while also suffering from a serious viral infection, but probably not dengue haemorrhagic fever. We were very conscious of prayer support from friends in Australia and elsewhere to whom we telegraphed details of their conditions. We constantly thank God for their recovery.

We left the Philippines with a wonderful sense of fulfilment and great joy, having been able to serve the Lord there at that time—despite the traumas of the final month. What the future held for us was by no means certain, but we were confident that the God who had guided us thus far would continue to lead us safely on for further service.

Chapter 10

Back in Australia: Hawthorn and Hobart, 1980–85

Hawthorn 1980–81

After 10 years away from corps or other appointments in Australia, we faced significant challenges in returning to ministry in our homeland after all our adventures in Zambia and the Philippines. We experienced significant reverse culture shock in returning from situations of financial deprivation to relative affluence—from places where food supplies were scarce to being spoilt for choice. Yet, we believed this move was the right thing to do, especially for our girls' schooling and cultural adjustments at that time.

The Army graciously gave us two months furlough from late November 1979 through until January 1980 at the unoccupied quarters belonging to the Malvern Corps, in Union Road, Armadale. Sharon, Jenni and Cathy were able to have six weeks of schooling at Armadale Primary before the school holidays commenced. What a contrast to come to a traditional red-brick school in Victoria with schoolmates having fair skin and Australian accents! By the middle of January we needed to move to the quarters of the Hawthorn Citadel Corps a little further north than Malvern, but still in the eastern part of Melbourne where our leaders had appointed us as the corps officers.

Hawthorn Citadel Corps was a large corps of some 300 soldiers and had been in existence for some 96 years. Its band, songster and timbrel brigades were well known for their musical excellence, and its uniform-wearing standards were amongst the highest in the Territory. The corps had been blessed with solid local officer leadership for many years. Our children commenced to enjoy a full programme of young people's activities offered by the young people's corps led by Young People's Sergeant-Major Carolyn Everett. Sonja also revelled in the home league (women's ministry) and especially seeing new members being attracted during the course of the year. It was both exciting and challenging to have a regular congregation for pastoral care and preaching week by week, with two public meetings on a Sunday. We rejoiced in promising signs of future development through the commencement of small groups using a series of Bible studies prepared for the centenary year of The Salvation Army in Australia.

Following their brief transitional experience at Armadale Primary School, our children were also glad to be able to settle into regular primary schooling in Australia at Auburn Road Primary School. Ian also taught two classes of religious instruction there each week according to the Agreed Syllabus drawn up by the Council for Christian Education in Schools. This allowed approved teachers from various denominations to present standard Christian education material at the different grade levels at schools, rather than each teacher deciding on their own curriculum such as working through the Gospel of Mark or the Gospel of Luke as Ian had experienced as a primary school student.

Aside from regular corps activities, Sonja accompanied the young people's corps (Sunday school) to Millicent in South Australia for a weekend. She was also a popular speaker at women's meetings around the metropolitan area—especially when describing some of our work in Zambia and the Philippines. Ian accompanied the songster brigade on an Easter weekend tour to Wollongong, New South Wales. This Easter event was led by the then Major Ian Cutmore, Training Principal in the Australia Eastern Territory, supported by some cadets. On the return journey south along the Hume Highway, the car in which he was travelling with Dell and Rex Harvey had a blowout. Dell was driving and, despite her best efforts, the car skidded around onto the median strip between the left and right hand carriageways and finished up facing the opposite direction. If no median strip had been in place on the dual carriageway, the car could very well have landed in the path of oncoming vehicles travelling north and we may all have been seriously injured or killed. Again, Ian was very conscious that the Lord was guiding and protecting not only him but also the other occupants. As Ian Cutmore later reflected when Ian told him what had happened, 'The Lord must still have things for you to do.' How right he was!

Back in Melbourne, Ian was involved as a representative of The Salvation Army at the Victorian Council of Churches on the Faith and Order Commission. With the permission of territorial leaders, he contributed 'Salvation Army' chapters in two books published by the Commission over the next few years, namely *Marriage in the Australian Churches* (1982) and *Initiation in the Australia Churches* (1984). He spoke at a number of service clubs about the work of The Salvation Army internationally.

With 1980 being the Centenary year of The Salvation Army in Australia many corps activities were directed toward reminding all concerned about the commencement and development of the Army in this land. Several events stand out in our memories. The first was the joyous flag-waving opening celebration at the Melbourne City Temple when the flags from all corps and social service centres in Melbourne and the immediate surrounds swept into the building behind the Hawthorn flag carried by Colour Sergeant Rodney O'Neill.

Our own civic service was helpful in developing relationships with civic authorities and groups of volunteers involved in the Red Shield Appeal. The Mayor of Hawthorn and representative councillors received the Centenary Charter, and endorsed our work.

The corps anniversary that year was led by Lieut-Commissioner and Mrs Frank Saunders, Captains Robert and Mrs Carol Saunders, Major and Mrs Neil Saunders and Mrs Captain Olwyn Avery. These good people not only provided links to the early days of the movement—for the Commissioner was a grandson of the pioneers—but served to renew our links with Robert and Carol Saunders, with whom we served in the Philippines in 1975–77.

Of course, the Centenary Congress in Adelaide was the climactic celebration. Over 10,000 local and visiting Salvationists gathered under the leadership of General Arnold Brown to give praise to God for the first 100 years of Salvation Army service in Australia. Events ranged from the Holy Spirit-directed opening prayer meetings through to joyful marches of witness, civic recognitions, brilliant musical festivals and tattoos, soul-stirring rallies, effective Sunday meetings and deeply challenging officers councils. The Hawthorn Corps musical forces—band, songsters, timbrels and drum corps—were all featured in the public events and made great impressions. A great rally on the Sunday afternoon was held at the Adelaide Cricket Ground. Throughout the Congress, many fresh consecrations were made, as well as quite a few first-time decisions being registered. Having officers and soldiers from both Australian territories together for the first time in living memory meant that we could sense something of the nationwide impact the Army in 1980, mutually encouraging each other in the Lord to further witness for Jesus in this land of then a mere 14 million people. We were particular thrilled to meet Cadet Alex Genabe who attended as a delegate from the Philippines. He had been one of our first-year cadets just before we left to return to Australia. We were able to have him share his testimony in a Sunday morning at Hawthorn before returning to his homeland.

The Christmas carols event was always a feature at Hawthorn Citadel, generating huge interest amongst corps members and the wider community. We also had regular links with Salvation Army social service centres around the area, including the nearby Lyndon Lodge for young men, and Allenby Lodge for women, then situated next door to our Salvation Army hall.

We have always been keen to raise the profile of The Salvation Army in any area to which we were appointed. Hawthorn Citadel building used to house the East Melbourne Divisional Headquarters as well as the corps. When we arrived at Hawthorn, the sign on the western side of the building indicated that it was still the 'divisional headquarters', even though that function had now moved to the Camberwell Corps building near the Camberwell Junction in Burke Road. Eventually, Ian secured permission from the corps council and the Hawthorn City Council to have a new sign placed on the western side of the building. Designed by Peter Connor, the words were simply 'Jesus cares'. We felt the words encapsulated the message of the Gospel and the mission of corps. The sign adorned the building for many years until well after the Hawthorn Citadel Corps left to move to Waverley and the building was sold to Swinburne College which had its main campus on the opposite side of Burwood Road to the hall.

Corps Sergeant-Major Gordon O'Neill had indicated to Ian on a number of occasions in 1980 that he was interested in retiring, but nobody seemed willing to take his place. Ian believed that a change would be of benefit to the corps, especially because there were now ideas of moving the location of the corps from Hawthorn to either Doncaster or Waverley. Divisional leaders were recommending a new site in High Street Road, Waverley. Most soldiers and adherents of the corps lived in one of those two areas, with very few living in Hawthorn. Because Gordon and his wife Jean resided in Hawthorn, quite close to the present citadel, they were very reluctant to support any move. Eventually, Ian gained the support of divisional leaders and sufficient of the corps census board members to make a change. He arranged a worthy retirement service for Gordon O'Neill led by the Territorial Commander, Commissioner Arthur Linnett.

Allen and Cheril Dewhirst were Salvationists from South Africa and relative newcomers to the corps. They lived in Doncaster. Ian proposed that Allen be installed as the new corps sergeant-major, and this occurred in February 1981. Allen came from a strong business and logistics background. He was able to sharpen procedures in many ways and help the corps move forward. Ian and Allen arranged for a survey of members in 1981 to see how much support there was to move the corps from its current location to a new area. That survey did not lead to a decisive recommendation at the time, but certainly prompted ongoing debate, analysis and reflection. The best decision in 1981 was to remain in Hawthorn for the time being. After we left, and Hawthorn celebrated its centenary in 1984, the corps moved to High Street Road, Waverley, when Captains Des and Margaret Veale were the officers.

The year 1981 was—as it is on many occasions in the second year of a ministry—something of a 'storm' year. Serious disagreements surfaced. Not everyone wanted the corps to move to another location. Although all the members of the drum corps wore uniform, not all of them were soldiers and some rationalisation was needed. Little support could be gained for Ian's vision of forming pastoral care cells so every corps member was part of such a supportive cell group.

We also realised that a number of names on our corps roll were 'inactive' soldiers. Holding census boards (pastoral care councils) every month helped us develop strategies to contact these people and see if they still desired to be Salvation Army soldiers. Had they had moved to other churches, or moved away entirely from the Lord? Our aim was to restore them to the fellowship of the corps if at all possible. However, the members of the census board and the divisional commander were reluctant to remove any names, so the roll probably stayed inflated. In these days of longer corps appointments, it would have been best to leave such a move until the third or fourth year—but appointments for more than two or three years were relatively rare in those years. If any action was to be taken, it probably needed to take place in 1981.

On a more positive note, a number of young people and a few older ones stepped up to become soldiers (full members). Local officers were appointed and each senior local officer encouraged to train an assistant so a succession of good local leaders could be maintained. We also installed a Salvation Army flag on the tower of the Hawthorn Citadel Corps, plus a set of lights controlled by a timing device to illuminate it at night. We also encouraged some soldiers to join us in the work of '*War Cry* evangelism'—taking copies of *The War Cry* to hotels in the district on a Friday night. Ian emphasised that the aim of the activity was not primarily to raise funds but to develop links with the patrons and provide spiritual or material assistance as appropriate. Money still came in, however. Because we were seeking first God's kingdom and his righteousness, we believed that the needed finances flowed to the corps (Matthew 6:33).

During this appointment, we came to realise that a number of Salvationists had become involved with Freemasonry while others had confused ideas about it. Many thought there was little difference between Freemasonry and a service club such as Rotary, especially because there seemed to be strong religious elements present. A few officers were still members and a cadet assigned to our next corps for practical out-training had become unfinancial to 'cover up' his membership during training. In the light of these anomalies and misunderstandings, Ian commenced some in-depth research on the topic over the next four years in order to provide helpful guidance to any who were members or considered becoming involved. As a result, he was able to present a lecture to cadets on the topic from 1985–91, 1994–97 and 2008–13. He pointed out some of the many problems faced by a Christian involved in a religious movement: in which Jesus is never mentioned when he is the only way to salvation;

that deliberately avoids the name of Jesus in its formal prayers; in which the Bible is placed on the same level as the Koran and other volumes of religious teaching—even in Australia; and which has as its ultimate aim the discovery of the 'secret name of God'—a name that combines that of the God and Father of our Lord Jesus Christ with Babylonian and Egyptian gods. [28]

Looking back over those two years, we now regret that we did not work to appoint an employee to act as a social welfare officer. Many needy people came to our quarters or to the hall seeking community welfare support. The corps could probably have afforded to pay for such a worker, but corps employees were relatively rare in the 1980s. Having also served in fairly deprived situations overseas, we were reluctant to spend too much money at all.

In the last few months of our term, some serious interpersonal relationship problems arose between certain families in the corps. The whole situation brought much grief to all concerned. Certain disciplinary action was needed and the divisional commander followed this through. As the corps officers, our role was pastoral.

We would have hoped to have stayed on into 1982 in order to help and provide ongoing pastoral care to the families involved and sort out some other challenges in the corps. Certainly, some new local officers were needed urgently and we managed to appoint these. In the event, our Army leaders determined that we should have change appointment and, in December, we received news that we were appointed to the Hobart Citadel Corps in Tasmania from January. Captains Reg and Pat Skelton would take our place. We left with heavy hearts, feeling our work was not quite finished. But God knew best and he was guiding. Eventually, we would rejoice in the opportunities at Hobart.

Hobart 1982–85

The year we arrived started with a rush of activity. On the day that schools resumed, the corps commenced a planned giving (stewardship) renewal programme with Captain Des Veale from Territorial Headquarters.

---

[28] The latest version of this paper *Engaging With Freemasonry* (2014), is available from the author on request at ian_southwell@yahoo.co.uk.

By the afternoon of that day, bushfires within 25 km of Hobart were burning out of control and racing toward the city's northern environs fanned by a strong northerly wind. As the smoke and smell of burning eucalyptus trees spread through the city, fear was palpable. Could Hobart be facing the same type of disaster that it experienced in 1967 when many lives were lost and homes destroyed? For the next four days, Ian's major role was coordinating a team of 44 relief workers who gave 750 hours of service and provided 735 hot meals, 4,000 sandwiches and 2,500 drinks—all of which were appreciated by the teams of weary firefighters who eventually controlled the fires. Little wonder that in the months ahead, Ian was involved with the disaster management programme for southern Tasmania.

The physical setting of our accommodation in Hobart was magnificent. Our quarters, in Forest Road, West Hobart, was on a hill about 120 m above sea level and overlooking a 2 km wide stretch of the Derwent River along which Hobart is built. Behind us was Mount Wellington, towering some 1,270 m and snow-capped for many months in the year, particularly May to September. We even experienced snowfalls around our quarters—quite a change after the years in the heat and humidity of Zambia and the Philippines. How exciting for our girls to handle real snow—a phenomenon about which they had only heard or read.

Although the corps was somewhat smaller numerically than Hawthorn, the spirit of the members was excellent. A fine team of local officers was headed by CSM Tony Foster who insisted on meeting Ian for lunch every Wednesday to discuss corps affairs and pray together. We rejoiced at a number of seekers during the year—some of whom became soldiers. Prayer and Bible study were considered to be important and there were many small group fellowships. Being directly associated with a divisional centre brought extra demands and Ian represented the Army at the Rotary Club of Hobart Town, the regional committee of the State Emergency Service, and the Tasmanian Council of Churches Faith and Order Commission. Other opportunities included special service such as broadcasting on a Christian FM radio station in Hobart. Our training at Salvation Studio in Zambia proved to be especially useful.

Sonja was busy looking after the growing family as well as the presidency of the local women's ministries including home league, women's fellowship, and morning coffee fellowship. She represented the Army on the Women's World Day of Prayer committee and was involved in visitation, meeting leadership, address preparation, and all the other activities of a busy corps officer.

As was common in the 1950s to 1990s, Sunday night salvation meetings were held weekly. Full corps participation was expected, with band, songsters and even young people attending. We felt it was very important to provide an opportunity for evangelical outreach, especially for holidaymakers who would come to Hobart and might look for a church to attend at least once on a Sunday. Few other evangelical churches seemed to have a Sunday evening service—concentrating more on an all-inclusive family service in the mornings. Our Sunday night services provided a good opportunity for outreach and also spiritual support for visitors. Occasionally naval personnel, or cruise ship passengers who were visiting Hobart, or others would attend. These gatherings were not always staid and serious. One night Ian was preaching on the feast of Belshazzar and the writing on the wall (Daniel 5:1–30). In his address, he asked the rhetorical question 'What will wipe out the writing on the wall?' A quiet voice amidst the youth present was heard to murmur, 'Liquid paper'—resulting in a burst of laughter among those nearby.

The Hobart Corps building site was L-shaped. The main corps hall faced Liverpool Street and the young people's corps building faced Harrington Street. On the corner was the Shamrock Hotel. Not long after we arrived, a vacant building in Harrington Street near the young people's hall was purchased for The Black Rose Sex Shop. Corps comrades were horrified. We immediately commenced to lobby for the change of use to be prohibited. Ian even went to the Planning Appeal Board to protest. He argued that alcohol-affected clients from the hotel who used the shop could pose a threat to our young people. While we gained some positive publicity for protesting, and the Planning Appeal Board members listened politely, they determined that there was nothing the Board could do. One commercial venture had been taken over by another. All we could do was to pray for the protection of our young and the conversion of the clients.

The normal busy corps programme was supplemented by preparations for the corps centenary celebrations in 1983. Committees were formed to plan numerous special events. Corps members were praying for new seekers and new soldiers as the result of the special efforts. In anticipation of great things happening from God, we ran at least one series of mercy seat counsellor training and planned to repeat this in later months and into 1983 just before the climax weekends.

Each division holds annual officers' fellowship retreats. In 1982 the fellowship series was in held in July. The Holy Spirit came very near as we studied God's Word and prayed together. Major Richard Guy, the Divisional Commander, invited Ian to speak about his concept of the multifaceted nature of the experience of holiness. God blessed that evening session with a significant moving of the Holy Spirit. Was this to be our special ministry as it was for one of Ian's heroes, Samuel Logan Brengle? Certainly, as result of that presentation, we were invited to conduct a holiness seminar at the New Norfolk Corps later that year and at other corps in the following years. God was indeed preparing us for a special ministry in the decades ahead.

Sharon and Jenni settled into Ogilvie Girls High School in New Town; and Cathy into Forest Hill Primary School just down the hill from our quarters. Having had pet dogs in Zambia and the Philippines, we eventually obtained an Irish setter named Shaun. He served as a companion and, if needed, protection for the children. The girls also acquired a white mouse, appropriately named Squeaky.

As planned, 1983 was a year full of excitement and activity building up to a climax in November and December as the corps celebrated its centenary. In January, we held a thanksgiving service at St David's Cathedral, Hobart, to mark the commencement of the 100th year. The event was planned by Corps Secretary Robert Mourant and Ian in cooperation with divisional staff and the centenary committee. The dean of the cathedral, the Very Rev Jeffrey Parsons, conducted the service, with Colonel William Roberts, the Army's Chief Secretary, as guest speaker. The State Governor, Sir James Plimsoll, the Lord Mayor of Hobart, Alderman Douglas Plaister, members of parliament, heads of armed forces and representatives of most churches were present for this excellent start to our celebrations. Prior to the service commencing, the corps comrades marched from the Elizabeth Street Mall to the cathedral with full police and civic cooperation. This was in dramatic contrast to the early days of The Salvation Army in Hobart during which Salvationists were imprisoned for marching in the streets and conducting open-air meetings.

In February we were visited by a modern music group called 'Crossroad' from Melbourne. Their rhythms and Christian witness challenged our youth and the wider community to which they ministered.

In March we journeyed to Launceston for the State Congress marking the Centenary of the Army in Tasmania. Launceston and Hobart commenced a month apart in 1883, becoming the 33rd and 34th corps in Australia, respectively. Three weeks later, Hobart Corps held a community festival at the historic Anglesea Barracks in Hobart. Many community groups took part in conjunction with our corps sections. The climax was a recital by the Sixth Military District Band, Moonah Corps Band, and Hobart Citadel Band. We also had our first links with The Philippine Cultural Society which performed several traditional dances at the festival. The members of that society were delighted to find that we had lived in the Philippines and could greet them in Filipino.

Easter time brought a visit by the Newton Citadel Band from New Zealand. Their music was excellent. Best of all, a school friend brought to the meetings by our daughter Sharon made her decision for Christ on Easter Sunday night. By early 1984, Debbie had been enrolled as a soldier.

Sonja's parents visited us in late April and who better to lead the Anzac remembrance service than Colonel Garnet Palmer. As previously mentioned, he had served as a Salvation Army welfare officer and senior representative in the Middle East during the Second World War.

After much discussion and prayer over almost a year, the corps decided to buy an 18-seat bus to transport children to Sunday school and adults to meetings. Within a fortnight an outstanding second-hand bus became available at a reasonable price. A non-Salvationist contact from the centenary Cathedral service with an appropriate drivers' licence offered his services as a bus driver, subsequently making his personal decision for Christ. In June, our family attended The Philippine Independence Day celebrations organised by The Philippine Cultural Society, and Ian was one of the guest speakers.

In May we were involved in our first ecumenical Pentecost event. Following the successful centenary Cathedral service, Ian was invited to be a member of the organising committee. Brief services were held commencing at 2.30 pm in Wesley Uniting Church, St David's Anglican Cathedral, St Joseph's Roman Catholic Church, St John's Presbyterian Church, and The

Salvation Army Hobart Corps. Then the congregations walked to Franklin Square for a 3 pm service of celebration and thanksgiving for the coming of the Holy Spirit, and for our unity in Christ. Refreshments were provided at St David's Anglican Cathedral Centre.

Throughout the months of 1983, the members of the Hobart, Moonah and Howrah Corps were involved in preparation for the Gowans and Larsson musical 'Glory'. This musical was based around the events that took place during the commencement of The Salvation Army in seaside Folkstone, England, as related in Edward Joy's book *The Old Corps*. As such, the musical seemed especially relevant for presentation during the centenary of the commencement of a corps in the port city of Hobart. Ian accepted a cameo role as 'Mayor Crook' who incited a group which would become a 'skeleton army' to attack and exterminate the fledgling corps. 'Drive them into the harbour or else into hell! Take their blessèd flag and tie it around their necks and hang 'em!'[29] Nine months of rehearsals led to three public decisions following the performance and one other seeker—a stage hand—on the Sunday before. Perhaps more would have responded on the night if Ian had changed out of his 'Mayor Crook' costume before giving the invitation to unsaved attendees to accept Christ. We were especially delighted to be able to enrol Sharon as a Salvation Army soldier in that month of August, too.

Sonja attended the inter-territorial Brengle Institute in Melbourne in August and September 1983 and found it to be a spiritual highlight. Following a brief furlough, Ian flew to Melbourne to teach classes in doctrine, world religions–Islam, and Old Testament at the biennial refresher course for officers. Cadets Peter and Lyn Lindstrom, and their daughter Jane, joined us for part of their training to be officers during a three-month period. They worked well and seemed to enjoy the opportunities presented.

Well-known Australian Salvation Army composer, Captain Howard Davies, was the special guest for a musicians weekend in October. His visit was a stimulus to the corps musicians. Unfortunately, Ian was only present for part of the weekend as he and Jenni had caught a virus which resulted in them both contracting pneumonia. Sonja's nursing skills were pressed into service caring for them both. Five weeks off duty and a further two

[29] John Gowans and John Larsson, *Glory* (London, Salvationist Publishing and Supplies, 1977), p 91.

weeks of part-time work were needed for Ian to overcome the ill health he experienced. We praised God for a complete recovery—but Ian had to learn some lessons. In retrospect, he realised that he had lost as many days away from active service as he had not taken at least one day off per week. Our bodies need to follow biblical principles!

Because of the good committee work during 1982 and the first nine months of the 1983 by a fine team of local officers led by CSM Tony Foster and the Centenary Planning Committee Secretary, Bandmaster Kevin Mansfield, the run-up to the centenary climax in December was smooth despite Ian's enforced absence. We were thrilled to see parents of new Sunday school children attending the excellent young people's anniversary which was a feature of the first weekend led by Majors Carl and Val Schmidtke. The Schmidtkes were former officers at Hobart. On the second weekend of December, Commissioner Eva Burrows, Territorial Commander, was the guest for the final celebration weekend. Events included a civic reception, Friday lunch-hour march of witness and open-air meeting, corps dinner, musical festival, and outstanding Sunday meetings at which two young people and one adult were seekers.

In an entry in his prayer journal dated 23/11/83 after his period of ill health and the centenary celebrations, Ian wrote: 'Prepared to spend all of (my) active service in corps work if this was God's plan (as) evangelist, pastor, teacher, encourager, administrator. (I) may (also) have contributions (to make) in training, literary, counselling and administration. The Lord will guide.'

Our last year in Hobart, 1984, was exciting and we felt we could have stayed for another year or two. A number of new converts became soldiers and other attenders linked up as adherents. Among the new soldiers were some women from the Army's Elim Sheltered Workshop in West Hobart. Ian regularly conducted chapel services at Elim over our three-year term and many of these ladies had made decisions for Christ either there or at corps meetings which they attended regularly. Sadly, many could not read or write—but they could understand what it meant to be a Christian. So Ian conducted a simplified form of recruits' class with them. Eventually he persuaded the corps census meeting to accept a number of them as soldiers. How thrilled they were to be accepted! Some had been Christians and meeting attenders for years, but had never been invited into soldiership.

Sonja also conducted recruits' classes in Dutch for a lady who had come from Holland. The Netherlands Territory kindly provided Sonja with the *Orders and Regulations for Soldiers* and copies of the *Articles of War* in Dutch so the whole process would be totally understood by this first-generation immigrant.

In early 1984 we had a visit from Lieut-Colonel John Clinch, the Field Secretary. He realised that Ian was rather stressed and suggested that, no matter what, we should take time off each week. Ian's illness the year before also served as an important reminder and John Clinch's words and practical suggestions were really a prompting from the Lord in guiding us on safely. As a result, Ian dedicated Monday mornings to writing a series of articles which were eventually typed up by Mrs Elizabeth Foster and published in *The Officer* magazine on the multifaceted concept of holiness. Late in the morning, we would take a packed lunch and then sit, sleep or walk by the Derwent River enjoying the fresh air and sunshine. We still managed to be home when our girls arrived back from school. That change of schedule helped to make that final year at Hobart one of the most productive of our officership so far. We felt much more refreshed by following the biblical principle of a day of rest per week.

After three very productive and satisfying years at Hobart, we received farewell orders to return to Melbourne and positions on the Officer Training College staff. Ian was to become the Education Officer (director of studies), teaching first-year doctrine, some second-year Bible units, and Christian ethics, as well as coordinating the work of other teachers. Membership of five other executive boards and councils would certainly increase his administrative involvement and experience. Sonja would also be on the teaching staff with responsibility for Church and Salvation Army history.

A new building scheme to improve the office, toilet, and recording room facilities had been drawn up but not commenced by the time we left Hobart. In the event, the corps eventually relocated to a new site in Elizabeth Street, which provided an even better facility. Sharon, Jenni and Cathy all did well at school, meaning that when eventually we moved to Melbourne, Sharon and Jenni could easily fit to Mac. Robertson Girls' High School in South Melbourne, with Cathy at grade six at Moonee Ponds Primary.

God was leading us all safely on.

Chapter 11

Australia: Education, training and administration, 1985–92

Our tasks at the Officer Training College in Melbourne, of course, were not dissimilar to the work undertaken in Zambia and the Philippines, but different in the sense that many more cadets were being trained and the staff numbers were much higher than in either of the other countries. When we arrived, there were 33 second-year cadets in residence with 24 first-year cadets due to commence training about a month later in February 1985. Between the two sessions they had a total of 33 children. Eleven officer staff with about 14 children lived on the college, with eight other officers, including us, living elsewhere. Major Robert Moulton from Canada was the Training Principal. Initially we resided in Moonee Ponds.

At that stage, the training college building was situated at 303 Royal Parade, Parkville—a very different structure to the red-brick training college building at 68 Victoria Parade, East Melbourne where we had trained. The Parkville building had originally been a hotel/motel and was now converted (in true Salvation Army style) so that the bar became the library and the basement carpark a chapel.

The residential en suite rooms of the old hotel provided adequate accommodation. Some of the function rooms on the first floor had been converted into classrooms. The dining room on the 10th floor provided a magnificent view of the city, Port Phillip Bay and the university area in which the college was situated.

On Sundays, Ian was usually involved in supervising cadets and their fieldwork particularly observing their approach to leading meetings and giving messages from the Bible. Sonja sometimes accompanied him, but more frequently stayed with our girls who initially attended Moonee Ponds Corps and later Camberwell Corps because of the change of quarters. The quarters in Moonee Ponds was really too small for three high school-aged youth. The Salvation Army was very sympathetic to that situation and the new quarters which we occupied from 1986 was less than a kilometre from Camberwell Corps and about the same distance from the Bethany Eventide Home where Ian's mother became a resident. Helpfully, it was about 6 km from the Inala Senior Citizens' Village where Sonja's parents were living. So the Fairmont Avenue, Camberwell quarters placed us in a strategic position at this time as both sets of parents were into their 80s and needed to accept that some of their previous activities might have to be scaled back. At least we felt their grandchildren were close and could see them more easily than at any other time in our officership service.

As mentioned at the end of the last chapter, our two elder girls had gained entry to Mac. Robertson Girls' High School, having returned to Victoria from Tasmania in 1985. Sharon completed her year 12 Higher School Certificate (HSC) examinations in November and achieved entry to the University of Melbourne in the Arts faculty. Jenni completed year 10 and chose subjects that fitted her interests in science and mathematics. She also enjoyed music as a form of relaxation and as a potential study option. Jenni was enrolled as a soldier during our year in Moonee Ponds and became an active songster at Camberwell when we moved there. She was also involved in the coffee shop run by the corps on Saturday night, finding much pleasure both in prayer support and counselling. We rejoiced at the number of youth attracted to the Camberwell Corps through the contacts made during those Saturday night activities. In 1986 Cathy completed her first year at Canterbury Girls High School in the district where we were living. The transition from primary school to high school always brings challenges, but Cathy settled in well and was elected captain of her form, apparently becoming quite popular amongst her fellow students. She was a junior soldier, young people's singing company number, timbrelist and corps cadet.

When the then Commissioner Eva Burrows was appointed as Territorial Commander of the Australia Southern Territory in 1982, a gentleman associated with the Army wrote to her. He challenged the idea that a woman could be appointed to lead a church and have responsibilities over men. Rather than replying herself, as she would have been quite able to do, she asked Ian to do so. When she was elected General in 1986, Ian adapted the reply he gave at that time into what her early biographer, Wendy Green, described as 'a reasoned article which was published in Army journals for the sake of any critics who doubted whether a woman could, or should, assume leadership... [Ian] argued from Scripture and the early church as the Army "mother", Catherine Booth, had done when she fought the self same battles at the end of the previous century.'[30]

As it turned out, 1987 was a year of the unexpected! Whilst we deliberately planned not to go too far from home for holidays in January because Sharon and Jenni were recovering from surgery to their feet, we did not expect to be spending extra time visiting hospitals until Ian's mother broke her leg. Further periodic trips to hospital became standard practice in January and February.

With the new academic year, we settled into the training college with a full load of teaching Bible, doctrine, ethics, preaching, and church history between us. We successfully arranged a Mature Age Training Course for auxiliary-captains and envoys, and received back the second-year cadets who had returned from their out-training placements. Then we received farewell orders! Ian was appointed as Assistant to the Field Secretary and Sonja as Secretary to The Salvation Army Medical Fellowship (formerly the Nurses Fellowship). Captain Jim Weymouth succeeded Ian as Education Officer.

From a fairly public role, Ian now had to adjust to the preparation of conference agendas, surveying divisional budgets, secretaryship of certain boards at headquarters, and helping organise the Brengle Institute (spiritual retreat for officers focusing on holiness teaching). His involvement at the Brengle Institute was in an administrative rather than a teaching role he would have really preferred. However, the experience was useful in learning about the preparation needed for such events.

---

[30] Wendy Green, *Getting Things Done, Eva Burrows: A Biography* (Basingstoke, Hants, UK; Marshall Morgan and Scott; 1988) p. 141.

He continued representing Salvation Army leadership on various interchurch agencies and committees, developing guidelines and position papers on different issues. At the end of the year he was involved in arranging transportation and luggage movements for officers who were farewelling from one appointment and going to another. Ian certainly enjoyed teaching a 10-week in-depth course on Romans during the second half of the year. The 22 soldiers from the metropolitan area who attended were enrolled for a second semester of the College Bible School. Preparing and presenting a similar one-semester course on 1 Corinthians was another pleasure for him.

Meanwhile, Sonja busily created new interest in the reconstituted Salvation Army Medical Fellowship. Men who were involved in healthcare could now be members—not just female nurses. She aimed to appoint secretaries for the Medical Fellowship in each division.

In our new roles, we enjoyed the opportunity of sharing in the organisation of commissioning for the 'Messengers of Peace' session of cadets. We had been involved in 15 months of their training, coming to know and respect each of them. Although not on the training college staff, we had the privilege of arranging for the counselling of seekers over the weekend, and the more mundane matter of organising grants for the newly commissioned officers' travel expenses. All this gave us other opportunities to be close to them as a group before they scattered across the Commonwealth of Australia.

A highlight of 1988 was celebrations to mark 150 years since Thomas Southwell and his family emigrated from Robertsbridge, East Sussex, England, to the then Colony of New South Wales. The event had been planned for a number of years. More than 1,200 Southwell descendants journeyed to Canberra in March for the reunion, which included the launching of a book about those pioneers and some more recent history of the family. Thomas and his wife Eliza were enthusiastic Christians, converted in the Methodist Church before leaving England. They held worship services in their home long before any nonconformist churches were established in what was to become the Canberra District. Ian was privileged to be asked to arrange and conduct the united family service of worship and thanksgiving in the Union Building of the Australian National University on the Sunday. Six hundred and fifty people attended.

The Anglican priest who offered prayer, the Uniting Church minister who brought the Bible message, a Catholic layman and Sonja who both read from the Scripture, were all family members. The Salvation Army Band from the Canberra City Corps provided musical support, and Ian included a children's story with a Gospel message emphasising the importance of spreading God's light and love in the world as did Thomas Southwell.

We also attended the 1988 Bicentennial Congress in Sydney in May held to coincide with the settlement by the British at Sydney Cove in 1788. The united Salvation Army event provided opportunities to spend time with Ian's Aunt Grace and Uncle Roy still living in Campsie, plus Salvationists from around the country. We even managed to fit in a sessional reunion with members of the 'Messengers of the Faith' who attended.

With the advent of personal computers in the 1980s, and the importance of being able to use them, we both felt it was necessary to gain some knowledge in this area. So from February to June 1987, we had undertaken a special course on computer software packages at what was then the Royal Melbourne Institute of Technology. The course helped remove some of our uncertainties in using the new technology. As result, we bought our first small home computer and a multipurpose software package. The word processing package was most helpful in preparing notes for divisional commanders' conferences and women's services conferences as well as lecture notes for the next year's holiness convention. Cathy had learnt about computers at school and was using the computer effectively for her history assignments. Sharon and Jenni taught themselves over the summer and one computer was definitely not enough in the family.

Toward the end of 1987, the Territorial Commander, Commissioner Donald Campbell, probed Ian about the possibility of us taking over the leadership of the Adelaide Congress Hall in 1988. We did not feel at ease about such an interstate move at that time and communicated that to our leaders even though we always stayed open to the possibility of a change of appointment. We were learning much and enjoying our present roles. In the event, we stayed at Territorial Headquarters.

Ian was thrilled to again teach a course on Romans for some soldiers at Camberwell Corps and a few officers studying the book as a post-commissioning subject during 1988. While he had taught this programme in 1987 as part of the College Bible School associated with the Officer Training College, this year his lessons were audio-recorded for use by others enrolled for the subject with the Territorial Education Department. Sonja was pleased that the interest in The Salvation Army Medical Fellowship[31] continued to grow under her secretaryship. Her bimonthly newsletters were well received. The members responded to the projects being undertaken and the flow of relevant medical information she sent out through its pages.

At the end of 1988, we received news that Ian had been appointed as the Divisional Secretary (second-in-command) of the Melbourne Central Division from 11 January 1989 and Sonja would remain in her role with the Medical Fellowship. Ian continued to be involved in the Victorian Council of Churches Faith and Order Commission.

Ian's appointment as divisional secretary provided opportunities for much learning and unexpected challenges. His task involved supporting the Divisional Commander, Major Hillmon Buckingham, in all administrative functions of the division. These included management of divisional headquarters, responsibility for divisional finances, overseeing and auditing corps finances, advising on property work within the division, and as a stand-in for the divisional commander in his absence. This last task became particularly relevant when, a few months after Major and Mrs Buckingham's furlough in New Zealand, they were again called to their homeland because of the critical illness of a grandchild. This necessary three-week absence overlapped the divisional officers' fellowship, leaving us with the task of providing spiritual refreshment for 56 officers over a three-day period. God was good and the prayer support of our fellow officers wonderfully provided mutual encouragement for all attending as well as spiritual sustenance for the Buckingham family.

Ian grasped every opportunity to be involved in preaching and teaching—albeit as 'extracurricular' activities. He taught subjects at the holiness conventions for Salvationists in January of 1989 and 1990. He also presented the Bible studies for a five-year review seminar for officers

---

[31] An international fellowship of dedicated medical personnel, encouraging a Christian witness and application of Christian principles in professional life while at the same time being involved with practical application in hospitals, clinics and various other places of medical care.

based on 2 Corinthians. He recorded his 10-lesson series on 1 Corinthians which, like the summer series on Romans, was used by officers and others undertaking relevant correspondence study through the Territorial Education Department. Together we conducted meetings at a number of corps throughout the Melbourne Central Division, the Kaniva Corps at Easter and the Horsham Corps for Self Denial Appeal Sunday.

One of Sonja's great thrills came from representing the Territory at The Salvation Army Regional Consultation on Health and Healing in Hong Kong in 1988. The consultation was chaired by Lieut-Colonel Dr Paul du Plessis with whom we shared service in Zambia from 1970 to 1975. Sonja acted as recommendations secretary and gave her own brief report on the work of the Medical Fellowship in Australia. As Sonja's return fare to Hong Kong had been paid by the Army and we had two weeks annual holiday left unused, it became reasonable for us to meet in Singapore. We spent two delightful days with a session-mate, Major Margaret Newdick, and then flew to the land of Sonja's birth—Indonesia. Three days in Jakarta gave us an opportunity live at the Officer Training College, give a lecture to the cadets on spiritual leadership, and present a freezer to the college made possible by cadets in Melbourne. We also visited a few places of interest, and reconnected with a family friend of Sonja's who still lived there. The room in which we slept at the college was one of those which Sonja and her parents occupied as they lived on the premises when her father was the public relations officer from 1950 to 1953. From 1947 to 1950 they had lived at the same address, 55 Jalan Kramat Raya, Jakarta, but in a different building when they were in charge of 'The Open Door' recreational centre for Dutch military personnel. Understandably, memories came flooding back to Sonja during our visit.

We also spent five days in Bandung after taking some three and a half hours journeying by train from Jakarta to the city situated 800 m above sea level. At least the elevation made the temperature a more bearable 24°C to 30°C daily. We were able to stay at the elderly citizens' complex run by the Army at which Sonja resided as a girl during school holidays some 35 to 40 years before. Also we visited a number of corps and Army centres and spoke at several Sunday meetings, THQ prayers, a Medical Fellowship meeting, and the gathering for officers' children accompanied by Lieut-Colonel Johannes and Augustina Watilete. Many who attended these gatherings remembered Sonja and her parents. Although we had a busy programme in Indonesia, we felt quite rested and refreshed for a return to Australia. Regular early afternoon siestas proved beneficial to us as they had in Zambia and the Philippines. Above all, we delighted to share in fellowship with such attractive and warm people.

Despite our change of appointment to Melbourne Central Division in 1989, we were able to live in the Fairmont Avenue quarters in Camberwell for another year. That was another instance in which we felt God guiding us. Normally we would have moved from Camberwell so that we lived in the division in which we were serving. Major surgery for Sonja at the end of 1988 meant it was not opportune to pack and move at that time and we were grateful for the understanding of our territorial leaders. We commuted to Fairfield Corps on Sundays so we soldiered in the Melbourne Central Division. A particular thrill toward the end of 1989 was Cathy's enrolment as a senior soldier at Camberwell Corps where she continued to attend.

In 1990 Sonja took over the role of League of Mercy Secretary in the Melbourne Central Division and concluded her period as the Territorial Medical Fellowship Secretary. Before handing over that role, she arranged an excellent series of seminars on medical/ethical topics such as stress, euthanasia, Alzheimer's disease, and in-vitro fertilisation as part of the annual Melbourne Congress during that year. Her work with the League of Mercy provided her with insights into this aspect of the Army's caring ministries. Meetings with League of Mercy secretaries from corps around the division helped in melding effective leadership across the division. She busily conducted training classes for prospective League of Mercy (community care) workers who would be involved in visiting hospitals and residential homes in their own time to bring the Gospel and render practical aid.

As well as the usual work of a divisional secretary, Ian developed a proposal to install computers at the divisional headquarters with the support of the new Divisional Commander, Major Doug Davis. Ian aimed to have all finance records processed on the system electronically from July 1991. Word processing and database facilities were included. At that time, before the Army's international intranet system was established, he suggested a system of filing computer-based correspondence. In addition to the business aspects of the appointment, Ian was involved in teaching at a soldiers and friends holiness convention, a six-session course on counselling seekers at Williamstown Corps and a Bible study on 2 Corinthians again for the officers five-year review seminar.

Sonja's stepfather, Colonel Garnet Palmer, needed a lengthy period in hospital following a gall bladder operation with a subsequent change to high-care accommodation, and to a single medium-care hostel room for her mother. Within days of Sharon's 21st birthday in July, Ian's mother sustained another fracture of the femur of her right leg—a repetition of a break in 1987, which did not heal completely, despite the support of metal plates. A new plate plus a bone graft were needed to overcome the problem. Four months later her leg failed again resulting in a much longer recuperation period. Between these two incidents, Ian had to be admitted to hospital for the removal of his gallbladder, and another groin hernia correction. Prior to that surgery, we spent a week of furlough in Sydney helping Ian's Aunt Grace and Uncle Roy finalise their affairs in Campsie, NSW, before moving into an Army retirement hostel in Altona, Victoria. Ian's cousin, Marion Dodds, helped in the process. How glad we were to be so close to our relatives during those times of transition! Again, we were very conscious of God's guidance and the support of his people.

We were also very aware of the Lord's presence in the move to Bundoora in 1990 and the opportunity to be soldiers of the Macleod Corps—although the move was not without some pain. Sadly, the rooms in the quarters in Bundoora were not large. Sharon moved to accommodation near the university in January 1990. Jenni moved with us while still trying to find the most suitable university course. Science Engineering did not suit her, even though she had achieved the excellent Year 12 scores required for entry. Eventually she moved into humanities, focusing on politics, women's studies, and philosophy at the University of Melbourne. Cathy also moved with us and played trombone in the band, teaching Sunday school, being a corps cadet and Bible study member. Ian played baritone when not away specialling and Sonja sang in the women's voices.

During 1991 we were delighted to meet again with Captain Mrs Raven Salegumba from the Philippines. She had been selected as a delegate to the special Administrative Leadership Training Course run by the Territory annually in Melbourne for overseas leaders with potential for holding more senior positions. During the year we also conducted a local officers seminar at Wodonga, Northern Victoria, focusing on mercy seat counselling and explaining the Army's position on the sacraments. Ian also taught at a church growth conference for officers and soldiers from five divisions at Dookie College in Northern Victoria.

Ian recalls that, during these years, the Territory received a visit from Major Terry Camsey, originally from the United Kingdom and the Republic of Ireland Territory but then stationed in the United States. From about 1985, the major had been involved in teaching church growth in the USA and he shared some of his insights in Australia. One of Terry's quotations stands out in Ian's mind and he recalls it as follows: 'Living things multiply. The fruit of the cell is another cell. The fruit of an organism is another organism. The fruit of a person is another person. The fruit of a cell group is another cell group. The fruit of the congregation is another congregation. The fruit of the corps is another corps. The fruit of the division is another division. The fruit of a territory is another territory.' Major Camsey's illustration helped to crystallise for Ian some important teaching about church growth in such a way that he felt he could both explain and apply it more easily in the future.

As well as counselling at the holiness convention, Sonja was involved in organising further training seminars for League of Mercy members. These seminars were designed to give them encouragement and provide training in topics such as bedside evangelism, grief counselling, and a special one on HIV/AIDS which focused on providing Christian support to the increasing numbers of persons with what was then a terminal disease.

After three years in that appointment and the various extra activities outlined, Commissioner Dinsdale Pender, the Territorial Commander, gave us farewell orders to become divisional leaders in Western Australia, with Ian as Divisional Commander and Sonja as the Divisional Director of Women's Organisations.

Another adventure in service was about to begin!

Chapter 12

Western Australia, 1992–94

We felt tremendously privileged to be appointed as leaders of the Western Australia Division commencing in January 1992. That year the division was to celebrate the centenary of The Salvation Army's commencement in Western Australia in 1892. From earlier chapters, readers will recall that Ian's grandfather, then Lieutenant George Lonnie, was a pioneer officer at Southern Cross in 1893 and Coolgardie in 1894. He then served in other corps in that state, including Geraldton and Perth. In 1921, after appointments in South Australia, New Zealand, New South Wales, Queensland and Victoria, he returned to Western Australia as divisional commander with his wife, Jennie, and daughters Ivy and Ian's mother, Florence. As mentioned earlier, Florrie came back to WA as Divisional Home League Secretary when Ian's father, David, became Divisional Commander from 1955–57. It was from Perth that David was promoted to Glory in 1957.

The Western Australia Division covered a vast area. Port Hedland, the most northerly of the 30 corps and six outposts in the division, was 1,600 km in a straight line from Albany, the most southerly corps. Kalgoorlie, the most easterly from Perth, the capital city, was 600 km away. We needed to travel by air to visit Port Hedland and Karratha. Much more travelling was carried out by road. Many of those highways were familiar to Ian from 1955–57.

Five hostels, a youth camp, two community centres and a women's refuge were also in the area of responsibility of the division. Specialist social services and family support, correctional services, senior citizens, alcohol rehabilitation and childcare were, at that stage, under the separate direction of Major Robert Cassidy, the State Social Services Secretary. How little we knew that, a year later, the situation would change and Western Australia would become a 'state command' incorporating all of those officers, employees and centres. Our headquarters in Perth was about 3,000 km by air from Territorial Headquarters in Melbourne.

All three of our daughters stayed in Melbourne to continue their studies. Obviously, we were concerned for them and our elderly parents who were still alive at that time. We looked forward to visiting them during times of divisional conferences and similar territorial events. At that stage, air travel was relatively expensive and seen almost as a luxury. As we write now in 2016, air travel is much less expensive and regularly used for interstate travel.

In the first few weeks after our arrival, Armadale Corps in the outer south-eastern part of Perth conducted a telemarketing scheme to replant their outreach. This was a first for Western Australia and, on Sunday 8 March, a celebration service was held which those contacted through the telemarketing calls had been specifically invited to attend. The corps had been operating for six years and was situated in a fast-growing suburb of Perth. Captains John and Winsome Mason, who had been cadets when we were on the training college staff, were the corps leaders. They planned to enlarge the existing corps building. Rather than doing that immediately, they considered telemarketing and moving temporarily into a local community hall for their Sunday morning services. This allowed them to keep the existing place of worship for a night meeting which became their holiness meeting and the venue for their other weekly activities. By and large the strategy worked, and the numbers of attendees grew. Approval was given for Armadale Corps to construct a large multi-purpose building which served as a recreation centre, community centre, and worship centre. This was completed by the end of 1993.

Because a territorial review was to be held at the end of 1992, it was necessary for Ian to undertake inspections at every corps before October, with parallel home league and women's fellowship reviews undertaken by Sonja. The Salvation Army in Western Australia certainly owned some excellent properties and some very large blocks of land. Officers who had led the division previously, such as Lieut-Colonel Brian Morgan, certainly had visions for growth. The buildings constructed in the decade before our arrival consisted of multi-purpose structures planned with the future in mind.

Our Divisional Headquarters shared the same building as the Perth Fortress Corps. The corps had moved from its historic site in Murray Street, City, out to William Street, Northbridge, just north of James Street. Of course, this was the area in which Ian attended the then Perth Boys High School as a teenager. Our quarters was near Lake Monger, Wembley, and we soldiered at Floreat Corps.

The division held a well-planned, multi-event Centenary Congress spanning some nine days in April 1992 with Commissioner and Mrs James Osborne, the National Commander of The Salvation Army in the United States as guest leaders. The Melbourne Staff Band also came to support, as well as the Territorial Leaders, Commissioners Dinsdale and Winifred Pender. The Staff Band was used to good effect in open-air witnesses and concerts, reminding the general public of the presence of The Salvation Army and its ministries.

Another notable event was a successful home league camp conducted by the Territorial Home League Secretary, Major Rosemary Haines, in May. We were also able to journey back to Melbourne and visit relatives while attending a leadership conference in June. Ian also travelled to Victoria for a planned giving training course at Kallista in August and a divisional commanders meeting in October.

Toward the end of the year, we received official notification of the administrative restructuring to take place in Western Australia. All social services would come under our jurisdiction as State Commander and State Women's Ministries President from January 1993. The social services consisted of family support services, correctional services, three senior citizens residences and three men's residential centres connected to our sobering-up intake and assessment programme. An adult rehabilitation centre was also included, together with Red Shield Industries consisting of a sheltered workshop and 11 family stores. A family crisis centre with two residential units, a women's centre including emergency accommodation for women escaping from domestic violence and a sheltered accommodation for the intellectually handicapped made up the rest of the social services component. In addition, we also inherited an employment training centre and a telephone counselling service. Fortunately, the former State Social Services Secretary, Major Robert Cassidy, was appointed to remain as State Programme Secretary. This change provided some huge challenges and State Headquarters was now administering the 95 active officers, multiple employees and coordinating a much wider programme than was the case for field operations alone.

Because of very limited prior consultation and explanation to all concerned before the announcement, many of the social services officers felt disenfranchised and uncertain. Lines of communication were not quickly established or understood. Some corps officers expressed the opinion that the emphasis on evangelism was being diluted because so much time was involved in integrating the social services with the total state programme. We all had to work out how to serve our Lord more efficiently and also to develop sufficient support for our officers and other workers. The Divisional Secretary, Major John Jeffrey, became the State Secretary and continued as a good support in supervising the administrative side of the state division. No officer for personnel support, such as a personnel secretary, was appointed in those first years of the state command. In order to augment the pastoral work for officers, Ian asked retired Colonel Gordon Fischer to act as a pastoral care officer. Some officers felt that Ian was abdicating his responsibility of looking after officers. On the other hand, Ian believed it was a matter of an appropriate delegation to try to achieve what needed to be accomplished during the transition. It was impossible to provide the same level of support under the state command arrangement as when we had simply been divisional leaders.

Life was certainly not dull in the first part of 1993 for other reasons, too. Colonel Garnet Palmer, the only 'grandfather' our children knew, was promoted to Glory on 29 January at 91 years of age after a long illness stemming back to a gallbladder operation. Sonja flew to Melbourne to be with her mother for the funeral and some of the adjustments that necessarily followed. Our friend from Zambian days, Major Gwenda Watkinson, journeyed from Melbourne to conduct the home league camp. Then we conducted divisional farewell meetings for Commissioner and Mrs Dinsdale Pender who had been appointed as territorial leaders to the United Kingdom and the Republic of Ireland Territory. These meetings took place in the middle of the Home League camp programme, and officers had to return to Perth for councils and public meetings on that day. Fortunately, Sonja was able to work this requirement into the camp arrangements.

While carrying the suitcase for the territorial leaders to the airport, Major John Jeffrey hurt his back, which already was causing him some concern. X-rays indicated two slipped discs. His legs could no longer hold him. John's wife, Judith, was in Melbourne for a church growth conference and intended to return via Adelaide to minister to her mother who was unwell. While all this happened, Major Robert Cassidy, who was third in charge under the state command system, and his wife were on holidays in Broome. They could not be called back. This basically left us with most State Headquarters officers away and all their jobs to do.

We were also due to go south to visit Pingelly, Narrogin and Katanning corps to conduct reviews and home league revisions. In the event, Sonja travelled alone to these places, staying in motels as needed. She really felt she was on safari!

Sonja's mother visited us during this year and it was sad to see her physical decline, including hearing loss and loss of short-term memory. She was also working through the grief of Garnet's decline in health and promotion to Glory earlier in the year. We wished we could have been living closer to her, but our girls were keeping an eye on her and on Ian's mother also.

During our term in Western Australia, we tried to follow the emphasis of the Territory on planting new corps. In consultation with a regional planner, Graham Collins, who also was a Salvationist, we targeted the Merriwa area north of Perth, putting in place all the preparations for a new corps planting. We secured land for an eventual hall and purchased accommodation for the incoming officers that could double as an initial small building for worship until a full hall was constructed. Lieutenants Paul and Wendy Hateley were appointed to Merriwa in January 1994—a cause for much rejoicing. In the meantime in 1993, we managed to plant an outreach at Catherine Street, Maylands, where the Army had an Employment Plus programme (as it was called then). Plans were also put in place for an opening at Port Kennedy, Warnbro. Graham and Margaret Collins, having been warranted as envoys, moved to Ellenbrook where they set about sponsoring a new opening. Ian also conducted mercy seat counselling training courses for helping seekers before the congresses in both 1992 and 1993, and enjoyed the opportunity of sharing the knowledge he had accumulated in that ministry over many years.

The State Headquarters building had been purchased about four years previously during the term of Lieut-Colonel Brian Morgan. It had been originally designed as a purpose-built TV studio complex. The ground and first floors were soundproof and all natural light was excluded. As the original owners became victims of an economic downturn, The Salvation Army purchased the building because divisional headquarters and the state social services headquarters had outgrown the premises they then occupied. A number of changes were needed internally so the ground floor could house the Perth Fortress Corps. THQ hoped that the second floor could have been rented to raise some money to pay off the purchase, but nobody seemed to want it. During 1993, at the suggestion of Major John Jeffrey, the divisional offices were moved from the windowless first floor of the building to the second floor where there were windows that allowed us to have natural light. We hoped that the first floor could have been rented out, but that did not happen either.

Early in September, we conducted an officers fellowship, including field and social services officers. This meant that over 100 officers were present. Preparing for that event took months of prayer and planning that God blessed wonderfully. We also had our first Women's Bible Conference in September. Major Barbara Mouchemore, the guest speaker for the Bible conference, stayed on as a lecturer for the first ever lay holiness convention for the state. The territorial holiness conventions for Salvationists each January were always held in Melbourne and, of course, travelling there was very expensive for Western Australian delegates. Fourteen Salvationists attended our convention, including two from interstate. Ian was one of the lecturers. Although he did not stay overnight at the venue, he drove in from the office each day for his classes. Both of us attended the evening activities. This was a valuable opportunity to encourage the spiritual growth of our soldiers.

In 1993 a large bequest came to the Territory to be used for study and development of officers. Our leaders, in their wisdom, saw fit that every officer should have the opportunity of a two-week study tour of Israel arranged through the Biblical Resources Study Centre, situated between Bethlehem and Jerusalem. Each individual officer who wished to attend was required to pay $1,200 toward the tour personally, the balance coming from the bequest. The personal contribution was really very small considering that the study tour would include two weeks accommodation, all meals, the tour around Israel, and a full study programme on the Gospels and the life of Jesus. Needless to say, all the officers in the group planned to see a little of Europe as well after the study tour. Because the general change announcements were to take place a week after the tour, and we wanted to visit Israel, we were permitted to travel to Europe earlier and join the rest of the party in Rome before flying into Tel Aviv.

Ian was appointed as assistant leader alongside our friend, Major Valma Ray, who was then the Education Secretary for the Territory. We were able to visit historic parts of London, its monuments and cathedrals, and a changing of the guard at Buckingham Palace. We travelled to Stonehenge, Salisbury Cathedral, and the beautiful city of Bath, famed for its hot springs, ancient Roman architecture, and baths, of course. Ian was aware of many of these sites these from his visit in 1974 for the International Training Principals Conference. We enjoyed visiting them together this time. The following week we visited Sonja's surviving family members in Holland who she had not seen since 1947. Most lived in or around Voorburg, The Haag. What a wonderful reunion that was and how strong were the family bonds after all those years! And equally amazing was how Sonja recalled the Dutch learned in her formative years yet had rarely spoken during the past 38. She recognised all her aunts and uncle. We were able to visit the Rijksmuseum and view the great Rembrandt paintings as well as taking a trip down Amsterdam's canals.

Our visit to Rome gave us opportunities to see some of the many historical sites, including the Vatican and related museums. Unfortunately, Sonja sprained her ankle on a spiral stairway in the Vatican. Because of the long siesta in Rome from midday to 4 pm, it was difficult to get a pressure bandage to give her ankle some needed support. We certainly hoped she would be fit enough for the Israel study tour. God was good and she improved rapidly once the ankle was strapped.

In Rome we met the other 25 officers who had booked for the tour. From there we travelled to Israel by plane. The guide for the field trips from the Biblical Resources Study Centre was a young Jewish Christian who had accepted the faith eight years previously. He was an enthusiast who gave us some new insights into many biblical events. How wonderful to visit places such as Mount Carmel and from there to view Mount Tabor and Mount Gilboa! While taking in the magnificent view, we were able to hear again the story of Elijah and God's victory over the prophets of Baal. We were able to view the huge Jezreel Valley, scene of so many battles throughout the centuries, and the ancient site of Megiddo. We visited Nazareth, Capernaum, Caesarea Philippi and the Golan Heights. The group was accommodated at a resort on the eastern shore of the Sea of Galilee and we took a boat ride across it—no storm at sea this time! We visited Elah Valley, where David defeated the giant Goliath. Being so familiar with the Bible stories, we felt as if we had 'come home'.

In Jerusalem we were privileged to share in a biblical meal based on the Passover meal. This latter was a very special and moving experience, particularly when we closed the occasion with Albert Orsborn's song:

My life must be Christ's broken bread,
My love his outpoured wine. …

My all is in the Master's hands
For him to bless and break;
Beyond the brook his winepress stands
And thence my way I take,
Resolved the whole of loves demands
To give for his dear sake.[32]

Having visited wine and olive presses during our tour, we better understood the symbolism in relation to the suffering of Christ and the challenges his followers must face as well.

Our accommodation in Jerusalem was in the Old City at a Maronite convent near the Jaffa Gate. This allowed us to visit all the traditional sites in and around Jerusalem even though many were reconstructions after demolition by the Romans in AD 70, the Crusades and destruction during other conflicts such as the more recent World War I. On the last Sunday morning we attended the Protestant service at the beautiful and

[32] Albert Orsborn, *SASB* (2015), Song 610.

peaceful Garden Tomb. Here we sat facing the door of the tomb on which were the words, 'He is not here, He has risen.' The thrill of that truth filled our eyes with tears of wonder and joy. Ours was a living faith in our risen Christ who had conquered death. We shared in this anticipation of his ultimate victory.

The week after our return to Perth, we received a phone call from Territorial Commander, Commissioner John Clinch. We were each given our new appointments as of January 1994, Ian as Assistant Secretary for Personnel—Education and Training. This was to be a new position in the Territory which involved the coordination of all education and training programmes for officers, cadets and soldiers from the 'cradle to the grave'. At that time, every department ran its own training programmes independently. Sonja was given the responsibility of Territorial Sponsorship Secretary. Her appointment, based in the Public Relations Department, involved arranging sponsorship by the Army of deprived children in Third World countries. The numbers of such children had grown to hundreds in recent years.

Majors John and Judith Jeffrey succeeded us as State Leaders in Western Australia.

Photos 2 1975–1998

(Top left) Travel by canoe to an open-air meeting on Mindoro Island, the Philippines
(Top right) Enrolment of junior soldiers at Quezon City 2 Corps, the Philippines, 1977
(Left) Sonja teaches cadets about children's ministries
(Below) Ian as producer/conductor of the musical 'Jesus Folk', 1976

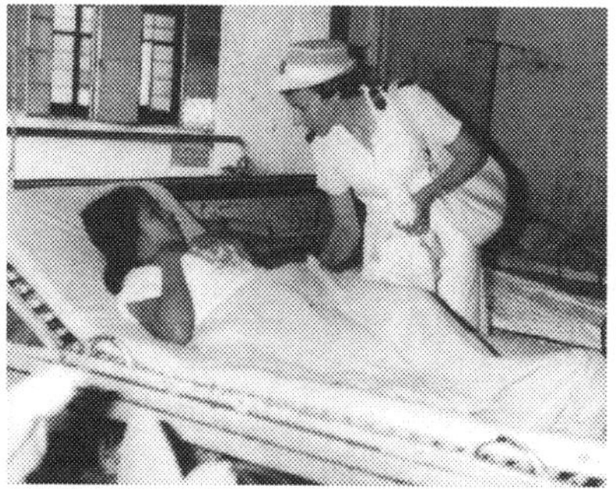

Sonja involved in Christmas Cheer distribution at Quezon Institute [tuberculosis hospital], c. 1975

Combined sessions and staff, the Philippines, 1979

Plane crash in Manila, 1978

Cadets minister to survivors after the plane crash

(Left) Hawthorn Citadel 1980 with message: 'Jesus Cares' and our Army flag
(Above) Sonja conducts enrolment of a new Dutch-speaking soldier in Hobart, 1984

(Top left) Family from left Ian, Sharon, Cathy, Sonja, Jenni, and Grandma Southwell, c. 1980
(Top right) Ian and Sonja with, from the left, Sharon, Cathy and Jenni c. 1989
(Right) Ian (right) with some of Melbourne Central Divisional Headquarters staff, c. 1989, led by Major Hillmon Buckingham (left, back) with DYS Major Kevin Grigsbey (left, front}
(Below left) Welcomed to Perth by Majors Alan and Val Laurens [Public Relations Officers], Major John Jeffrey [Divisional Secretary], and Majors Robert and Betty Cassidy [State Social Service Secretary], 1992
(Below right) A 25th wedding anniversary cake and flowers from our girls in 1992 to share with the WA headquarters staff

(Top) Sonja with staff members at Geelong Conference Centre, 1997
(Middle row left) On the Israel Study Tour, 1993
(Middle row right) Internet set up for distance education at Geelong Conference Centre in 1996 with Majors Wayne and Jeanette Ennis, and Ian's secretary Belinda Carter
(Above left) The Clean Life March, Seoul, 1998, with Territorial Leaders, the then Colonels Lee, Sun-duk and Cho, In-sun, staff and cadets
(Above right) Baby dedication, with translator, Major Kim, Dong-jin, at Sudaejon Corps, Korea

Chapter 13

Australia: Education and training—again, 1994–97

We certainly did not expect a change after only two years in the Western Australian appointments, and our leaders were sensitive to this. However, the appointment fitted uniquely into Ian's teaching background and our joint commitment to world mission. So we believed that the Lord again was leading us in this direction. He had never failed in his guidance to that point and we trusted him for the future. We accepted these appointments as from him and had a sense of peace about them.

Extra bonuses came from the fact that we were back in Melbourne for Cathy's wedding to Darren Elkington on 29 January 1994 at Macleod Corps. This was a great occasion, with both of them testifying at the reception to God's guidance in their lives. Cathy had just completed the first two years of a three-year Bachelor of Nursing qualification and planned to spend a year as a nurse before entering the Officer Training College with Darren in 1996. Also, our new quarters in Blackburn South was situated conveniently near our elderly mothers in Camberwell and Blackburn South.

The vision of territorial leadership of coordinating the education and training programmes throughout the Territory was a very worthy one. Unfortunately, it was somewhat difficult to accomplish.

When Ian came into the position of 'coordinator', in-service education including post-commissioning studies and distance education were organised at Territorial Headquarters by the Education Secretary who was responsible to the Secretary for Personnel. This was the position previously held by Major Valma Ray up until early 1994. She would soon be leaving Australia for another overseas appointment and this would be one of Ian's major hands-on tasks. Ian felt it was an honour to be appointed to a position his mother held in 1958–59 on her return from Western Australia. Majors Wayne and Jeanette Ennis were already tutors in the Department and were supported by a team of retired officers and others with backgrounds suitable for tutoring the variety of distance education courses then offered.

Major Valma Ray had done some excellent work during her leadership of the Department. She surveyed the newly commissioned officers over a number of years to discover what they perceived as their further educational needs immediately after Commissioning. Rather than ongoing in-depth Bible studies, they generally felt they needed more skills in areas such as time and self-management now they were away from the tightly structured training college programme. The second need was negotiating skills—how to communicate effectively and, if needs be, negotiate with corps members, employees and their Army leaders. As a result she proposed and implemented an in-service programme of post-commissioning seminars to be held in the second and fourth year of officership. These served as a means of fellowship for newly commissioned officers, many of whom were appointed at significant distances away from divisional headquarters support, and to help them complete the Army's requirements in regard to their post-commissioning studies. Distance education study assignments completed both before and after those seminars could provide any evidence needed by territorial leaders that the officers had satisfactorily completed their post-commissioning requirements. This change took place before the Officer Training College moved to have their programme recognised either as a vocational training course or part of a recognised theological degree.

Major Vic Poke, a friend and session-mate, had been just appointed as the Training Principal at the Officer Training College. Traditionally, the principal reported directly to the Chief Secretary rather than the Secretary for Personnel and certainly not to the territory's Education Secretary.

Major Robert Paterson had been appointed the Director of the Geelong Conference Centre (GCC)—a newly purchased in-service training centre situated in Eastern Park, Geelong. This was to be the venue for the post-commissioning in-service training programmes, Brengle institutes, officers fellowships, mature-age officer training courses (that used to be held at the Training College for auxiliary-captains and some envoys), plus five-year and 20-year reviews seminars for officers prior to promotion to captain and major respectively. It was hoped that employee training best offered in a residential setting could also take place at GCC. The reviews at five and 20 years gave officers at these points of service opportunities to reflect on the previous years, have interviews with senior leaders and be assessed to determine if their progress warranted confirmation of their officership and promotion to higher ranks. Ian was very pleased to participate in these seminars and the teaching provided, even though it meant him living at GCC several weeks each year.

Obviously, each of those centres felt they had their own particular roles to fulfil and some resistance was experienced in trying to achieve coordination. In addition, the Officer Training College was already working to have their programme accredited in some way so that cadets could receive government financial support that would allow them to make some financial contribution to their training. Such contributions would help to lift the financial burden on the Territory and also provide the cadets with a recognised training certificate—possibly a Certificate Four in Salvation Army Ministry in addition to The Salvation Army Certificate of Officer Training. Achieving that goal meant a fairly radical rewriting of the curriculum in terms of the competencies in knowledge, skills and attitudes required by newly commissioned officers. How would that fit in with the traditional pattern of officer training which emphasised spiritual growth and servant leadership? What would that mean for post-commissioning and similar courses traditionally offered by the Territorial Education Department, for instance?

While Ian was busy working through these areas, Sonja mastered the computer-based record-keeping and financial packages used to monitor the thousand or so children in Third World countries sponsored by the Territory. The flow of correspondence and finance to children in the Army's care in other lands needed constant checking. As it was, many hundreds of children were currently without a sponsor and Sonja developed new advertising materials in the hope that others would be attracted to give—at that stage $15 per month—to help a child. For a time, Sonja was also the Acting Assistant Territorial Home League Secretary.

Mrs Colonel Johanna Palmer, Sonja's mother, had lived a wonderful life in the service of God. Her courage and fortitude were particularly evident in Indonesia during and after the World War II. Unexpectedly, she was promoted to Glory in June 1994. The funeral service gave opportunities for Sonja, especially, to remind those present of her mother's faithful service. Then, Ian's mother fell and suffered yet another broken leg in late September, necessitating a lengthy time in hospital and rehabilitation. We were glad to be nearby to give some support. In retrospect, God was guiding again.

We did receive a probe from Territorial Headquarters toward the end of 1994 about the possibility of us moving down to the Geelong Conference Centre. It would make leadership of seminars easier. We felt strangely ill at ease about the suggestion and responded to our leaders accordingly. In August 1995, we understood why. In between all the normal events of organising studies within the Territory and trying to coordinate the total education programme, Ian's mother, Lieut-Colonel Mrs Florence Southwell, also went home to be with the Lord just two months after her 90th birthday. We had planned a special party for her birthday in June, but an abdominal emergency required urgent surgery in hospital a week before the event. She never fully recovered. After a month in hospital, she was moved to the nursing home at Inala Village for additional care. Following a collapse and readmission to hospital on 14 August, she was promoted to Glory the next morning. We were glad to be able to stay with her during the night, reminding her of the promises in Scripture which she had loved throughout the years and singing some relevant and assuring songs. We were overwhelmed with expressions of gratitude to God for her life and influence coming to us in the weeks following.

Being still resident in Melbourne, it was easy to attend the official closure of the Fairfield Corps in November 1995. The number of corps in the north of Melbourne, planted when owning or driving a vehicle was a rarity, needed to be rationalised. Many of the corps were ceasing to be financially viable as the soldiery aged. The Territorial Commander, Commissioner John Clinch who, with his wife Beth, had entered training from that corps, conducted the ceremony. Readers will recall this was the first corps in Australia that Sonja and her family attended after coming from Indonesia in 1953. Ian's mother soldiered there from 1959 until 1993, well after she moved to Bethany Senior Citizens residence in Camberwell. We both sang in the combined songster brigade for the occasion. As an officer who entered the Training College from Fairfield, Ian was privileged to hold the Army flag for the closure ceremony.

We were also pleased to be able to attend Cathy's Bachelor of Nursing graduation ceremony in 1995 and know that she would gain some good experience at the Repatriation General Hospital before she and Darren entered officer training in 1996. They were both very involved in the Macleod corps. Our other daughter, Jenni, completed her Bachelor of Arts degree with excellent results, especially in her politics subjects. Sharon moved away from historical research, in which she had gained an honours degree, to study psychology subjects at Monash University. Professional counselling work was now her long-term goal rather than archaeology. We were delighted that they had all achieved professional qualifications and were commencing to make positive contributions to the community.

During 1994 and 1995 we had the delight of meeting officers from around the world who came to Melbourne for the Administrative Leadership Training Course (ALTC). As mentioned earlier, this course was offered by the Australia Southern Territory through International Headquarters (IHQ) for emerging leaders in grant-aided territories. Ian was appointed to coordinate the course during those two years. For instance, we were pleased to renew our links with Major Wesley Curameng with whom we had served in the Philippines. Other delegates came from South Africa, Indonesia, India Northern and Nigeria. All the delegates benefited from the month in Australia and we enjoyed the opportunity to accompany them to South Australia for the state congress in Adelaide in 1994.

Another interstate visit took us to Tasmania to be guest leaders and Bible teachers at the annual officers fellowship. During the visit, we were pleased to view the new facilities at State Headquarters and the Hobart Citadel Corps. Best of all, we were able to meet some who had been our co-workers at Hobart in 1982–85 and spend time with them.

Together, we hosted a home Bible study at our quarters on Wednesday evenings in between the various courses Ian was facilitating. We were able to soldier at the Box Hill Corps during those two years, then led by Majors Raymond and Aylene Finger. Ian was invited to conduct a two-evening seminar on spiritual gifts. He was also able to attend a reunion of classmates from Northcote High School. We chose to attend in Army uniform and this provided opportunities for us to witness to God's goodness throughout the years.

Toward the end of 1995, we took a restful and educative visit to the Snowy Mountains in New South Wales. The scenery around Mount Kosciusko, the highest mountain in Australia some 2,225 m above sea level, was magnificent. Lakes, dams and power stations of the Snowy Mountains Hydroelectric Scheme provided many photo opportunities and also new information about one of the engineering wonders of the world. Sonja recalled her visit there some 30 years earlier. We returned via the south-eastern section of the Snowy River that had not been diverted by the scheme to rivers in the west of the Great Dividing Range.

At the end of the year we were told that the Education Department would definitely be relocated from THQ to the Geelong Conference Centre (GCC). We felt the time was right to move there. God gave us that assurance—especially in the light of the events in 1994 and 1995.

We were delighted to have an excellent staff at GCC. They were so willing to work for the success of the centre, both as the primary in-service training centre for the Army and also as a commercial venture for self-funding. Early discussions led to the adoption of a mission statement that the centre would be 'A serene place of learning, inspiration and renewal where we delight in giving quality service'. For the six committed Christians on the staff including Majors Wayne and Jeanette Ennis and us, the spiritual inspiration and renewal of all those attending courses was our greatest desire. As an innovation in 1996, we commenced staff prayers, sometimes combining these with devotional periods of particular courses. Our prayer, of course, was that all our staff members would make their commitments to Christ.

Residing at GCC meant that it was somewhat easier to coordinate a wide range of courses. These included: the post-commissioning seminars, a worship seminar, five-year reviews, the four-week Mature Age Training Course for auxiliary-captains and envoys spanning four weeks, a preaching seminar with the Rev. Dr Gordon Moyes from Sydney Central Mission, and a course for middle managers organised in conjunction with Lieut-Colonel Warren Golding, Secretary for Business Administration. Major Wayne Ennis and Ian taught subjects towards the Army's Certificate of

Bible Knowledge on Tuesday evenings to appreciative soldiers from the Geelong Corps in both 1996 and 1997. The numbers of soldiers and friends studying by correspondence was maintained. As another innovation, we set up a worldwide web homepage and an email address so that lessons could be sent out and responses received via that medium. The first candidates lessons arrived from Western Australia for assessment that way.

Ian was given the opportunity of preparing the Easter series of devotionals for the Army's publication *Words of Life* published in the United Kingdom. He did the writing in 1996 and the series was published in the Easter edition for 1997.

Sonja also had other activities as well as the day-to-day running of Geelong Conference Centre. These included membership of a government committee investigating prostitution in Victoria, the Army's Public Questions Board (now the Moral and Social Issues Council), and the Territorial Literature Council. Ian represented the Army on the Faith and Order (Unity) Commissions of the Victorian and National Councils of Churches as well as being a member of the Education and Training Council, Training College Council, Candidates Board, and the Territorial Strategy and Planning Council. These were all enriching experiences that were preparing us for wider responsibilities.

We were thrilled to attend the welcome to cadets in February 1996 when Cathy and Darren became cadets of the 'Messengers of God's Love' session. Cathy was the representative speaker for the cadets from her division at that meeting. Cathy and Darren thoroughly enjoyed their first year of training and were appointed to Alice Springs Corps for practical out-training at the commencement of 1997. It was also a special thrill to be told by Commissioner John Clinch about our promotion to the rank of lieut-colonel in 1996.

The year 1997 was particularly satisfying as far as the management of the Geelong Conference Centre was concerned. Under Sonja's close supervision, many physical improvements were made to the buildings and surrounds. The paving of the roads was repaired and road signs placed in Eastern Park, making it easier for people to find this special centre. Both of us undertook the Certificate Four in Workplace Training and Assessment programme at Gordon Institute in Geelong on the assumption that this would help us in teaching at the Officer Training College where

Salvation Army courses were now recognised as accredited tertiary and further education courses. The move to become accredited at degree level was another decade away.

In April, Ian attended his first spiritual retreat at GCC led by Major Raymond Finger, and what a wonderful time it was. There were periods of directed study, walking with the Lord and with the Word. Raymond gave each participant an IADOM medallion to remind them that 'It All Depends On Me' for one's personal spiritual development. We cannot do that for others. All we can do is to provide them with the environment and resources so they can grow. Their response is up to them. Also, Ian was challenged again with the words of Isaiah 40:31 'They who wait on the Lord will renew their strength… They will mount up with wings like eagles, walk and not be weary, run and not faint.' On a Walk with the Word overlooking Corio Bay, Ian saw seagulls effortlessly 'resting' on the wind—uplifted by the air. He recorded in his journal that he heard God saying, 'Allow my Spirit to lift you.' For the dedication time at the conclusion of the retreat, Ian took a small nut and two feathers as a symbol of dedicating himself and his 'wings' to the Lord to be lifted for service.

A couple of medical examinations that year showed both of us were quite fit for service—including service overseas. Commissioner Norman Howe, our new Territorial Commander, enquired toward the end of June about our availability for overseas service and we answered positively.

During that year a number of international visitors came to Geelong Conference Centre. One of these was Commissioner Fred Ruth, the International Secretary for South Pacific and East Asia. We thought he was examining the centre and checking facilities with a view to holding a possible international conference of leaders or zonal conference at the venue. However, he also probed us about our interest in returning to overseas service and we thought that could probably be to the Philippines where we had served earlier. Lieut-Colonels Robert and Carol Saunders, friends from our days in the Philippines, also visited. Rob was the current Chief Secretary and Carol the Territorial Secretary for Women's Ministries and Territorial Home League Secretary in the Korea Territory. We thought they were just examining the conference centre and we were pleased to show them around. They shared something of their work in that Territory—especially teaching the Servant Leadership Training Course which Rob had been trying to encourage the Korean officers to undertake. Always being interested in leader development, Ian showed quite a deal of enthusiasm for such a project. He had already been trying to record video resources for this course using the studio then situated at GCC.

On 15 August 1997, however, we received a phone call from Commissioner Norman Howe asking us to ring the Chief of the Staff of The Salvation Army, Commissioner Earle Maxwell. The Chief was staying at a certain hotel in Colombo, Sri Lanka. During that conversation, Commissioner Maxwell broke the news that Ian was to become the Chief Secretary (second-in-command) and Sonja the Territorial Secretary for Women's Organisations in the Korea Territory, effective 1 November. The news was not to be released until 1 September.

Following the announcement of our appointment to Korea, we discovered that a relative, Major Linda Southwell, had served in Korea for 20 years from November 1921 in variety of appointments. These appointments included service at Territorial Headquarters, Seoul Boys Home, as Assistant District Officer, and finally Trade Manager. She returned to Australia in 1941, just before the commencement of the hostilities of the World War II in the Far East.

The weeks following that phone conversation with the Chief of the Staff became particularly busy. We commenced some language studies by means of taped dialogues and grammar lessons—especially because we learned that very little English was spoken in Korea. We set about trying to learn as much of the geography and culture of the country as possible. Finalising the appointment in Geelong and taking some furlough also had to be fitted into those weeks, as was packing those goods we would take to Korea, and arranging storage of other items or distributing the balance to family members. Some uncertainty regarding our visas for Korea became a serious matter of prayer during October. The Korean Consulate office in Sydney misplaced the applications we had made, and they consequently missed being placed in the diplomatic bag to Korea. Wonderfully, our visas eventually came back to Sydney from Seoul on 24 October, barely a week before we were due to leave.

Because Cathy and Darren were to be commissioned in early December, we received special permission to fly to Korea, be welcomed at the commencement of November and then return almost immediately for the commissioning weekend in Melbourne. Our newly issued visas meant we could enter and leave Korea and then re-enter again. Around that time we also learned that some money from the estate of Ian's Aunt Grace would help to make that trip back financially possible. So did a freewill offering from Cathy and Darren's session-mates at the training college, who were concerned that we might miss out on the important event of their commissioning.

During July 1997, Sharon married Frank Sanders. He was a citizen of the USA and taught English as a second language in Melbourne to university students. Some of his students were Korean and Frank arranged for us to spend a very informative hour or more with them. Having almost completed a further major study in psychology, in 1998 Sharon began the postgraduate training needed to become a psychologist. We were pleased that she was in a settled position before we left.

Some other family matters also fell into place during 1997. After a long succession of casual jobs, Jenni gained a full-time position at a technical and further education (TAFE) college as an administrative officer in social welfare. This work was multifaceted in the field that interested her, and we knew she had secure employment and accommodation before we left Australia.

God's timing was perfect, as usual!

So, after almost four years back in education and training work, we said goodbye to Geelong Conference Centre and our Territory, and flew to Korea. The next stage of the adventure in service was commencing.

Chapter 14

Korea, 1997–99

Korea was the first country in which Ian had lived and worked where Christianity was a minority faith and English was not understood by the majority. Sonja, of course, had lived with her parents in the Netherlands East Indies (now Indonesia) and was more familiar with that situation.

Soon after our arrival we enrolled to undertake two hours of language studies on Friday afternoons so that we could gain a grasp of the language and the script. Most of the road signs were in Korean—just occasionally they would have an anglicised version beneath them in small print. How grateful we were that in the early 15th century King Sejong presided over the invention of a phonetic script called *hangŭl* for the Korean language. Based on the sounds and the grammar of Chinese, *hangŭl* was infinitely simpler than the Chinese characters and language structure. As result, literacy in Korea had increased greatly. By learning the sounds associated with the distinctive Korean characters, we were at least able to read the road signs and sing from The Salvation Army Korean Song Book in meetings. Ian's pocket dictionaries became Korean-English and English-Korean.

We were also blessed that some officers were appointed to assist us as translators in our ministry. Major Hwang, Sung-yup had trained in Australia and so he understood English and some Australian idioms as well. Major Kim Dong-jin was another and, still later, Captain Kang Jong-gil. Each of these was invaluable in translating correspondence coming to Ian's desk in Korean and, of course, translation of his replies back into Korean. We were particularly blessed to have Envoy Joy Johns from the Australia Eastern Territory as the Private Secretary to the Territorial

Commander. Having served in Korea for a number of years, she had a good grasp of the Korean language and fulfilled more or less complementary roles as translator and secretary for the Territorial Commander and his correspondence. Joy also was the translator when Ian needed to have his daily discussions with Territorial Commander Colonel Lee, Sung-duk about business matters of the Territory. The colonel respected her as a highly confidential person and was not prepared to allow junior officers to be party to the discussions that he and Ian might have. Colonel Lee had limited abilities in spoken English, although he could certainly understand more than he could speak. His wife, Colonel Cho, In-sun, who was the President of Women's Ministries for the Korea Territory, was not so restrictive in regard to her translated conversations with Sonja.

On the basis of what Lieut-Colonels Robert and Carol Saunders had shared with the leaders in Korea about us from our time of service together in the Philippines, Ian was given a Korean name roughly transliterated as Nahm-goong, Ee-uhn; and Sonja the name Nahm-goong, Sun-nyuh. The surname comes first. Nahm-goong meant 'South Palace'—because a palace is always near a well. Eu-uhn meant 'word of authority' because Ian had been a teacher. Sonja's called name meant 'womanly angel' because Sonja's previous occupation had been a nurse. Somewhat flattering for both of us and fairly close to the phonetics of our names!

We tried desperately to learn the names of the officers at headquarters, feeling it was important to be able to call them by name and so relate to them. Many had the family names of 'Kim', 'Kang' or 'Lee'. More complicated still was discovering that women retained their own name after marriage so it was a matter of trying to place couples together where different surnames applied. However, we soon learned that Koreans preferred to be addressed by their job title such as 'territorial commander', 'secretary for personnel', 'divisional commander', or 'corps officer' and so on in preference to their rank or name. Job title was very important in the hierarchical systems of this country with Confucian foundations and a majority Buddhist religious background. So Ian was always addressed as 'chief secretary' rather than by his rank or his name.

Little wonder that when the Asian economic crisis struck Korea not long after we arrived in 1997, and people lost their jobs, the newly unemployed were disillusioned. All of a sudden these dismissed workers had lost their statuses. They were almost 'no-persons'. As result, a number of men committed suicide by throwing themselves into the Han River or by taking some other drastic course of action. In response to this, The Salvation Army set up drop-in centres to which those who had lost their jobs—especially men—could come during the day. They could leave home with their briefcase as though they were going to a job and come to The Salvation Army centre. There they could view any job advertisements in the newspapers or through the internet before returning home at the usual time, thus giving their neighbours the impression that they were still employed.

This same economic crisis also caused many families to fracture. Women were considered to be very low-class citizens within Korea. Few had opportunities for a full secondary education and rarely any tertiary education at that time. As result, some men acted quite aggressively toward their wives. When the wives of these unemployed men discovered their husbands had lost their jobs, they vented their anger by returning the aggression. As a result, some of these men became homeless. In response to this, The Salvation Army set up accommodation centres where these homeless men could live at least until such time as they regained employment and put their lives back together again. Once more we saw the principle at work: 'Where there's a need, there's The Salvation Army'.

Our accommodation was a double apartment on the fifth floor of a hillside building owned by the Army for housing THQ officer staff. To save electrical power, no lifts operated in the building, but the view over downtown Seoul was worth the climb. That daily climb—especially when carrying groceries—certainly helped to keep us fit. Whilst we were easily able to view THQ from our raised elevation, it could take 15 minutes to drive there because of the traffic and the special system of turns and U-turns needed along the route. As with the Philippines years earlier, driving was on the right side of the road rather than the left, and all the vehicles were left hand drive.

At the time we were there, Seoul had a population of 11 million and was the capital of a nation about the size of the state of Victoria, Australia. The nation of South Korea or, more correctly, the Republic of Korea, had a population of 45 million people. Fifty kilometres to the north was the most heavily armed frontier in the world—the Demilitarised Zone

(DMZ) between North and South Korea. North Korea described itself as the Democratic People's Republic of Korea—although the political system in South Korea was much more democratic than in the North. We visited the DMZ on a Saturday in the depth of winter (temperature: -14°C) and the truce village of Panmunjom that straddles the border. The tensions there were palpable.

We found great growth had taken place in The Salvation Army over the 90 years of its existence on the Korean peninsula—especially since the end of the World War II. From 1,041 soldiers on the Army's rolls in 1946 (over 8,000 in the north of the country had been lost during the war years and the resulting separation), the Territory now had 38,000. From 44 corps then, they now had 222. All the elements for church growth were evident: believing prayer (early morning, late at night, every day of the week at corps buildings), regular home Bible study groups, and faith goals. Officers' councils were spent in reviewing past successes and committing to new goals for the year ahead. Long-term appointments for officers were common. Many corps officers served in appointments for more than a decade and they rarely moved unless they asked to do so. Officers and soldiers made sacrificial offerings to build the kingdom and places of worship. We discovered several officers who had sold their wedding rings and the gold rings given on the first birthday of their children to achieve such goals.

Good church growth teaching had been given—much of it dating back to the time when the then Major Paul Rader was involved with the Territory. He served on the Officer Training College staff before becoming the Training Principal, then the Territorial Education Secretary, and eventually Chief Secretary. Major Rader had studied church growth principles at doctoral level at Fuller Theological Seminary in the USA. Other Protestant churches in Korea were also applying effective church growth principles about the same time. Many Salvationists were encouraged to plant new corps or outposts. As a result, a number of corps had been commenced by local officers and soldiers at their own initiative. For instance, the late Corps Sergeant-Major Kim, Ki-chul and his wife, Sergeant Lee, Jae-ok planted five corps and two outposts. These grew from meetings they held in their homes as they moved around the country to his various teaching appointments. Courses were developed by the Territory and refined to equip Salvationists for this task.

Each year in spring, the Army would take to the streets. Marching down a major road in Seoul, for instance, THQ staff and officer trainees would carry banners encouraging people not only to spring-clean their houses but allow God to clean up their lives. We were delighted to join them on these Clean Life marches.

Because all men had to undergo compulsory military training due to the threat from North Korea, men and women Salvationists alike all wore their Salvation Army uniforms proudly. They understood the military metaphors in Scripture and those inherent in the organisation. We were delighted to conduct Spiritual Days with cadets. At the conclusion of the in-college training, those about to be ordained as ministers of religion and commissioned as officers always recite the Army's doctrinal statements. The Koreans did so loudly and with military precision. Because the verb in the Korean language is the last part of every sentence, the word order of the Korean statement of doctrine number seven, for example, would be something like the following: 'We … repentance toward God, faith and our Lord Jesus Christ and regeneration by the Holy Spirit are necessary for salvation … believe!' They almost shouted the word 'believe!' for each of the 11 Articles of Faith to demonstrate their conviction. Most dramatic and challenging for the listeners!

What a delight it was to meet so many dedicated Salvation Army officers and soldiers as we travelled around the country. We usually engaged in such journeys on two weekends each month. Typically, this meant a Saturday train journey with one of our translators to a large city such as Taegu, Taejon or Pusan where the local divisional commander met us and took us to prearranged corps or social service centres within driving distance. We greeted the officers, and enquired after their families. The officers briefed us on the work of the corps or centre while we enjoyed light refreshments, usually consisting of fruit and green tea. Often we sat on cushions on the floor and at very low tables. Following the briefing and refreshments we offered prayer for the officers, their family members and their ministry. We took photographs of each place to remind us of the people and the situation—and some, such as Kil-hyn Corps led by Envoys Lee, Hyang-ho and Kim, Soon-deuk, were very deprived. Then we travelled to the next centre. After being accommodated in a hotel on the Saturday night, we spoke at the Sunday morning meeting in one of the corps. Knowing just a little Korean helped us build a rapport with the congregation and the officers. Lunch followed at the corps or a restaurant, usually sponsored by one of the corps local officers, before perhaps a visit to another corps and being returned to the railway station for the train trip back to Seoul. Sometimes we spoke at an afternoon meeting as well. In that way we visited around 70 corps in the first year and met many other officers in councils. We rejoiced at the responsiveness of the various congregations to the messages we brought from God's Word.

One of the most moving occasions was an afternoon visit to the site in Chinju near Pusan where Senior-Major Noh, Yong Soo was martyred during the Korean War. He defied pressure by the Communist forces to renounce his faith. Holding his Bible in one hand and his Salvation Army song book in another, he had apparently shouted, 'By believing you can have life!' before he was shot dead. Subsequently, the soldiers of Chinju built a magnificent corps building in memory of his sacrifice—a very different building to that at Kil-hyn Corps. A motion picture about Major Noh's life entitled *The Blood of the Martyr* carried the story of his heroism around the world after the Korean War and acted to encourage personal dedications and corps growth.[33]

Officers councils were held twice a year and we were responsible for speaking at two sessions on each occasion. During April 1998, at the social officers councils, a third day was added after the usual reports and goal-setting for a holiness focus that Ian was delighted to facilitate. His notes were translated, but the officers were shocked to be involved in group discussion and other modern learning strategies instead of hearing a succession of lectures. Teachers are held in high esteem in Korea and tend to demonstrate their knowledge by lecturing in the style endorsed by Confucius. Ian tried to introduce the officers to thinking for themselves, hearing what the Scriptures revealed and testing out some alternative ideas.

The executive officers councils in October that year also gave opportunity to introduce another module from the Servant Leadership Training Course from IHQ. We experienced a few challenges in translating

---

[33] The motion picture version of the story suggests he shouted, 'Whether I live or die matters not: Jesus lives!'

the textbook and dubbing the script to a supporting video. In all of these situations, relying on translators was absolutely essential. About the only events we could attend without a translator were the Seoul Rotary, the American Chamber of Commerce or one of the English-speaking women's groups. Aside from Rotary, these others were not regular events.

Cultural adjustments were a great challenge. Culture shock tends to occur in any situation when a disparity is found between what one expects and what one finds in reality. We have already mentioned the matter of job title being more important than personal names. The multiple levels of the Korean language and the place then accorded to women were also linked to the strong hierarchical nature of society. Nevertheless, the Army had made much progress since the pioneer officers needed to build partitions down the centre of their halls to keep men and women from seeing each other at worship. Much more freedom existed in the 1990s. We are gratified to note that, at the time of writing, a very capable woman officer, Kim, Nam-sun, who was the manager of a senior citizens' residence when we were in Korea, subsequently served as the Territorial Social Services Secretary and Secretary for Programme with the rank of lieut-colonel.

Our other main role was international communications. This involved interpreting letters which came from overseas such as International Headquarters and trying to craft suitable responses from the Territory. Again, Ian valued the help of various translators and Envoy Joy Johns in this task. When Joy went on homeland furlough in November 1998 much routine work came to Ian's desk and Sonja was involved also.

Although the women's work in the Territory was extensive, the role of Territorial Secretary for Women's Organisations in the Territory was not a demanding one, so Sonja was mainly involved as the Secretary to the Medical Fellowship—a very active group in Korea that arranged distribution of medicines and occasional all-day medical visits to doctor-less villages. After the busy appointment at the Geelong Conference Centre, Sonja found teaching English classes weekly to cadets at the Training College, other similar classes for headquarters staff during lunch hours and after work, plus leading an English language Bible study, gave her some satisfaction. Following extensive floods in August 1998 that claimed the lives of over 200 in Seoul, Sonja was able to tell territories overseas about Army involvement in providing dry bedding, instant noodles, clean drinking water, and clothing to thousands of survivors who were forced from their homes. As a result, significant donations to help defray Army relief work expenses were willingly offered and gratefully received.

A major event in 1998 was the Zonal Conference in May. Being early spring, the weather was most pleasant. The conference brought together Territorial Commanders, Chief Secretaries and equivalent leaders from all territories, commands and regions in the South Pacific and East Asia Zone to Seoul under the leadership of General Paul Rader and the International Secretary, Commissioner Fred Ruth. Ian chaired the organising committee, and the event was a great success. All concerned gave excellent support. General Rader wanted the conference held in Korea to emphasise the significant growth of the Army in that country. The purpose was achieved. In addition, President Kim, Dae-jung officially received the delegates, awarding the General a special medal for the service given to the Korean people and around the world. One of the recommendations of the conference was that 'Korea story' be published in one of our Army journals. Ian eventually prepared an article which appeared in *The Officer* magazine in February 1999. He also contributed an article on Korea to *The Historical Dictionary of The Salvation* Army edited by Major John G. Merritt and published in 2006.

We certainly felt the separation from our children during that first year in Korea. However, we were delighted that Cathy and Darren, having been eminently successful in their training work, were appointed to Kingborough (formerly Blackmans Bay) in Tasmania early in 1998. This appointment was like a homecoming for Cathy after the three years we spent as a family at Hobart and its environs from 1982 to 1985. On the weekend of their arrival, bushfires closed the road between Hobart and Kingborough. The officer who was to conduct their installation meeting could not travel through the fire zone and the meeting was postponed. Instead, Darren, Cathy and their corps members provided welfare relief to firefighters and others negatively affected by the fires. We wished we could have been closer, but were delighted when we learned of their efforts.

After a time in the office of the Fine Arts Department of the University of Melbourne, Sharon moved to an administrative position at Trinity College on the same campus. In her spare time, she worked to complete a postgraduate degree in counselling, linking her courses to some studies in natural medicine and the adherence to diet of those with food intolerances. Frank worked part-time in the International Office of the University of Melbourne and taught English as a second language at Holmes College. Jenni did well during her first year in administration of the social welfare unit at Barton Technical and Further Education College in Moorabbin which was currently the subject of a merger with other similar institutions. At least we were reassured that they all had secure jobs and seemed to be enjoying their work. In those pre-Skype days, we tried to set up personal email accounts so we could communicate with them more easily than by air letters.

We were delighted that we could be involved in some important property work in Korea. A site that would eventually become a new territorial headquarters needed consolidation of a number of plots of land and slowly this was achieved. In the south of the country at Mount Paekhwa, a conference centre was also set up which could accommodate 1,000 people if needed.

As often happens in appointments, the second year in Korea provided some challenges. Ian was disturbed about a number of administrative and procedural matters, and shared his concerns with the Territorial Commander. The now Commissioner Lee, Sung-duk, did not seem to be as concerned, but Ian's approach triggered some tensions.

Nevertheless, we experienced several notable successes in Korea during 1999. One of these was the inauguration of the HIV/AIDS care and prevention team of enthusiastic officers, funded by AusAid to raise awareness of Salvationists and those in the residential social services centres about the disease. We hoped the work would spread to strategic areas around military camps and red light districts. Sonja was also delighted that the Medical Fellowship was able to visit another doctor-less village one Saturday, providing immediate health care and referrals to a nearby hospital for those rural workers who would otherwise not seek help.

The 90th Anniversary of the Territory was held in March 1999 with the Chief the Staff, Commissioner Earle Maxwell, and Commissioner Wilma Maxwell as guest leaders. This was a most memorable event, especially for the ready responses in rededication by many Salvationists as they looked forward to serving Christ in the next decade that would flow into the new millennium. After the congress, Commissioner Maxwell asked us about some of our thoughts of work around the Southeast Asia area.

Later we received a phone call from Commissioner Fred Ruth indicating that Colonel James Lau, Officer Commanding in Hong Kong, was very ill with a recurrent brain tumour and not expected to live. He asked us our opinion about certain matters and sensed our concern for the work in China. Late in June, Colonel Lau was promoted to Glory. Lieut-Colonel Kang, Sung-hwan and his wife, Lee, Jung-ok, who was the Secretary for Personnel when we arrived in Korea, had been sent to Australia Southern as Assistant Chief Secretary to learn more about Salvation Army administration. They were now available to return to Korea and take our places. All this led to an afternoon phone call from General Paul Rader appointing us in charge of the Hong Kong Command. He emphasised the strategic nature of the work, particularly in view of the progressive opening up of the People's Republic of China (PRC) and the fact that Hong Kong was now part of that nation—no longer a British colony.

A visit by the Hong Kong Command Band and Songsters to Korea late in July 1999 assured us that we would be very welcome and would have little difficulty communicating in this new area of responsibility. Much more English was spoken than in Korea and the Hong Kong Salvationists seemed very friendly.

So, after just 22 months in Korea we were packing again and, under God's guidance, moving to the next stage of our opportunity to serve him—in China.

Chapter 15

China, 1999–2003

Our contacts with the members of the Hong Kong Command Band and Songsters before we left Korea had been most reassuring.

As expected, we were warmly welcomed and made to feel very comfortable by the newly appointed General Secretary, Major James Ling and his wife, Major Fona Ling. Lieut-Colonels Ian and Mary Begley, retired officers from Australia Southern who had come to Hong Kong to provide oversight for the Command's finances and business matters, also helped with the settling in process. Our quarters, on the upper floor of Pink Villa in the New Territories area, had a beautiful view over the estuary of the Pearl River into the South China Sea facing Tsing Yi and Ma Wan Islands. Majors James and Fona occupied the ground floor. Crossing the Tin Kau Bridge and using an excellent set of freeways could take us quickly to Command Headquarters (CHQ) in Wing Sing Lane, Yaumatei, Kowloon. At least we could drive on the left side of the road again.

Commissioner Lim, Ah Ang, a former International Secretary for South Pacific and East Asia, now retired and living in Singapore, conducted our welcome and installation meetings at Kowloon Central Corps. During the afternoon officers councils on 17 September, we learned of a devastating earthquake in neighbouring Taiwan. The Salvationists on that island used to be part of the Hong Kong and Taiwan Command but, with Hong Kong becoming part of the People's Republic of China (Mainland China) in 1997, IHQ took the decision that Taiwan should become a separate region. Ian dispatched Major On, Dieu-Quang and Major Tony Ma, Yeung-mo, who both spoke Mandarin, to investigate the situation and report back. They confirmed that more than 2,500 people had been killed in the earthquake. Salvation Army properties were not badly damaged. However, our personnel there were in a state of shock like everybody else and apprehensive about possible aftershocks. Relief supplies and personnel were needed, especially to care for the survivors in the Puli area near Sun-Moon Lakes, and also provide support for our Salvationists in Taiwan who were trying to cope with the situation.

From our limited pool of 36 active officers, we allocated two at a time to support the Regional Leaders, Australians Majors Dennis and Patricia Rowe, and Salvationists in Taiwan. Through the Army's international network, other reinforcements from Indonesia Territory, Singapore and Malaysia Command and International Headquarters joined us. Ian visited Taiwan in October to see for himself something of the good work that was being done. In the weeks immediately after the earthquake, the people of Hong Kong generously donated sleeping bags, tents, food and medicine and funds to The Salvation Army, and these were put to good use. Proceeds of a celebrity concert held one Sunday night organised by our Public Relations Department (Envoy Simon Wong) and China Development Department (Envoy Alfred Tsang) generated over HK$12,000,000 (AU$2.5 million) in pledges. During the concert, uniformed Salvationists were among the volunteers on phone duty receiving pledges. Plans were put in place for projects to help many survivors whose homes and livelihoods had been badly affected by the quake. In 2000 we were able to return to open a village reconstructed with donations channelled through The Salvation Army and provide supplementary food supplies to the survivors.

Early in our appointment we quickly moved to grasp the ministry situation of the Army. Corps (church) ministry in the Hong Kong Command was relatively small. The Command had 19 corps, two outposts, 1,700 soldiers, six cadets in training and about 40 officers. However, a wide variety of educational and social service situations compensated for the lack of obvious corps ministry. The Command had six schools—including a large secondary school, four primary schools and a special school for students with disabilities. Other ministries included seven kindergartens, 15 pre-kindergarten nurseries, 16 residential centres for children and the elderly, and some 60 other centres. These latter included crèches, children's and youth centres, centres for the handicapped, a home-help programme, and centres for the homeless. Seven thrift stores helped fund the multifaceted social service programmes.

In addition, outreach was taking place in the People's Republic of China with at least 30 different community development programmes at the time we arrived. These projects included primary health care, water supply projects, and health education. We also supported integrated micro-enterprise projects such as poultry and pig-raising to lift the standard of living of unemployed and poverty-stricken minorities—especially in the western and southern regions of Mainland China. Such projects were funded through donations given to The Salvation Army in Hong Kong through International Headquarters Development Services, AusAid from Australia, NORAD from Norway, and similar groups.

Just over a month after arriving in Hong Kong, Ian spent a fascinating fortnight being introduced to some of those projects in Mainland China. In the company of Envoy Alfred Tsang and Mrs Puisi Chan, both of the Command China Development Department, he was able to open a 20-bed hospital/clinic/teaching centre funded by AusAid in a desperately poor area of the Yi minority tribe in Meigu County, Sichuan Province, South Central China.

Ian was also involved in the opening celebrations for the Lusing Village in Hubei Province to the north. Yangtze River floods devastated the area in 1998. Over a period of some weeks, Hong Kong Command helped feed the many people displaced. As a result, The Salvation Army was asked to rehouse some of the survivors. Funding was arranged to assist in providing basic housing, and now each of the 295 houses in the village displayed a Salvation Army Red Shield on its address plate containing the Army's name in Chinese characters: 'Save the World Army'. The main street was called Hong Kong Avenue in gratitude for support from Hong Kong. The town square, where the opening ceremony was held, was named 'Rader Plaza' as a tribute to the world leader of The Salvation Army at that time. Because the Chinese characters for General Rader's name also meant 'encouraging good virtue', the plaza should provide an ongoing reminder of part of the Army's ethos.

During the trip, Ian also met some of the leaders of the China Christian Council in Nanjing. This was the body that supervised the official churches in Mainland China for the Patriotic Three-Self

Movement—Self-Government, Self-Support and Self-Propagation. He visited a seminary where 160 theological students were training for Christian ministry and also toured Amity Press which produced three million Bibles in Chinese and related languages annually. His government 'minder' told him, 'There is no need for anyone to smuggle Bibles into Mainland China because they are being produced here on the spot and inexpensively. To smuggle would be dishonest and very un-Christian!'

Sonja was supposed to join Ian on this trip to the People's Republic of China, but instead made an urgent journey to Tasmania, Australia. Cathy needed to undergo an emergency caesarean delivery in giving birth to our first grandchild, Stephanie Grace Elkington. Stephanie was six weeks premature. Both mother and daughter recovered, although Stephanie needed to stay in hospital for a further three weeks until she was considered close enough to full term. Sonja was glad she could travel there to support Darren and Cathy. We had already planned a brief furlough in Australia over Christmas and so we had the thrill of conducting Stephanie's dedication at Macleod Corps on Christmas Day and be 'at home' in Melbourne for the turn of the century.

The year 2000 was an exciting one for the command because we celebrated 70 years since the Army officially commenced in Hong Kong. In consultation with other leaders in the command, we decided on the theme 'Celebrate and Move Forward'. All wanted to celebrate the good things God had accomplished through the Army in the past, but also move on to new victories in the future. Heads of departments and leaders in education, social services and corps ministry were involved in setting Specific, Measurable, Agreed, Realistic and Time-sensitive (SMART) goals for the years ahead. Our experiences in Korea of setting and monitoring such goals in a similar culture provided helpful preparation.

As we had in the Philippines and Western Australia, we commenced emphasising corps planting. Before he was promoted to Glory, our predecessor, Colonel James Lau, had appointed newly-commissioned Lieutenant Sara Tam Mei-shun as pioneer officer to the Special Administrative Region of Macau in June 1999. In March 2000, we officially inaugurated the work in Macau in the presence of Dr Luis Amado de Vizeu, Minister for Youth Education. We then opened the rented premises for the Iao Hon Corps in the presence of Mr Carol Chan of the United Evangelical Church, more government officials, CHQ senior leaders and the Hong Kong Command Brass Band. Ian recommended to IHQ that the command be renamed 'Hong Kong and Macau Command' and this occurred in August of that year.

Our work in Hong Kong, Macau and Mainland China was greatly assisted by a fine citizens advisory board chaired by the Honourable Dr David K.P. Li, Chairman and CEO of the Bank of East Asia (BEA). The board advised on what was allowable or wise in those transition years after the return of Hong Kong, Kowloon and the New Territories of the People's Republic of China. The members also assisted in promoting our various Army projects and rehabilitation work.

At the suggestion of one member, Ian's diary became an electronic Palm organiser—including an English dictionary and several versions of the Bible.

Aside from Macau, however, the command had not planted a new corps in nine years. Some corps had been un-officered or combined with other centres. So that year, Chaiwan Corps at the Ann Wyllie Memorial Primary School was reactivated with assistance of a second-year cadet couple. A new outreach was commenced at Cheung Kwan O (East Kowloon) with other cadets and the then Divisional Commander, Major Gideon Lam. Plans were put in hand to open another centre in Tung Chung, Lantau Island, where the Army's next primary school would be opened in due course. Even though retired officer couples led two corps, we believed God was going to raise up more workers to lead all the corps centres.

Existing corps were not neglected either. The command completed the purchase of a disused picture theatre for the Kowloon City Corps near the site of the old Kai Tak Airport. In true Salvation Army conversion-style, this theatre that used to show pornographic movies was now sanctified for use to proclaim the Gospel! When we arrived in the command, the need for larger accommodation for that corps was obvious. Some of those attending Kowloon City Corps could only follow what was taking place at the Sunday morning meeting through closed-circuit television connections to other rooms in the building. We discovered many of the corps halls were more than 80 per cent filled on a Sunday morning—a great challenge.

Our command kept good relations with the neighbouring territories, commands and regions. Manila Central Corps from the Philippines came for our anniversary. Eventually officers from the Philippines were appointed to Hong Kong to lead the English-speaking Corps on Hong Kong Island. This corps mainly catered for Filipina women doing domestic work for wealthy households in Hong Kong. We installed Major Gillian Downer as acting regional commander and later Lieut-Colonel David Bringans as regional commander in Taiwan. Our command continued supporting the rehabilitation the Puli area of Taiwan for some years after the earthquake. Women from Singapore joined us for a women's camp. Sonja and her team from the women's department arranged the camp that drew 180 delegates. Retired General Eva Burrows was the special guest speaker and 15 seekers were recorded.

We were privileged to participate in the International Leaders Conference in Atlanta USA in June and then the Millennial Congress in the same city. What wonderful times of blessing and inspiration these events provided and for Ian another time of spiritual renewal. This was our first visit to the USA and we spent a fascinating two weeks following the congress on furlough in Washington DC and New York. We saw many sites, including viewing, from the top of the Empire State Building, the Twin Towers of the World Trade Centre, which were subsequently destroyed in terrorist attacks on 11 September 2001.

Returning to Hong Kong, we decided to emphasise encouraging Christlike character, clear communication of the Gospel and compassionate care, together with General John Gowans' emphases on saving souls, growing saints and serving suffering humanity.

In October we were both able to visit some more of our Army community development projects in Mainland China. These included animal husbandry projects in Hebei and Inner Mongolia provinces. In the latter area, an initial herd of 160 cashmere goats (with yellow, red and blue ear tags numbered SA01, SA02 and so on) had grown to 350. Another project was tree-planting to help conserve topsoil of an area that was denuded of trees and badly eroded. We witnessed a cistern-digging project where the whole village was enlisted to dig the reservoir, with the Army and sponsors to pay for the concrete to line the cistern and for piping to carry water to the village houses. Without such water projects, women in many villages in Mainland China, at that time, sometimes needed to carry heavy buckets of water several kilometres from distant wells to their homes several times a day. Government officials were delighted with the help provided by the Army. These officials also gratefully remembered the relief work following the disastrous earthquake in 1998. We saw schools with plaques reminding students and their parents that the centre had been rebuilt with the help of the 'Save the World Army.' Wherever possible we took opportunities to explain our Christian motivation for service.

We travelled on to view community development projects in Yunnan province—deep in the south of Mainland China near the Tibetan border and only accessible by kilometres of unmade roads. Assisted by AusAid and donations from money raised by the Self Denial Appeal in the Australian territories, the Hong Kong Command was able to share in building a much-needed school. Sadly, no water supply was included in the initial project. We had to trust that it would be included in a follow-up project. The Army was also able to install a simple electricity system, help with animal husbandry projects and microcredit loans, and install an improved water system in another village. Again, we found government officials in the area very positive in their attitudes to the Army. We were building good relationships. Having our Chinese-language Salvation Army Red Shield on a number of buildings provided us with openings for helpful conversations.

Life for the Chinese in these western area provinces was very challenging. Many of the women were engaged in agriculture whilst their husbands were in the cities trying to earn money on construction projects. In order to reduce the size of the population, the government had decreed that couples should only have one child. Most wanted a boy. If that child, a boy or girl died, then there was little chance that the couple would be supported in their old age. Both the men and the women were hard workers. The hands of the women we met in the rural areas were large and calloused. They were amazed at Sonja's small and soft hands. Our microcredit programmes were designed to move these women out of poverty. In one project, they had been taught cloth painting and embroidery. The work they did was so good that the proceeds of selling this—some items overseas eventually—enabled these women to improve their standard of living and to provide education for their one child. With the money raised, some of the women were able to buy treadle sewing machines. Using these machines they could make garments and curtains for houses and in that way raise more money for food and their child's school fees. Our hearts were touched as we mingled with them and we were so pleased that our programmes had done something positive to help them.

As our relationships developed, we found many of the government officials quite open to spiritual matters. At the various banquets to which we were invited, we bowed our heads and silently asked the blessing on our food. As we continued to do this over the course of the next few years, we found that government officials were prompted to ask, through our translator, 'Colonel, would you ask the blessing on the meal for us all?' Of course we would! The officials also realised that we were people of strong principles when we politely refused to accept the gifts of cigarettes they offered to us or the glasses of wine that were on the banquet table. They also learnt that we required strict accountability for the use of any funds we entrusted to them for projects. We would also not receive any gifts of money unless they could be officially receipted. Of course, we also indicated we expected that standard to be maintained by our employees and other representatives in Mainland China.

We were also able to maintain links with former officers—those who served in Mainland China before the Army was officially banned during the Communist revolution in the 1950s—their children and their grandchildren. They mainly lived in Beijing or Shanghai. In January and October 2000 we were able to share evening meals with those in Beijing. Although they regularly worshipped at one of the official Three Self Movement churches in the city, they were proud of their Salvation Army heritage. At their request, we were honoured to conduct a devotional meeting and dedicate two young children—great grandchildren of early day Army officers in China. A small Salvation Army flag was carefully removed from its hiding place in the room and pinned up on the curtain. Together, we sang some well-known Army songs in Chinese, dedicated the children and opened God's Word. We were greatly moved.

At the same time we were striving to develop good relations with the Beijing Christian Council and the China Christian Council in Nanjing. Later, Ian had the opportunity to preach at the Chongwenmen Church (a former Methodist Church building) in Beijing in January 2001 to a congregation of about 1,500. This opportunity only came about because of the specific invitation by the pastor of the church. (We were told his mother had been a Salvationist and used to play a timbrel when the Army was active as a church.) Some of those who crowded into the church were only able to follow the service by a closed-circuit television line into the basement because of lack of space in the main church auditorium. We again reaffirmed how delighted we were that three million copies of the Scriptures were being published in Chinese and distributed by Amity Press each year, funded by donations to the Bible Society.

In all our travelling around the China and the surrounding areas, we always wore a small cross on the left lapel of our uniforms. If people seemed mystified about the uniforms we wore, or the metallic bar on our epaulettes carrying the Chinese characters for 'Save the World Army', we would point to our crosses to communicate we were Christians. Generally they seemed to understand. One man who Ian met in China quietly showed him the similar small cross he was wearing—but *under* the lapel of his jacket.

Ian was a member of the delegation of Hong Kong church leaders to North Korea in July 2000. 'Like Mainland China 20 years ago,' remarked one of his companions. Poverty, limitations on communication, the all-pervading cult of the Great Leader, Kim, Il-sung and his son, the Dear Leader, Kim, Jong-il, were lasting impressions. The delegates from Hong Kong rejoiced in some signs of improving relationships between North and South Korea and viewed this as an answer to prayer. The group visited a noodle factory that had been funded by gifts from South Korea and Hong Kong, realising that such facilities were important for the nourishment of people in such a deprived nation that directed much of its resources to building and training their military forces. Following a visit to the Demilitarised Zone from the north, the group moved to areas where it was alleged atrocities had been committed by United States troops during the Korean War. The North Koreans were chanting (as translated for us), 'We will fight the American aggressors.' From their point of view, the war was not over. No peace treaty had been signed. Only an armistice existed and they were ready for hostilities to resume at any time.

The delegation visited two churches and was both encouraged and concerned. We were glad that worship was being conducted and God's Word opened, but there were so few young people. Ian had been carrying his Salvation Army cap with him on the trip. Inadvertently, he left it in the church after one of the services. This gave him an excuse to return without a minder and, after collecting his property, he walked up the aisle slowly repeating the words in the limited Korean he remembered: 'May God bless you all!' And people smiled.

In November 2000, we enjoyed a God-glorifying anniversary congress led by General John Gowans and Commissioner Gisèle Gowans. All corps, schools and representatives of each social service centre marched with their particular Army flag on anniversary Sunday afternoon. This was the first time since the handover of Hong Kong to Mainland China in 1997—and for many years before—that The Salvation Army had conducted a march of witness. During the anniversary celebration, the General 'topped off' the new Kam Tin Corps Hall and Community Centre in the New Territories. The building was not quite ready for an official opening, but at least the 'topping off' indicated new growth in the Command. The General opened a new integrated social ministry at Mong Kok, Kowloon, amid a set of 41-storey high-rise apartments. That ministry included a residence for 132, a day centre, and a nursery. Regular Sunday outreach commenced there soon after with the Financial Secretary, Captain On, Dieu-Quang, as the leader. We rejoiced at good support provided by Mrs Victoria Kwok and her team of 1,300 social service employees—most of whom were not Salvationists and many who were not-yet-Christians. Each social centre had an Army flag, and the Command developed a chaplaincy programme which we hoped would lead residents and any not-yet-Christian staff to faith in Christ. During the Congress Sunday morning meeting, Ian was privileged to publicly enrol 59 new soldiers, with the General bringing a special greeting to them before opening God's Word. Twenty-seven seekers were recorded at the conclusion of that meeting.

Christmas and New Year 2000/2001 was spent in Tasmania, Australia, with Cathy and Darren and our precious grandchild Stephanie. The visit once again provided opportunities for us to meet people with whom we had served at Hobart Corps from 1982–85 as well as share in Cathy and Darren's final weeks of ministry before they moved from Kingborough Corps to become associate officers at Box Hill Corps in Victoria. We expected to be in Melbourne to help welcome them, but a phone call from Hong Kong on the return journey caused a sudden change of plans. The General Secretary, Major James Ling, who had been covering Ian's position as well as his own during our homeland furlough, had been diagnosed with nasopharyngeal cancer. James had experienced some cancer problems in the facial area about 18 years before, but all his doctors believed these had been fully cured. On reflection, we realised that he was having increased difficulty hearing what was being said to him, especially by those people who were on his left side in conversations such as in board meetings. A speedy return to Hong Kong was essential to reduce the pressures he was feeling and to reassure the Command of continued stable leadership.

The next 10 months were coloured by variations in James's health situation and necessary pastoral care during periods of hospital treatments, returns to home, more chemotherapy, crises, some recovery, and ongoing assessments. During these months, we were greatly supported by Lieut-Colonels Ian and Mary Begley, who returned to the Command once again for six months through to June, and then Lieut-Colonels Edward and Mary Schmidtke on to November. Both couples were colleagues from Australia Southern and Ian and Eddie were well-experienced administrators—easily able to fulfil the role of Assistant to the Officer Commanding. With the need for Eddie and Mary Schmidtke to return home before the end of the year and the reality that Major Ling would not be able to continue in a leadership role in the foreseeable future, the General decided to appoint Majors Barry and Arlene Dooley from USA to be the new General Secretary and Command Secretary for Women's Organisations from 7 January 2002. Major James Ling was placed on indefinite sick leave with Major Fona Ling caring for him while preparing for a requested corps appointment at some stage in the future. In the event, James Ling was promoted to Glory before the end of the year, much to the sadness of the Hong Kong Command. This was a second significant national leader lost to cancer in the past three years.

Having the support of Ian Begley and Eddie Schmidtke in the Command during 2001 meant that Ian was able to travel to Mainland China and Macau several times The first trip was with the delegation of Hong Kong Christian Council heads of churches at the invitation of the State Administration for Religious Affairs. What a delight it was to see thousands of Chinese attending multiple services in churches at Shenyang in the Liaoning Province of north-eastern China. Theological colleges training pastors for Chinese and Korean ministries were overflowing. Government officials were coming to accept that Chinese Christianity was really indigenous since no overseas missionaries had been in the country for 50 years. 'We used to think that when a person became a Christian they ceased to be Chinese,' confessed one official. 'Now we see Christianity is indigenous.' Our delegation thanked the Lord for good foundations laid all those years ago by pioneers from overseas and the continued work of the Holy Spirit in the lives of those Chinese nationals who had committed themselves to Christ. Truly, nothing can stop the Gospel!

While denominations in Mainland China had been officially eliminated and absorbed into the official Patriotic Three-Self Movement Church, some remnants still remained. One church leader in the Liaoning Province told Ian how several groups met in his church during the week. 'Some groups,' he said, 'celebrate communion using a single cup; others use small individual cups. Others used real bread and still others use wafer biscuits. One group meets on Saturdays!' Ian wondered if he was suggesting a group with a Salvation Army style of congregation would also be welcome to use his facilities!

We had been praying about how we could provide better support for the former officers and their families in Mainland China as well as establishing a network for an eventual official return to Mainland China as a church. Ian had approached a number of officers in the Command about moving to the Mainland, but all were reluctant for various reasons. Some were genuinely afraid because they remembered the excesses of the Communist Revolution and the later Cultural Revolution. On the journey through Mainland China with the heads of churches, however, Ian met Lieutenant Jeremy Lam, Yin-ming on holidays from Hong Kong. Jeremy seemed most at ease in the People's Republic and was fluent in Putonghua (Mandarin). Ian felt a spiritual nudge. Could Lieutenant Lam be the officer most suitable to be appointed to Mainland China? Despite the fact that Jeremy had been commissioned only recently, he was prepared to accept the challenge of becoming the official project officer (PO) based in Beijing—and also to act as the unofficial pastoral officer (PO) for the former officers and their families. As such, he became the first commissioned officer of The Salvation Army appointed to Mainland China since 1949.

We both travelled to International Headquarters in London for an orientation experience for leaders such as ourselves early in May. Three days of intense observation and discussion gave us good insights into the working of the nerve centre of the Army—even though the actual offices were temporarily located at the William Booth Training College in Denmark Hill. The earlier International Headquarters at 101 Queen Victoria Street was being demolished and rebuilt. How we wished we had had such an orientation when we were first appointed to Korea four years earlier! The paid trip to the UK provided good reasons for us to take a week of uninterrupted furlough to visit Sonja's aunts and cousins in Holland, and take a further week in Switzerland catching up with Lieut-Colonels Rodney and Jacqueline Bates in Bern. We served with them in Zambia from 1970–72. What beautiful scenery they introduced us to around Lake Geneva and the Jungfrau region of lakes and alps!

Barely having arrived back in Hong Kong, we accompanied the now Commissioners Robert and Carol Saunders on a visit to Army operations in Mainland China. The new International Secretary and his wife were well received by church and local officials. They were also able to view our community development and agricultural projects in Hebei and Inner Mongolia provinces. Commissioner Saunders was permitted to preach, as Ian had done, at the Chongwenmen church in Beijing. They also visited some former officers and their families who emphasised to the international leaders that they 'never quit!' being Salvationists. We returned to Hong Kong in time for the cadets covenant day, commissioning ceremony and appointments service for six new officers. Parramatta Songsters from the Australia Eastern Territory were the guest musical group. The week before the commissioning, the songsters visited and ministered to capacity crowds across the border in Guangdong province as well as visiting Army facilities in Hong Kong

In harmony with the Command theme for the year of 'Move Forward with the Spirit', we were involved in holiness teaching and counselling retreats for officers and soldiers within a week of the commissioning. Majors Ray and Cathy Harris from Canada were the guest facilitators covering the biblical/doctrinal/historical and prayer aspects respectively of the life of holiness. Ian was delighted to have the opportunity to teach about the person and work of the Holy Spirit. Captain Ian Swan, Training Principal, coordinated the programme.

In July, Ian travelled to Kuala Lumpur with 22 other Salvationists from around the world, including nine from Hong Kong, to be part of the Chinese Congress on World Evangelisation (CCOWE) meetings. Immediately following, he chaired the first Salvation Army Chinese Ministries Conference in Singapore, with 18 delegates. Hong Kong Command organised the occasion. A number of significant recommendations were made to Army leadership, and the Hong Kong Command was challenged to provide resources for Salvation Army Chinese ministries around the world as far as possible. Good bonds of fellowship were formed and new networks established.

Sonja did not travel to Kuala Lumpur or Singapore as she was intently involved in finalising the annual women's ministries camp for the Command. What a great occasion that was! One hundred and sixty delegates filled the accommodation, with 20 more present on Sunday to focus on God who creates, controls the world and re-creates the lives of those who trust in him.

In August, Ian travelled with 16 volunteers from Hong Kong to inaugurate a tree-planting project in the almost treeless Chinese province of Inner Mongolia. Originally planned for the same area in which the Command brought relief supplies earlier in the year, the lack of suitable seedling trees and a locust plague also caused the plans to be changed. So the team planted trees in the same area in which we ran our community development programmes. Ian signed a memorandum of understanding for the Army to assist in building a new school in a deprived area to serve about three villages. Conditions were so bad in one of the villages that the school buildings had been condemned as unsafe. The 24 children at this one-teacher school of several grade levels were currently taught in the very confined space of the teacher's own house.

As planned, new corps outreach centres for the Command were commenced in Tseung Kwan O in East Kowloon and in Tung Chung on Lantau Island. The latter started meeting in a recently opened school sponsored by the Army and named in memory of a benefactor, Mr Lam Butt Chung. The Lam Butt Chung Memorial School had a capacity of 1,600 students. This school had been allocated to the Army in a new housing area near the Hong Kong International Airport. When it was opened, the school already had 900 pupils enrolled. The Command bought accommodation for officers as we expected the Army would serve in that area for a long time to come.

As 2002 commenced, we welcomed our new General Secretary and Command Secretary for Women's Ministries, Majors Barry and Arlene Dooley. Because they had served in Hong Kong previously, they were a great support and helped us move the Army forward in many ways.

Ian was an active member of Rotary during his years in Hong Kong as he had been in Korea. In 2002 he was elected a Paul Harris Fellow in recognition of the work of The Salvation Army in Hong Kong and the People's Republic of China.

In February we travelled again to Mainland China. During this visit, we saw some of the projects completed over the years by The Salvation Army China Development Department. Residents in some of the villages in Shandong Province were so grateful to have water flowing to their homes. Previously the village women had to walk considerable distances to collect water from wells to bring supplies to their homes. Now they have more time for other activities and to raise money for their families. Families in that area of Mainland China survived on as little as 200 RMB (AU$50) a month at that time. In another town, we saw the results of an income generation programme commenced by the Army in 1996. In this project women learned to undertake embroidery work that was later incorporated into sheets, curtain drapes, cushion covers and similar items. From the humble beginning with a seeding fund of a few thousand dollars from AusAid and The Salvation Army in Australia, this project had grown to a multimillion RMB industry. The products were being sold in Walmart stores in the USA and elsewhere. The women involved were now earning up to 500 RMB (AU$125) a month for their families—a small fortune for them. Although Shandong was one of the wealthier provinces of China, the diet tended to lack protein. Deep-fried scorpions and deep-fried cicadas were on the menu during our meals!

In February 2002 we shared in the Zonal Conference for Salvation Army leaders in Geelong, Australia. Geelong Conference Centre was the venue of the conference and we were delighted to return to the centre at which we lived and worked for almost two years before our appointments to Korea in 1997. Many staff members from those years were still working there and they were pleased to meet us again. The conference, led by General

John Gowans, brought together leaders from the South Pacific and East Asia region. It provided a forum for exchanging ideas and dealing with issues affecting The Salvation Army. During an evening session, Ian shared with the conference delegates about the Army's current work in Mainland China.

General Gowans had recently introduced the concept of short-term commissions for those Salvationists giving service to the Army for an agreed period of time without becoming commissioned officers. He took what had previously been the commissioned rank of lieutenant and allowed this to be granted to those men and women who offered for short-term service of three to five years. After this time these lieutenants could be considered for entry to the officer training college and eventual commissioning as officers in The Salvation Army with the rank of captain—the same rank that would now be given on commissioning to all those who successfully completed in-college training at a school for officer training. Ian had been asked to present a paper on 'Flexible Training for Lieutenants'. In doing so, he emphasised the importance of ensuring that these leadership recruits had the necessary knowledge, skills, attitude and spirituality required of spiritual leaders in corps or social services work. In this way they could also gain recognition for prior learning if they ever desired to move on to become commissioned officers.

In the event, the use of an officer rank to describe the position of a non-officer worker became confusing and difficult to administer in many territories. Similarly, the idea of cadets being commissioned directly as captains created difficulties in following through the previous five-year review system that had to be successfully completed before consideration of promotion to captaincy. As indicated earlier, in the five-year review system, commissioned lieutenants needed to demonstrate their dedication to lifelong learning, reflect on their service, and consider whether officership was really God's will for them. General Shaw Clifton officially scrapped the plan for short-term lieutenants in 2008. As we write in 2016, however, the Australia Southern Territory has been given the opportunity to implement an 'auxiliary-lieutenant' scheme for men and women who might be considering ministry opportunities within The Salvation Army through the avenue of short-term service. Hopefully these auxiliary-lieutenants will continue to be encouraged to develop the competencies required for fully commissioned officership in due course if they eventually decide to follow that path, and as a result receive some credit for service given.

Our visit to Australia in February 2002 coincided wonderfully with the birth of our second grandchild, Nathan Jeffrey Elkington. Our daughter, Cathy gave birth on the very day our plane arrived in Melbourne. We were delighted to spend time with Cathy and Darren as well as granddaughter Stephanie and our new grandson. Because we chose to take three weeks holiday immediately after the conference we had the privilege of dedicating Nathan to God at the 9.30 am meeting at Box Hill Corps on 18 March.

Of course, it was a privilege to share time with other family members as well. Sadly, Sharon and her husband Frank had decided to separate in October 2001, but continued to be friends. Since then, Sharon had busily engaged herself in writing a family history especially for Stephanie and Nathan. She found good support at a local Anglican church where she became a member. Jenni was working with the Domestic Violence and Incest Resource Centre in Fitzroy, doing both research and publication work. We were also able to spend a day with Sonja's sister Joan and husband George, together with members of their growing family of grandchildren.

During the latter part of 2002 the International Secretary, Commissioner Robert Saunders, visited Hong Kong and China to conduct a Command review—the first one while we were in charge of the Command. This was a helpful exercise. So was a visit by our Legal and Parliamentary Secretary from International Headquarters, Major Peter Smith. He travelled to Macau to talk to our solicitors about modifying the registration of The Salvation Army to fit in with normal Salvation Army requirements internationally. We were also involved in registering our Salvation Army trademarks (name, crest and red shield) in Hong Kong and Macau, and attempting to do the same in Mainland China. The need for registration had been highlighted because an organisation commenced that described itself, in Chinese, as 'The Cat Salvation Army'. The aim of this group was to rescue stray cats! Understandably, we did not want prospective donors confusing that organisation with ours. Sadly, we were not able to register our name or trademarks in Mainland China. There was only one army there, namely the New People's Army! In November, two members of the international audit team from IHQ, Lieut-Colonel John Rowlanes and Major K.C. David came to verify the work undertaken in Hong Kong and the People's Republic of China. Their review was in addition to the annual audit undertaken by commercial auditors in Hong Kong—a basic requirement within The Salvation Army worldwide.

We were involved in a number of interchurch activities. One of the most exciting was the opportunity for Ian to preach at the Cantonese, Putonghua, and English services at the Ward Memorial Methodist Church, Kowloon on Ministry of Healing Sunday. The congregations seemed most appreciative of Ian's messages. He also presented a paper on Salvation Army officership to a forum on clergy ministry arranged by the Hong Kong Christian Council.

During September, we travelled to Indonesia. At the invitation of the Territorial Commander, Commissioner Johannes Watilete, we spoke at Sunday meetings and conducted officers councils and holiness retreats in Java and Central Sulawesi over a two-week period. For Sonja, this was a very important visit to the country of her birth. In her classes at the retreats, Sonja focused on the person and work of the Holy Spirit, while Ian concentrated on different aspects of the holy life.

Tensions in Sulawesi were palpable, however. Christians were under significant persecution at that time. A bomb exploded at the Maranatha Bible College near our Army hospital in Palu. Survivors became patients at the hospital. A day later an employee found a bomb under the electrical substation of the hospital. Fortunately, the police who were called defused the bomb before it exploded. These events took place during the week we arrived in Indonesia, but before we set foot in Palu en route to the venue for the holiness retreat in the more remote district of Kulawi.

We were delighted to see the enthusiastic Salvationists in Indonesia. Despite the persecutions against Christians in some areas, the Officer Training College in Jakarta was overflowing with 84 smartly uniformed and enthusiastic cadets. This new structure at 55 Jalan Kramat Raya in Jakarta was magnificent. What a difference to the original buildings which Sonja's father obtained for The Salvation Army after the Second World War and where Sonja lived from 1947–53. They were also in a much improved state than when we visited the property together in 1988. Significant among the buildings was a new and very large hall for the corps still situated there.

We planned to take a final week of holiday in Bali on the way home, but a phone call from Hong Kong on the final day of the holiness retreat in Kulawi changed our plans. The call alerted us to a tragic accident in Mainland China. A minibus carrying seven people, including some of our staff, left an unmade road in Anhui Province, plunging 70 metres into the valley below. Major Carolyne Frazer from New Zealand, Miss Jocelyn Ma from our China Development Department, the driver and one other person were killed. One of our officers, Captain Tommy Chan, was seriously injured. We needed to return to Hong Kong quickly. Our visit to Bali was limited to an overnight transit stop to take a connecting flight. However, we were there long enough to understand something of the situation, and yet be thoroughly surprised at the devastating and disastrous bomb blast two weeks later that ripped through part of the entertainment district of this holiday island. In solidarity with our comrades in New Zealand, Ian obtained permission to fly to Christchurch, New Zealand, to attend the funeral of Major Frazer. He returned home in time for funeral services for Jocelyn Ma.

Early in November, we celebrated our biennial congress. This year our special guest group was the Southern California Divisional Band from USA, with conductor Kevin Larsson and tour leaders Lieut-Colonels Alfred and Sherryl Van Cleef. Band members were top-quality players from corps bands around Southern California. We provided opportunities for them to play in our schools, in outdoor settings, in concerts and Sunday meetings. The Van Cleefs brought excellent messages to officers and soldiers alike. Many seekers were recorded on the congress Sunday morning. During the afternoon soldiers and friends rally, Ian introduced the next year's Command theme, namely 'Moving Forward in Faith for One'. The idea was that each soldier should aim to win one new disciple for the Lord in the coming year. In addition, we hoped that each corps would have faith to commence one new open group, welcome one new family into the corps, and recruit one new candidate for officership. Only in this way, we felt, would the Army grow while moving into the future. To help remind our Salvationists of the theme, we distributed bookmarks containing the four goals in the shape of a number one (1).

On the Monday following the Congress, we travelled with the band to Guangzhou Province and the City of Guangdong (the former Canton) in Mainland China. There they presented a service of Christian music to an overflowing congregation of 1,800 in one of the larger churches in the city. The church choir of 70 members also participated. Understandably, the band was thrilled with this highlight of their tour.

On 7 November, we received a phone call from General John Gowans indicating that, as of March 2003, Ian would be the Secretary and Sonja the Associate Secretary for International Training and Leader Development at International Headquarters in London. As such, we would be responsible for supervising the training of leaders internationally, liaising with various zonal secretaries and the Chief of the Staff on all aspects of the training work for officers. We were also to support and conduct training courses as appropriate, and to arrange in-service training for International Headquarters staff. Some new aspects for training including flexible training—about which Ian had spoken at the Zonal Conference earlier in 2002—were to be encouraged. What an opportunity! All the training and experience of the years seemed to focus beautifully into this appointment. How we thanked God for his timing of the opportunities that this presented in what was to be our final active-service assignment.

Having served as associate officers in Box Hill for the three years while Darren worked to complete his bachelor of theology degree, Cathy and Darren were appointed to Carrum Downs Corps on the south-eastern fringe of greater Melbourne in January 2003 as corps officers in charge.

In a rearrangement of appointments as we were about to leave, Major Alfred Tsang who had been re-accepted as officer a year or so earlier, was installed as General Secretary with Lieut-Colonels Tan, Thean Seng and Patricia Loo Lay Saik from Singapore Malaysia Command appointed to succeed us as Command leaders.

A number of men from Inner Mongolia representing the People's Republic of China came to Major Tsang's installation. What a thrill to learn that the following day some of them knelt at the mercy seat and committed their lives to Christ with the help of Captain Jeremy Lam. This event seemed to us to be a wonderful seal on our ministry in Hong Kong, Macau and the People's Republic of China.

Chapter 16

To the ends of the earth, 2003–2007

The year 2003 was one of transition, training and travel.

One of the recommendations of the Army's International Conference of Training Principals in 2001 was that agreed competencies should be the basis for the training of officers—especially as training staff and their leaders considered flexible options for training. It had become clear that one programme of training did not suit everyone—especially when Salvationists came into candidateship to become officers from a variety of educational backgrounds. Educational attainments by young people were increasing as their school systems improved and people stayed longer in formal education. As a result some cadets may even have already experienced previous theological education or other professional training. At that time very few officer training colleges around the world had sufficient staff available to teach a complete externally-recognised university-level degree course in theology. However, certain staff members were highly qualified and the numbers of these were increasing. What recognition could be given to prior learning? How could training staff arrange to build on the knowledge these trainees already possessed and stimulate them to want to gain more?

Of course, we remembered the situation in Hong Kong. Most cadets there already had a full secondary education. In that Command, our highly qualified staff led by Majors Ian and Wendy Swan were able to teach the curriculum at such a level that by the time cadets were commissioned as officers they could be credited with at least one third of a bachelor degree in ministry from Bethel Bible College in that special administrative region of China. These newly-commissioned officers were then able to complete the degree as part of their post-commissioning studies in the years following. Such an arrangement greatly motivated life-long learning amongst the officers.

Academic theological education has never been the only, or most important, aspect of Salvation Army officer training. Salvation Army officers need firstly to be spiritual leaders, who are deeply in love with God. They also need to be fully committed to alleviating human suffering in Christ's name and serving God within The Salvation Army. They should be passionate about leading men, women and children to commit their lives to Christ, as well as having the diligence and skills to work wisely and well. Officers should know how to visit people in their homes, in hospitals and social services institutions; and supervise the administrative aspects of a Salvation Army corps (church). In most of their early appointments, they would need to be able to do such administrative work themselves, but always with the objective of training other Salvationists to undertake these tasks. Undoubtedly, all officers need a good grasp of the Bible and Salvation Army theology so that they can effectively teach and train their people in God's truths. They would be expected to encourage home Bible study groups and other means of spiritual growth amongst soldiers, adherents, young people and seekers.

What we understood General John Gowans and his successor, General John Larsson, wanted us to do during our appointment at International Headquarters was to develop definitions of the competencies that would be required for commissioning cadets as Salvation Army officers in each territory and culture. No matter what their academic background, they needed certain competencies in knowledge, skill, attitude and spirituality in order to be effective leaders. If they could demonstrate those competencies, they could receive the internationally accredited Salvation Army Certificate of Officer Training and be commissioned and ordained. If not, they would either not be commissioned or would be directed to remedial programmes. The Army needed competent, confident and Christlike leaders. Our training programmes should be designed to develop and nurture such leaders.

If increasing educational standards in a country—and expectations of local Salvationists—encouraged degree-level studies, and staff was available to offer these in biblical studies or theology, then this was certainly possible. Alternatively, cadets with advanced academic standing could have their training enriched by undertaking courses at nearby theological colleges. In other words, officer training could be flexible in length and content—tailored to individual cadets rather than demanding that every officer cadet go through exactly the same programme everywhere in the world.

How different this was to when we trained as officers! Of course even then some flexibility was possible. For instance, as noted in Chapter 6, Ian was allowed to undertake the final year of a postgraduate academic degree in education during his second year of training. This was the exception rather than the norm, however, and nothing systematic was organised.

With that mandate, and by adapting suitable materials developed while seeking accreditation for the training programme in Australia Southern within a competency-based vocational education system, we were then able to confidently move around the world. Our primary task was encouraging competency-based training for Salvation Army officers in as many territories as we could. We also linked this with teaching the Servant Leadership Training Programme and offering holiness seminars to encourage practical and spiritual growth. Perhaps this was as close as we could come to the ministry of Samuel Logan Brengle about a century before in The Salvation Army. In the June, August and November after our arrival in London, we visited our Salvation Army training programmes in East Africa; at the William and Catherine Booth College in Winnipeg, Canada; and in the Eastern Europe Command in Moscow, respectively.

In Eastern Europe, Ian conducted a seminar with training staff about their programme. This Command had a very flexible programme at that time, with 34 cadets, all in corps appointments, scattered around the Command. The challenges were immense as the staff tried to equip them for fully commissioned officership. Many of these cadets had already served as corps leaders, and a few had planted corps prior to commencing formal training. The Command needed some form of assessment to determine if these cadets had, in fact, qualified to be commissioned as officers.

As well as working on this matter of competency-based training, our responsibility in the International Personnel Department of International Headquarters (then led by Commissioner Keith Banks), was also to develop an orientation programme for new territorial commanders, chief secretaries, officers commanding and general secretaries and their spouses This programme of about one week's duration would allow newly appointed leaders to visit International Headquarters and meet the General, the Chief of the Staff, and the International Secretary of the zone in which they were appointed, together with the zonal staff. In addition, they would meet the international secretaries for business administration, programme resources, and those in the office of the Chief of the Staff to discover the other support facilities International Headquarters could provide. How we wished we had had such a detailed orientation when we were appointed as the Chief Secretary and Territorial Secretary for Women's Ministries in Korea in 1997 rather than a fairly short one so late in our term in Hong Kong and Macau! Over the next three years we developed quite a polished programme that served incoming leaders very effectively, which we augmented with visits to the Territorial Headquarters of the United Kingdom and the Republic of Ireland Territory to view an example of a well-organised, multi-department headquarters. Initially these orientation programmes were held at William Booth College in Denmark Hill while IHQ was still temporarily situated there. Once the new IHQ building was opened in central London in November 2004, the programmes were based at 101 Queen Victoria Street. During several orientation programmes we even managed to fit in an afternoon visiting some Salvation Army historical sites especially for those delegates who had not attended a session of the International College for Officers.

During 2004, we organised eight orientation programmes at International Headquarters for new territorial leaders. We facilitated three training leaders conferences—three days for European leaders at William Booth College, London, in February; six days for South Asian leaders at 'Surrenden', Coonoor, Tamil Nadu, India in June; and two weeks for African training leaders during September and October in Accra, Ghana. For the second of these we were supported by Commissioner Lalkiamlova, the International Secretary for South Asia. The last of these was supported by Lieut-Colonel Joan Dunwoodie, the Under Secretary for Africa. Their presence added to the significance of the occasion for those attending and allowed other leaders from IHQ to understand what we were doing. Such conferences gave us excellent opportunities to emphasise the importance of competency-based training, encouraging the delegates to specify—and then focus on—the knowledge, skills, attitudes and spirituality newly commissioned Salvation Army officers needed in each of these diverse geographic areas. The competency list for officers in South Asia is attached as Appendix 2 (pages 245–250) in this book as a sample of the types of lists produced by the participants during our various training leaders conferences during our four years in the department.

We always travelled in Salvation Army uniform when on Army business. Those fellow passengers waiting in airport lounges, or sitting near us on flights, who knew the Army felt confident to share their problems with us. Some even allowed us to pray with them if that was appropriate. Our uniforms also provided opportunities to explain about the work of the Army and our Christian motivation to those less familiar with The Salvation Army. We rejoiced at the many opportunities we had of witnessing for our Lord as a result.

In company with the International Secretary for Personnel, Commissioner Keith Banks and later Commissioner Lyn Pearce, Ian presented a lecture on leader development at each session of the International College for Officers during our time at IHQ.

In May, we attended a part of the International Conference of Leaders in New York at which leader development was discussed—again emphasising the importance of competency-based training. During the following two days we visited The Salvation Army Officer Training College in the United States Eastern Territory and saw something of the excellent work that was being undertaken. In July and August, we visited Nigeria to conduct a Salvation Army Management Training Course with about 25 senior officers. We followed this course by leading a Brengle Memorial Institute (holiness seminar) for another 20 delegates. In addition, we had the privilege of speaking at meetings at Lagos Central and Igbobi Corps. Then, in December and the depths of winter, we held a review seminar for officers in the Eastern Europe Command who had completed between nine and 11 years service—officers from the first three sessions trained in Russia since Army work recommenced there in 1991. The delegates shared something of their calling and how God had guided them through the years. What a privilege to be part of this occasion!

As well as attending the Catford Corps on Sundays when possible, Sonja served as Recruiting Sergeant, Ian played in the band and we were involved in conducting seminars and Bible studies in that corps. We also led Sunday and some Saturday meetings at a range of corps in England.

Being based in London provided wonderful opportunities to visit the wealth of historic, scenic and cultural sites in England, Scotland, Scandinavia, Holland, Belgium, France, Switzerland and Germany on weekends or mostly on furlough. The Channel Tunnel or the Dover-Calais Ferry provided easy access to Europe for train or car travel. In so doing, we were also able to meet colleagues with whom we had worked in various appointments internationally.

While making a visit to Sonja's relatives in the Netherlands, we journeyed to her parents' home corps of Vlaardingen, near Rotterdam. Later we extended the journey to Amsterdam. In that city we discovered the Netherlands Institute for War Documentation. To our delight, the staff of the Institute helped us find Sonja's father's debriefing report after his internment during the Second World War in what was then the Netherlands East Indies (now Indonesia). Other prime source material for an account of the Van Kralingen family was also available. All this inspired us to try to capture the story of Sonja's parents and to share it more widely. As usual, we explored other art galleries and museums in Amsterdam before journeying to Paris, exploring its famous sights, art galleries and museums.

On another occasion we visited Salehurst and Robertsbridge in East Sussex. As mentioned earlier (in Chapter 11), Ian's great-great-grandfather, Thomas Southwell, left there with his wife, Eliza, and two children in 1837 to travel to the colony of New South Wales. Ian's great-grandfather, William Southwell, the third child of the family, was born in New South Wales soon after their arrival. We found the graves of Thomas's father and other relatives in the church graveyard.

What a delight it was to return to the Philippines Territory in May 2005 for our first visit since we left in late 1979! We rejoiced at the growth of numbers of corps and officers during the intervening 26 years. Several of 'our cadets' were now significant leaders. We conducted a Progressive Training Seminar with THQ staff and divisional leaders, and then another week focusing on officer training and assisting development of new training staff.

A second trip was made to the National Training Seminar in Los Angeles in early July. One hundred and thirty training staff from the four USA training colleges together with some representatives from Canada and the Caribbean met together. We were able to present a plenary session and a double workshop on competency-based training. At the end of July, we journeyed again to 'Surrenden' in Tamil Nadu for another South Asia Training Leaders Conference. On that occasion, we were able to build on the work done the year before and focus on refining the competencies needed for newly commissioned officers. As with the previous South Asia Training Leaders Conference, Commissioner Lalkiamlova, the International Secretary for the South Asia Zone, accompanied us.

Immediately following the conference, we travelled by train and four-wheel-drive vehicle to Nagercoil, Tamil Nadu, in India South-Eastern to visit the Officer Training College, meet the cadets and encourage the training staff. We were particularly appalled at the paucity of the college library there—as we were when visiting several colleges around the world in Africa and Asia. After three days in Nagercoil, we moved west to Thiruvananthapuram, Kerala State, to view the India South-West Territory Officer Training College, again encouraging the training staff and cadets. On our way home, we transited through the India Western Territory and visited our friend Commissioner Krupa Das in Mumbai who was unwell. The commissioner had been one of the delegates to an Administrative Leadership Training Course in Australia Southern when Ian was coordinating them.

In September 2005, we journeyed to the South America West Territory based in Santiago, Chile, to conduct a Servant Leadership Training the Trainers programme and review the officers training facilities. Facilitating the Servant Leadership Training programme was quite challenging because all our work had to be translated into Spanish. The participants responded marvellously, however, and the dedication service on the Sunday morning was most moving. The territorial leaders had arranged to have a large cross with a basin of water and towel at its foot as a powerful visual focus. Many recommitments to service were made that day. On the way to London, we economised with a quick visit to Brazil to discuss officer training and leader development with the Territorial Headquarters staff and training leaders.

In between all of those visits, we organised and ran a further seven orientation sessions for territorial or command leaders at International Headquarters in the year. Ian was also asked to run a special orientation programme at IHQ for Captain Gia Salarishvili from Eastern Europe Command who was being appointed to take charge of the Georgia region. As Gia had not attended the International College for Officers, Ian took him to Mile End in Whitechapel, East London where William Booth had commenced his ministry with the East London Special Services Committee which eventually transformed into the East London Christian Mission, the Christian Mission and The Salvation Army. How appalled they both were to find that someone had defaced the statue of William Booth erected on Mile End Road in memory of the Army's commencement. Gia wanted something done. Rather than just reporting the matter to the police or to IHQ and hoping someone else would take action, Ian and Gia purchased paint remover and cloths at a nearby hardware store and cleaned up the defaced statue themselves.

In September, Sonja received notification from the Australia Southern Territory that she would be retiring officially on 1 December 2005—just after her 66th birthday in November. This was actually a year overdue by their reckoning. She had worked on the assumption of retiring when Ian retired in July 2007. So this notification came as somewhat of a surprise. We were grateful to International Headquarters administration for accepting an arrangement that suited both IHQ and ourselves. From December, Sonja worked about four days a week as a retired officer. We could still take homeland furlough in March 2006 after which we would return to our appointment at IHQ till the end of June 2007. At that point we would finally return to Australia. How delighted we were to remain in UK and continue our worldwide ministry a little longer.

In the weeks leading up to Christmas 2005, we were again involved in the Catford Corps programme of carolling in all kinds of weather, in shopping centres, on streets and wherever people could hear the message. Additionally, we shared with General John and Commissioner Freda Larsson in a reception celebrating the investiture of a knighthood on Doctor Sir David K.P. Li. As mentioned previously, Sir David was the Chairman of the citizens' Advisory Board in Hong Kong during our service there.

We managed to fit in a visit to the Territorial Carol Concert at the Royal Albert Hall and, later the same week, *The Messiah* at the same venue. What wonderful Christmas events they were. One of the most exciting days for us was 26 December when we were able to drive around Whitechapel and the areas where the Army commenced rather than using public transport. We discovered many of the venues were in walking distance of each other. At least the statue of William Booth in Mile End cleaned up earlier that year was still undefaced! The visit highlighted for us how wonderfully God had taken a small group of his dedicated servants and grown a mission and a church that worked at that time in 111 countries and used 175 languages.[34]

In January 2006, we journeyed back to Zambia—the first time we had returned since 1975. We felt honoured to unveil memorials for the late Lieut-Colonel Leslie Pull and the late Brigadier Laura Dutton on Easter Hill outside of Chikankata. The school had developed well over the years and now had a computer laboratory. And what a different training college was situated in Lusaka compared to the very simple one in which we worked in the 1970s! This Zambian trip was particularly precious because we met a number of our former students who were making significant contributions in that country and elsewhere. What saddened us was the sense among the Chikankata students that, because of the prevalence of HIV/AIDS, many of them would not live to old age despite their good education.

Then we flew on to Kenya to lead the Servant Leadership Training Programme and conduct in-service activities for officer training staff. We also shared in a regional congress at Nakuru, led by our Australian friends, Lieut-Colonels Lyndon and Julie Spiller, who were the Chief Secretary and Territorial Secretary for Women's Ministries. On the journey we saw a sign on the wall of an agricultural supply store showing a seed and a seedling. The words on the sign read: 'Your growth is our goal'. What a good motto for our department at IHQ—and for every education and training department around the world. So we adopted it.

At the end of February, we returned to Australia for homeland furlough. What a delight it was it was to catch up with our family. We were able to attend a meeting at Box Hill Corps and speak at Carrum Downs Corps

[34] At the time of writing in 2016, the Army now works in 128 countries.

where Cathy and Darren were still the corps officers. During the visit we commenced negotiations to lease a unit at a retirement village in an eastern suburb of Melbourne in anticipation of our retirement. We tentatively booked our retirement recognition meeting for Box Hill Corps on Sunday, 15 July 2007. The house we reserved in the retirement village consisted of two bedrooms, a study and living room that we felt would provide us with quite adequate accommodation, although the space was somewhat smaller than we had at our quarters in the United Kingdom. However, the unit had a structural difficulty evidenced by a crack through the brickwork of the garage wall. We were assured by the village management that the foundations would be repaired and the wall rectified before we returned to Australia in June the following year.

Ian also had the privilege of visiting the United Arab Emirates (UAE), Bangladesh and Pakistan in April that year. He spoke at a Good Friday meeting in Dubai attended by a group of about 60 migrant workers—mainly Tamil-speaking Salvationists from India South Eastern Territory. Ray and Geraldine Boyd, from Ireland and Holland respectively, led the group. The Boyds pioneered the fellowship 24 years previously when they moved to UAE in connection with his work, and had nurtured it ever since.

Easter Day in Dhaka, Bangladesh, was exciting. Ian attended a sunrise service with about 6,000 other Christians in that predominantly Muslim country and spoke at a Sunday morning Salvation Army corps meeting in the city. His visit to the Officer Training College in Dhaka the following day and then in Pakistan later the same week helped the training leaders in those two countries catch up on matters discussed at the training conferences we had conducted in India. They had been unable to attend due to visa difficulties. During the Pakistan visit, Ian also attended Sunday meetings with the cadets outside Lahore, conducted a spiritual day for the cadets and spoke at a midweek service at the Lahore Central Corps.

In June, Ian visited Army training centres in Malawi and Zimbabwe. The enthusiasm of the Salvationists in both these areas was heart-warming. Both countries faced dire economic difficulties. Although Zimbabwe possessed sufficient raw materials to be prosperous, hyperinflation was then a problem. The price of basic foodstuffs almost doubled in the week Ian was there. At that time the Zimbabwean currency notes displayed expiry dates.

In Malawi, Ian had the opportunity of helping assess a number of envoys who had been serving as corps leaders, in order to determine whether they had the competency profile needed to be commissioned as officers. This was another outworking of the flexible training programme in a command where it was very difficult to bring all these trainees together without leaving so many corps in the region without officers. In the meantime, Sonja continued her work as Recruiting Sergeant for the Catford Corps and was delighted with training six recruits who progressed to soldiership during the year.

In August, we took some of the balance of our holidays visiting family members in the Netherlands—the last time before our return to Australia. This gave Sonja opportunities to conduct further research about the time she and her family spent interned in the Dutch East Indies through the Netherlands Institute of War documentation. Staff members were again most helpful.

The first 10 days of September were spent in the Democratic Republic of the Congo known to The Salvation Army then as Congo-Kinshasa and Angola Territory. Because of an unexpected change of flight at Brussels en route, we arrived in Kinshasa in almost total darkness on the evening of Friday 1 September. The change of arrival time meant that the officer assigned to pick us up was in a different area of the airport. This was one of a number of occasions when travelling in Salvation Army uniform was so beneficial even though our uniforms were summer-weight navy blue in comparison to the white uniforms worn in the Congo. The Congolese in the airport lounge gazed with much curiosity at the two fair-skinned Salvation Army officers who were looking lost. In broken French we said that we belong to 'Armée du Salut' (the French translation of The Salvation Army). Someone hurried to find Major Eugene Dikalembolovanga (abbreviated as 'Dikal') who was in another arrival lounge. How pleased we were to see him, and greatly relieved that he could drive us to our accommodation in the THQ compound.

On Saturday morning, Lieut-Colonels Onal and Edmane Castor, the Chief Secretary and Territorial Secretary for Women's Ministries, took us to a number of Salvation Army centres around Kinshasa. These included the William Booth University, Salvation Army schools, hospitals and maternity clinics. The visit provided a good opportunity to sense the scope of the work, the credibility of The Salvation Army and the vision of the early pioneers who obtained good areas of land for a wide variety of ministries in the 1930s. As Albert Kenyon's 1951 book and the subsequent film *Congo Crusade* had been major sources of inspiration to Ian as a corps cadet in Australia, being able to make this visit and contribute to the present-day work—even in a small way—was very special for him.

In the afternoon, we spent time with the Territorial Commander, Commissioner Ludiazo and Lieut-Colonel Castor discussing leader development strategies within the Territory. Before a meal with the Territorial Commander and Territorial President of Women's Ministries, we viewed the Training College site and the facilities for the Servant Leadership Programme.

On Sunday, we accompanied the Chief Secretary and Territorial Secretary for Women's Ministries to Kalamu Corps (a French-speaking corps in Kinshasa) where we both spoke. There were a number of seekers. In the evening, the Servant Leadership Programme opened with a meal with the delegates, and worship led by the Chief Secretary.

From Monday to Saturday we facilitated the Servant Leadership Programme—being translated sentence-by-sentence into French and using translation sets for simultaneous translation of delegates' questions and comments back to us. In the absence of the full set of translated notes, we used the initial day to talk about adult teaching methods and to prioritise goals for the activity. On most days, we commenced at 8.30 am with prayers and continued through until 8.15 pm, with breaks for lunch and an evening meal. On the Friday afternoon and evening, we gave the delegates some free time to model an appropriate use of recreation and balance in the programme.

In driving to and from the training college from THQ, we were very conscious of United Nations Organisation Mission in the Democratic Republic of the Congo (MONUC) peacekeeping troops in armoured vehicles. Following strife between the Democratic Republic of the Congo and five regional states, namely Angola, Namibia, Rwanda, Uganda, and Zimbabwe, these troops were assigned to maintain the ceasefire and facilitate the disengagement of forces. They were also present for the period when the country's first free and fair elections were held on 30 July 2006. A run-off for the election of president was due on 29 October—and we were there in September. Little wonder we sensed some tensions in the country!

Our overall impression was that the delegates were very responsive. They asked good questions, engaged in spirited discussion and deeply desired that the Army should grow despite domestic uncertainties around them. We were delighted to have three delegates from the Republic of the Congo (known by The Salvation Army as Congo Brazzaville) including their Secretary for Personnel, their Extension Training Officer and Secretary for Business Administration. The 19 other delegates came from Congo Kinshasa and Angola.

On the Saturday night, we led a devotional session to look again at the Scriptural basis of Servant Leadership, and all the delegates took the opportunity for recommitment. On Sunday morning, the final meeting gave opportunity for a number of delegates to testify, and for the Territorial Commander to bring a message emphasising the importance of servant leaders feeding God's flock. Again, a number of delegates also made special recommitments. After a final meal together, the delegates prepared to depart and that evening we flew back to London.

We felt that this was one of the most productive and positive Servant Leadership Programmes we had the privilege of conducting to that time. All the delegates were mature, with no less than seven and sometimes up to 30 years of service each. They were also chosen because they were seen to have potential to teach others. We believed that this event would be the commencement of a good forward movement for practising servant leadership at all levels in the territories. The delegates had great visions of what God could do through the Army in the days ahead. One of the greatest challenges was finding enough money to enable them and their leaders to accomplish these visions. Achieving financial self-support needed to be a territorial goal.

In the last week of September, Ian travelled to Canada to take part in the American Convocation on Higher Education in The Salvation Army. The key question for discussion that year was, 'What was the nature of William Booth's vision for a "University for the Study of the Science of Humanity"?' Has this vision been fulfilled in our training colleges or is there something greater that could be happening in these days? Should all our training colleges aim to be accredited as universities? Training leaders from all the Americas, plus representatives from two Australian territories, and social workers from Sweden, shared with leaders from International

Headquarters and Canada to look at these matters. Again, Ian highlighted the acute disparities he had observed between training for officers in financially independent territories and those that had to depend on grants from International Headquarters.

In early October, Ian visited Kenya again to speak at a conference of African leaders on leader development and training strategies, training resources and shared evaluations in our African territories.

Before a Servant Leadership Training Programme in Sri Lanka soon afterward, we were able to visit some of the areas affected by the December 2004 tsunami and see firsthand the excellent relief work carried out by Salvationists there in the following years. We also spoke at a corps meeting and visited some social service centres so as to understand the contexts in which the delegates were working. About 20 officers from around the country attended the course. Some also came from northern areas where they were constantly under threat from the Tamil Tiger rebels. One officer always had to be ready to move the children from the children's home she managed if hostilities broke out. The delegates were open to the prompting of the Holy Spirit as we progressed through the seminar to the time of rededication.

In January, February, March, and May 2007, we were able to lead further orientation sessions for new territorial leaders at International Headquarters. For the March orientation, we invited Lieut-Colonels Wayne and Myra Pritchard from Canada. They were in the process of being appointed as our successors and the experience helped them to gain some helpful understanding of the roles they would be fulfilling. Ian also chaired a committee working on developing a new computer database for international and territorial personnel records. The previous database was about 10 years old and needed upgrading.

While we were on international service, our children always tried to help us celebrate important life events. In 2007, they secretly notified both International Headquarters and the Catford Corps that we were celebrating our 40th wedding anniversary on Sunday 4 February. On the Sunday before, the Catford Corps prepared a special surprise luncheon. On Thursday 1 February our anniversary was recognised at prayers and a special morning tea at International Headquarters. Interestingly, we shared the event with Commissioners Robert and Janet Street (also in IHQ) who were married on exactly the same date as us, but in the United Kingdom. We were leading the meetings of Bristol Easton Corps on the actual wedding anniversary day and the comrades there added to the celebration. We took a day of furlough to stay overnight at Bath and then visit that ancient town before returning to London.

In the second half of March, we made our last international trip before returning to Australia. The Indonesian Territory had invited us to assist them in drawing up a list of competencies for newly commissioned officers as the basis of revising their training programme. The Territorial Commander, Colonel Ribut Kartodarsono, organised for us to meet training staff, representative headquarters officers, divisional personnel, corps officers and local officers. They outlined the usual tasks undertaken by officers in Indonesia. We then guided them through the process of determining the knowledge, skills, attitudes and spirituality needed in newly commissioned officers to fulfil their responsibilities. Toward the end of that first week Colonel Kartodarsono called a representative group of his cabinet from Bandung to Jakarta and they ratified these competencies. A working party then commenced the process of revising the curriculum to achieve them. We expected that the training staff members would complete the process in the following weeks and months.

Having spoken at Sunday meetings in Jakarta on the first weekend, we travelled to Bandung for the second weekend where we again spoke at meetings. We are privileged to lead special officers councils on the following Monday and business meetings with Territorial Headquarters staff on the Tuesday. Then we were able to commence the process of developing competency lists for each headquarters position. This was aimed at helping the Territory develop leadership profiles for each of these positions; and to assist personal growth, development, and deployment. We felt that this was one of the most successful visits we made to any territory, especially because of the excellent support for, and endorsement of, our work by the territorial leaders.

As mentioned earlier, while on homeland furlough in March 2006 we had commenced negotiations to move into a retirement village in Melbourne with the understanding that the structural fault in the foundations and wall of our selected unit would be rectified before June 2007. We were not prepared to sign a contract or pay the necessary ingoing contribution before that time. Despite our best efforts over almost 10 months, repairs were delayed. We started to reconsider our decision to move into that village. Through the internet, we surveyed other options. Then the owners of the village notified us that repairs would not be finalised until late July 2007. If the repairs were successful, we *might* be able to move in during September. We were booked to return to Australia to retire in June! Commissioner Lyn Pearce, our head of department at International Headquarters, suggested that we follow our trip in Indonesia by flying to Melbourne to sort out the matter.

After we arrived in Melbourne at 5 am on Saturday 31 March, our daughter Cathy took us directly to the retirement village. What we saw of the situation at the unit convinced us that we should neither make payments nor pursue residency. The garage wall now had two cracks instead of one. Because the carpet in the sitting room had been removed before fresh floor covering was laid, we saw the cracks in the concrete flooring as well. Further, we all sensed the floors in several rooms were not level—something we had not noticed a year earlier. So we commenced visits to estate agents that Cathy knew and surveyed details on about 14 sites—moving progressively further east to housing that we could actually afford. Cathy felt we should make a start on this day rather than waiting until Monday as we had intended. Besides, she could only make time on this day to drive and to provide another point of view. Next week she would be too busy with her corps work.

The early properties we saw were simply too expensive, rundown, or lacked the features we sought. However, they gave us a feel for current market values. Cathy drove us around and visited real estate agents for information, also keeping us hydrated and fed because we were still recovering from a three-hour jet lag and lack of sleep in the aeroplane the night before. By midday—and we felt more awake by then—we focused attention on about four properties. As we described what we wanted and why, one agent said she thought she had the unit we might be looking for in Croydon. We discovered why on both that day and during the next week. Cathy arranged a viewing for this property and about three others in the general area before the end of the day.

The second last property in Croydon was all that the agent said—and more. Of course, Ian had gained experience by assessing properties for the

Army in a variety of places. Normally, we would not make a decision on only one viewing. However, we had undertaken our preliminary research and the other properties viewed that day we could use as comparisons. This one fulfilled all the criteria we had for location, size, structural integrity, price, security and ambience. Two other parties were viewing the house as well. Surprisingly, we saw a Salvation Army calendar on the wall and a newsletter from the Inala Retirement Village which had, until recently, been owned by The Salvation Army. Although now owned by another company, The Salvation Army still currently held chapel services in that village. After prayer, discussion and viewing one other alternative, we returned to the agent and made what we felt was a reasonable offer late that day, leaving a holding deposit of $500. By 7.15 pm that night we received a phone call to say that our offer had been accepted.

The vendors, John and Jean Elstub, invited us for lunch the following Monday. During the meal, we discovered that they were committed Christians who commenced attending the Inala Chapel because John's father had been a resident in that village. John and Jean enjoyed the chapel's Salvation Army style of worship. Even after John's father was promoted to Glory, they stayed to sing in the choir, be involved in services in ways such as taking up the collection and generally making this their church. Little wonder we noticed a Salvation Army 2007 calendar and the Inala newsletter in the unit when we made our inspection on the Saturday. Despite owning this delightful, personally-decorated home, John wanted to move to a country area near their elder son and also the seaside where their grandchildren might like to visit. Through a Bible address given by The Salvation Army officer chaplain at Inala, Jean had finally become convinced that they should move. Apparently the house went on the market about the time we received the letter from the manager of the retirement village early in March. Although many people had inspected the unit, no-one had made an offer. The estate agent could not understand this, but felt 'there must be something going on'. John and Jean were convinced that the Lord was holding the unit for someone. We had met them briefly as we were leaving the unit after viewing it on the Saturday afternoon. Because we had been travelling internationally on Salvation Army business, we were still in uniform (albeit summer style with pullover suitable to the cooler part of the autumn day) when they met us. No wonder we could remember them smiling at us! John and Jean were convinced we were committed Christians who should have their house and water the seeds of Christian faith and fellowship they had been planting among their neighbours.

Unsurprisingly, by Thursday 5 April, we knew that the property and pest inspections showed no problems. Our solicitors saw no difficulties with the legal aspects. So on Saturday 7 April, we paid the balance of the formal 10 per cent deposit with full settlement due on 8 June—one week before we were due to leave the United Kingdom. Perfect timing yet again! What an example of being safely led by God! The rest of that second Saturday, and during the following week, we spent time on carefully selecting furniture so that we would have a bed, table, chairs, sets of drawers, washing machine and refrigerator for delivery before we arrived. After so many years, we were not surprised at the Lord's leading. We had experienced this in the past and now we were experiencing it again as we prepared for this special transition in our ministry.

Returning to London with great peace of heart, we were involved as faculty at the International Conference of Personnel Secretaries (late May and early June) at Sunbury Court. Before and after that event, we were graciously farewelled from Catford Corps and from International Headquarters.

Arriving in Melbourne on 17 June, we busied ourselves arranging pension payments, selecting a new corps at which to worship closer to our new accommodation in Croydon, and preparing for the welcome home and retirement recognition. The last named event was held as planned on Sunday 15 July at Box Hill Corps—Sonja's home corps—at which we were married before entering Salvation Army training college 40 years earlier in 1967. It was a wonderful time. Many friends, session-mates, colleagues and relatives came to greet us at the event. The meeting was conducted by Lieut-Colonels John and Judith Jeffrey, the Chief Secretary and Territorial Secretary for Women's Ministries, with whom we had served in Western Australia. The Box Hill Band and Mrs Mavis Sanders provided musical support. Kevin Lewis, who sang at our wedding, read the Scripture portion and brought greetings. Our Melbourne-based daughters, Sharon and Cathy, supplemented their own greetings by presenting us with a volume of messages collected from colleagues at International Headquarters, the

United Kingdom, Hong Kong, Korea and the Philippines as well as those from Australia who could not attend the gathering. We felt the occasion focused appropriately on giving glory to God for his goodness to us over 39 years of active officership and the years of preparation through which he guided us.

God had been so good to us!

Photos 3 1998–2016

(Left) Sonja on Medical Fellowship ministry trip to a doctor-less village, Korea
(Middle left) Saturday afternoon tea on visit to Kil-yun Corps, Korea with corps officers [right] and divisional leaders
(Middle right) Sonja with doctor giving pain-relief treatment on SA Medical Fellowship ministry trip to a doctor-less village

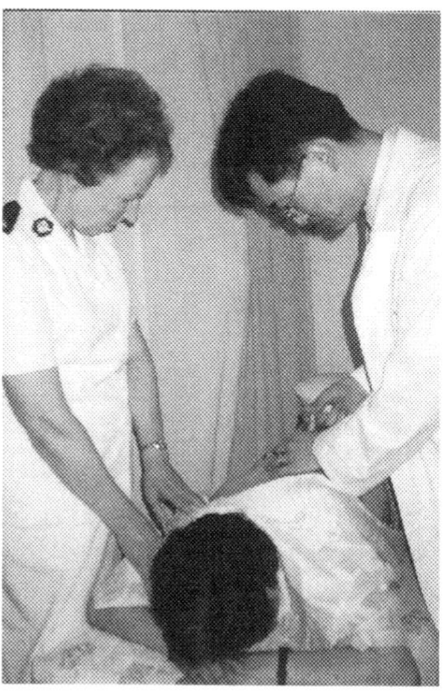

(Below left) Opening a 20-bed Salvation Army sponsored and AusAid-funded hospital/clinic in Yi minority area, Sichuan, PRC, 1999
(Below right) Delivering supplies to earthquake survivor in the Puli district of Taiwan now living in a house built by donations from The Salvation Army, in 2000

Minister for Youth Education in Macau speaks at the official inauguration of The Salvation Army in Macau, March 2000

A representative of the Uniting Evangelical Church shares with Ian in opening of Iao Hon Corps, Macau, SAR

With a team at a tree planting project in the almost treeless province of Inner Mongolia, 2001

Preaching in Chongwenmen Church, Beijing, 2000

Pastoral visit to a former Salvation Army officer in PRC with translation support by newly appointed Pastoral and Projects Officer, Captain Jeremy Lam, Yin-ming, 2002

Ian and Sonja with villagers in PRC who were digging a storage facility for a community development water project sponsored by The Salvation Army and AusAid

(Above) This sign we saw on the wall of an agricultural supplies store in Kenya became the motto of the Leader Development Department at IHQ
(Above right) Discussions of competencies for officers in the Philippines
(Right) Sonja speaks at South Asia Training Leaders Conference in Surrenden, Tamil Nadu, India, 2005
(Below left) Sunlit basin and towel for final session of Servant Leadership Training Course in Chile, South America West Territory
(Below right) Cleaning the defaced statue of Willam Booth on Mile End Road, London, 2005

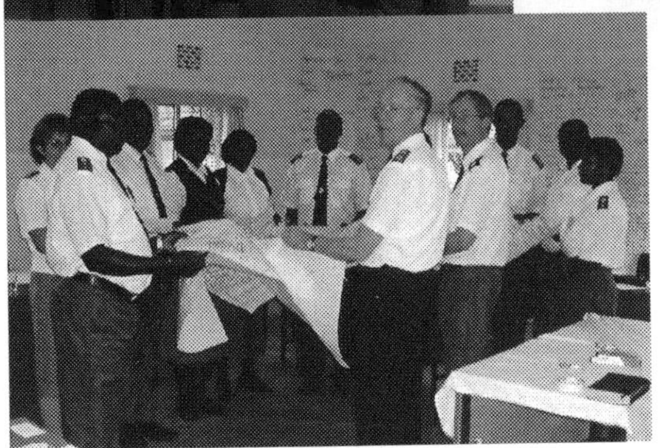

(Above left) Sonja with some of the many recruits she prepared for soldiership at Catford Corps, UK. Major Mary Scott [centre back row] was the corps officer during our time there
(Above) Ian preaches on Easter Hill, Chikankata, Zambia, during dedication of new memorials to Lieut-Colonel Leslie Pull and Brigadier Laura Dutton, 2006
(Left) Praying over the visions of delegates at the Servant Leadership Training Course in East Africa, 2006
(Bottom left) Sonja speaks at World Day of Prayer in Ringwood, 2010
(Bottom right) Ian and young helper cut the Maroondah Fellowship of Churches Pentecost Celebration birthday cake, 2015

(Top row left) Ian leads a Bible study during a divisional leaders conference in Nigeria, 2011
(Above) During the 2016 Congress in Hong Kong meeting a few of the delegates from The People's Republic of China.
(Left) Free Bible and information bookmark distribution with Mr Robert Woodward, Gideons Maroondah Camp, at Australia Day Ceremony 2016
(Below) Our family, December 2014

Chapter 17

The mission continues, 2007 onward

Some years before our adventures in Korea, Hong Kong, China and at International Headquarters, Ian was asked to prepare a lecture on the theology of retirement for a pre-retirement seminar in the Australia Southern Territory. In doing so, he found that the word 'retirement' and any related concepts occurred only once in most translations of the Bible. Very sensibly, this referred to the Levites who were involved in transporting the Tabernacle (Tent of Meeting) through the wilderness before the children of Israel entered the Promised Land. Male Levites from 25 years of age and onward were to take their share of doing the work at the Tent of Meeting—undoubtedly packing it up, carrying it to a new location and setting it up again as the pilgrim party moved from place to place. 'But at the age of 50, they must retire from their regular service and work no longer. They may assist their brothers in performing their duties at the Tent of Meeting, but they themselves must not do the work' (Numbers 8:23–26 *NIV*). While the heavy physical work could be handed over to others, these older Levites were to assist in doing other work around the Tent of Meeting as their physical strength allowed. Of course, when the Tent of Meeting found a permanent home in Shiloh, and the temple was built in Jerusalem years later, it consequently became easier for them to work to a greater age as did Eli and Samuel. In addition, Ian found many examples in the Scriptures of people such as Caleb who, at 85 years of age, was still enthusiastic about expanding his territory and taking possession of the Promised Land.

In truth, the work of God's servants never really ceases this side of eternity. The call to lead men, women and young people to Jesus and the availability to alleviate social need wherever it is found, continues. There is no discharge in God's war—only a change of roles according to one's physical strength. In the covenant we signed at commissioning—which we still display prominently in our bedroom—we individually promised to 'live to win souls and not allow anything to turn me aside from seeking their salvation as the first purpose of my life'. That promise continued to apply in retirement.

With this in mind, we settled very quickly into becoming active soldiers of the Ringwood Corps situated about 6 km from our house. At that time Majors Ian and Vivien Callander were the corps officers. We found this corps had very active outreach programmes. At that stage, the corps' modern-style 5 pm Sunday meeting was followed by a simple community meal attracting a number of people from the surrounding area. Also many lonely, elderly, or socially challenged people—some of whom came from local supported residential services—attended the corps Byways Programme on Wednesdays. The name 'Byways' arose from Jesus' Parable of the Great Banquet (Luke 14:15–24) in which the host encouraged his servants to go the 'the roads and country lanes' (or 'highways and byways' in the *KJV*) to invite people to the feast. Byways at Ringwood consisted of a weekly morning tea from 11 am, a nutritious two-course meal at 12 noon and a voluntary chapel service of about 30 minutes duration at 1 pm. Both Christian and secular music and songs, conversations around the table, prayers for those who were unwell, and recognition of birthdays, were all helpful in building relationships. Specifically the chapel service provided opportunities to share the Gospel with, or encourage spiritual growth amongst, those who voluntarily chose to come to the main hall—about a third of the approximately 100 regular attendees at the meal.

We also were invited to bring God's message at Ringwood and Carrum Downs (where Cathy and Darren were the officers), and at Ingle Farm corps in South Australia during the South Pacific Retired Officers Convention.

Ian was elected as the President of the World Mission Fellowship (WMF) at the end of 2007 for an initial two-year term, being re-elected in 2009. The WMF still provides prayer and practical support group for officers and non-officers from the Australia Southern Territory who are serving internationally. We had benefited from the fellowship members' prayers and practical interest from 1970 to 1979 and again from 1997 to 2007. We were glad to give leadership to this group supporting the next generation of those on the frontline of world mission from our Territory. As President, Ian led the WMF meetings in the Inala Village Chapel on the first Monday of every month other than January over those four years. In addition to the 40 to 80 people who attended the meeting in Melbourne, another 140 members around the Territory also pledged to pray regularly for reinforcement personnel and their children. The Fellowship raised funds for Christmas gifts for those serving in the most financially deprived areas. A monthly newsletter produced by the then Secretary, Major Tim Lynn, helped to keep the prayers well focused on the greatest challenges these personnel were facing. Tim eventually created a web-page for the Fellowship. Ian tried to spell out the mission of the Fellowship through the acronym GRIP. This stood for Giving, Recruiting, Informing, Praying—emphasising that we all needed to get a GRIP on world mission.

We enjoyed being in Australia for the Connections 07 Congress in Melbourne that brought together Salvationists from all around the Territory led by Commissioners James and Carolyn Knaggs. This was a great occasion of meeting together, worship, discussion and outpouring of blessing. In December we were involved in Christmas collecting at the Eastland Shopping Centre in Ringwood to support the local work of The Salvation Army. We were delighted at the generosity of the people.

From January 2008, we shared with Majors Brian and Irene Robertson, and Major Barbara Munro, in planning the 40th anniversary of the commissioning and ordination of the members of the 'Messengers of the Faith' session who trained as officers from 1967 to 1969. Eventually we chose a weekend in August when our session-mates, Commissioners Victor and Roslyn Poke (nee Pengilly) would be holidaying in Australia from their appointment as Territorial Leaders in Sweden. What a time of blessing and inspiration that was for all 21 who were commissioned in January 1969. We gathered at Elkanah Conference Centre in Marysville in Victoria. How we all rejoiced in the faithfulness of God and the vast opportunities he had given to so many of us to serve him in such a wide varieties of ways in Australia and several different countries over the years. In addition to our own international service, Majors Howard and Kathy

Smith had served in Venezuela; Lieut-Colonels Ian and Nancy Smith at International Headquarters plus trips to many countries by Ian as an international auditor; Major Margaret Newdick in Singapore Malaysia Command and at International Headquarters; and Commissioners Vic and Ros Poke in the United Kingdom and Republic of Ireland Territory, as well as in Sweden.

About the same time, Ian was asked to contribute to a book being compiled by then Cadet Kim Haworth. Titled *Famous Last Words: Inspirational Messages of Faith and Ministry,* the book grew from the inspiration of the Training Principal, Captain Stephen Court, who wanted the experiences of retired and some active officers to speak into the lives of cadets, officers and Salvationists by sharing their knowledge and wisdom through stories of ministry and faith. Adapting the phrase: 'Bring him home…' from the musical *Le Misérables,* Ian summarised our mission as that of bringing home the lost to Jesus. 'Bring them home!'[35]

At the prompting of Hian and Basil Beilby, two of the Byways leaders, Ian became the chaplain of Byways in 2008. Retired Bandmaster Noel Jones gave wonderful support in providing sensitive piano accompaniments for the chapel service led by Ian and others he invited to do so. For a time, Sonja took on a chaplaincy role for a craft group that met on Thursday mornings. On the third Thursday each month, we both attended a cluster group for Chinese corps officers at the invitation of the divisional leaders in Eastern Victoria Division, Majors Winsome and Kelvin Merrett. Four Chinese-language corps were situated in Melbourne at that time and the officers came together for coaching and encouragement led by Major Kelvin Merrett who held a concurrent THQ appointment in the Growing Healthy Corps Programme. On the occasions of Kelvin's absence, Ian led the group. As a result, we visited Sydney in October 2008 for the first Australian Chinese Ministries Congress. That event brought together about 220 people involved in Chinese ministries in Perth, Melbourne, Sydney and Tuggerah Lakes, NSW. Salvationists from Taiwan and Hong Kong (including their Staff Band) also attended.

Together we were able to make presentations about Salvation Army activities in Korea and China, as well as leading meetings at a number

---

35 Ian Southwell, in Kim Haworth, compiler, *Famous Last Words: Inspirational Messages of Faith and Ministry* (Melbourne, Salvo Publishing, 2008) p. 183ff.

of corps in Victoria. From 2008 through until 2012, Ian was invited to present lectures on leader development and time management at the Administrative Leadership Training Course that was still being conducted annually by our Territory each March. At Ringwood, Ian led a series of eight classes on helping seekers in meetings or elsewhere. Eventually that material was published as the first of the Stairways Series of books entitled *Born of the Spirit: Helping Seekers Enter and Grow in God's Family* released in 2009. A more extensive teaching assignment was to present six 90-minute lectures over four days (followed by discussion groups) on the principles of Christian giving at the Tri-Territorial Planned Giving Conference in August. The delegates present at the conference came from Australia Eastern, New Zealand and Australia Southern Territory plus one from Kenya, Ghana and Indian Northern. Eventually Ian brought together the material from that lecture series, and an earlier one he had presented in 1996, in a book entitled *Giving to God: A Response of Love*, published by Salvo Publishing in the Stairway Series in 2011.

In March we travelled to Welshman's Reef near Malden to visit Joan (Sonja's sister) and her husband George Stolk prior to conducting the launch of the Self Denial Appeal at Castlemaine Corps where they were soldiers. We then journeyed on to Adelaide to share a luncheon with the office-bearers of the World Mission Fellowship branch in South Australia. The major reason for that trip, however, was to conduct a memorial service around the fifth anniversary of the promotion to Glory of Envoy Bevan McDonald. Bevan had served as Financial Administrator for the Hong Kong Command for a couple of years when we were the command leaders. His unexpected promotion to Glory took place just after we left Hong Kong in 2003 and we had been unable to be present at his funeral.

We were also thrilled to attend the handover of some AU$75,000 collected by the Springvale Chinese Corps in June through to August to assist with relief of those involved in the earthquake in Sichuan Province, Mainland China. This was a wonderful way to celebrate the ninth anniversary of the corps, then led by Captain Jenny Fan. In August, Ian was privileged to share in conducting the funeral of Retired Corps Sergeant-Major Jim Shanks. Jim had been the bandmaster of Melbourne City Temple when we were the officers there in 1969.

A major highlight of 2008 was our visit to Hong Kong and Korea in September and October. We had been invited to Korea for the Centenary celebration of the Territory. Taking the opportunity of travelling through Hong Kong, we were able to meet many of our comrades with whom we worked from 1999 to 2003. What a delight it was to see the Lam Butt Chung Memorial School we opened in Tung Chung in 2001 filled with students and surrounded by an ever-expanding sea of 50-storey high-rise apartments. The school was providing a high standard of education in the area. The Tung Chung Corps that commenced its meetings in one of the rooms was continuing to grow as well. We were also pleased to see the new assembly hall at Shek Wu Special School for handicapped children at Sheung Shui, New Territories. To meet and share meals with the officers and friends in Hong Kong also was a wonderful privilege. Our friend, Commissioner Margaret Sutherland, visited Hong Kong at the same time just as Majors Jim and Marion Weymouth left the Command for appointments in Zambia. All five of us had previously served in Zambia at some time; then in Australia with Jim and Marion; and at International Headquarters with Margaret.

From Hong Kong we flew to Korea for the Centenary. The Congress was excellently planned, with General Shaw Clifton and Commissioner Helen Clifton providing good leadership. The Melbourne Staff Band and Box Hill Corps Modern Music Group provided great support as guest musicians. About 24 officers from overseas who had served in Korea such as ourselves were recognised at the World Mission Rally on the Friday afternoon. The Sunday morning activities took place in a stadium in Seoul designed to seat about 8,000 persons. Another 1,500 sat on polystyrene mats on the floor of the arena so they could be present. Apparently others watched on large screens outside the stadium. General Clifton clearly presented God's Word and many attendees made recommitments. In addition, pioneer officers were appointed to commence Army work in Mongolia. Concerts, displays and processions at Seoul Plaza ensured the Army was very visible in the capital city. Again, we felt wonderfully privileged to meet officers and comrades with whom we served from 1997 until 1999. Our return journey was via Sydney for the Chinese Ministries Congress mentioned earlier.

The activities of 2009 commenced with Ian speaking at the Ringwood Corps Men's Breakfast about China and the work of The Salvation Army in that country. Almost immediately after this, we were involved in supporting bushfire relief at Traralgon and Whittlesea. At least 170 people were killed and many thousands of houses destroyed or damaged by the disastrous bushfires in January, and especially during the days 7–10 February. In retrospect, how glad we were that we held the reunion of the 'Messengers of the Faith' session in August 2008 because the Elkanah Conference Centre was burned down when these disastrous bushfires raced through Marysville. Other fires were less than 50 km from Melbourne. The Army's work in providing comfort and material aid was deeply appreciated by survivors in many areas.

The year provided a wide variety of opportunities for celebration, challenge, and service. Our daughter Sharon's 40th birthday in July, granddaughter Stephanie's 10th birthday in October, and Sonja's 70th birthday in November, were all special occasions to thank God for his faithfulness to our family over the years. A representative cross-section of family, friends and colleagues came together at Ringwood Corps to celebrate Sonja's special occasion. This was the first major birthday party for her in Australia since her 21st!

Early in 2009, Cathy and Darren were transferred to New Zealand to be the leaders of The Salvation Army Corps at Whangarei in the North Island. In May, we were able to travel across to see something of their situation and then hire a campervan to travel around many areas on the North Island. We visited such historical sites as the Treaty area in Waitangi, Kerrikerri, the Kauri Coast, Auckland and Rotorua.

Before we knew that the family was going to New Zealand that year, we booked a bus tour through the heart of central Australia in late June and early July 2009. We followed through with that booking as well. We were able to view Coober Pedy, Uluru (Ayers Rock), Kata Tjuta (the Olgas), Alice Springs, Tennant Creek, Nitmiluk (Katherine Gorge), Katherine, Kakadu National Park, and Darwin over a period of three weeks. As a result, Sonja was able to make a sentimental journey back to Katherine Hospital where she served as a nurse in 1964 and 1965. The hospital had developed beyond recognition, as had the town. We arranged a dinner with a nursing friend from those years, Mrs Jan Forscutt, together with her husband, Jim. Unlike Sonja, Jan had lived in Katherine almost all those years. Jim had been a town councillor, eventually being elected and re-elected mayor for at least 16 of them. He was a great source of information about the town and obviously had positively influenced the development of that city over the years.

Later that year, the wife of the manager of a supported residential service in Ringwood made her commitment to Christ following a 'Christianity Explained Course' we conducted. For time she attended Ringwood Corps meetings. Being of a Hindu background previously, in early 2010 she asked Ian to conduct a house cleansing in her home. She signed a certificate stating that she 'voluntarily, and of my own free will, emptied my house of all idols, objects and publications associated with my previous religious beliefs as a witness to my new and exclusive allegiance to JESUS CHRIST'. On this basis, various household idols and other materials were removed and taken to the local tip.

Despite significant periods of travelling, we were still very busy in God's service in the Ringwood area. We became representatives of the Ringwood Corps for the Maroondah Fellowship of Churches—an ecumenical fellowship then representing some 13 churches in the district. Ian was initially elected as treasurer in 2009, becoming the president from August 2010 until the time of writing. Very early on in his presidency, Ian cast a vision of the Fellowship: *Affirming* fellow Christians, *Informing* about ecumenical activities, *Motivating* spiritual growth, and *Supporting* social action. Over the years this has been abbreviated to 'Affirming, Informing, Motivating and Supporting: Christians, churches, and the community'. Both the full statement and the abbreviation fit well around the acronym AIMS.

Moves to make Australia a more secular and multicultural society meant that potential citizens could swear or affirm allegiance to Australia using any 'holy book'—or none at all. As President of the Maroondah Fellowship of Churches (MFC), Ian shared his concerns about this with the members. They agreed with him, but were uncertain about what to do. While attending a citizenship ceremony near Ringwood Lake on Australia Day, 26 January 2011, we noticed that the Australia Electoral Commission was provided with a table at which they were enrolling new citizens as voters. If this group could have a table for such a purpose, why should not the churches have a table offering free Bibles? Eventually the Maroondah City Council agreed. The next task was to obtain low-cost Bibles. One of our MFC members had links with the local camp of Gideons International. This group, led by Mr Robert Woodward, was willing to grasp the opportunity and teamed up with us in facilitating the project. As result, and under our auspices, the MFC and the Gideons offer complete Bibles or New Testaments at no charge, together with information bookmarks about the churches in our district at each citizenship ceremony. We thank the Lord for the number of Bibles distributed during this and the succeeding years, together with the opportunity to greet new citizens on behalf of the Christian community. Over the years till 2016, the number of churches that are members of the Fellowship has grown from 13 to 18.

Ian continued his role of teaching at the Administrative Leadership Training Course until 2012. In addition, he became the corps representative to the committee of the Eastern Salvation Army Cricket Club which had a number of teams playing on Saturdays and practising a couple of nights a week. He even donned his cricket gear when one of the teams was short of players. Ian was also elected as chairman of the Owners' Corporation Committee for the set of units where we lived.

Ian's second book in the Stairways Series, namely *Prayer: The Communication of Love* was published in 2010. He had already taught much of this material at holiness seminars and similar spiritual growth events. As with the other books in the Stairways Series, this volume focused around the steps needed to develop relationships in general, and a loving relationship with God through prayer quite specifically. Ian based his approach around the affective domain categories outlined by David R. Krathwohl, Benjamin S. Bloom and Bertram B. Masia in the *Taxonomy of Educational Objectives: The Classification of Educational Goals, Handbook 2*. These categories were awareness and attention (receiving); response; commitment (valuing); organisation; and characterisation.

As an alumnus of the University of Melbourne, Ian offered to be involved in supporting current students as part of a welcome programme for overseas students designed by the university. The first couple we supported was from South Africa. They were committed Christians who attended a Pentecostal church in Richmond. Mark and Sandy Corneilse were delighted to be paired with a Christian couple such as ourselves. They enjoyed a meal at our home and we took them out to see the devastation of the February bushfires. Mark's area of postgraduate studies in educational measurement—one of Ian's postgraduate study areas as well. They invited us to Mark's graduation when he completed his degree a year or so later.

We were able to return to New Zealand in September 2010, especially to see our family. Ian conducted a Friday night and Saturday morning and afternoon seminar for about 12 corps members at Whangarei about helping seekers based around his then recently published book *Born of the Spirit*. He also brought the Bible message on the Sunday morning meeting the next day, as Darren had only just returned from earthquake relief work in Christchurch. The mention of Christchurch leads logically to mention the rest of the trip to New Zealand. After a few more days enjoying time with our family we travelled to Rotorua. This was the venue for the South Pacific Retired Officers Convention (SPROC). About 120 retired officers from New Zealand, Australia, Fiji and Tonga attended. We enjoyed Maori cultural exhibitions, reunions with colleagues, excellent Bible studies and even a lively debate. Ian led one of the debating teams. The delegates made excursions to some of the local tourist sites and experienced some moving spiritual moments.

From Rotorua we flew to Christchurch. That night a magnitude-5 after-shock—only 1/100th of the magnitude-7 earthquake which earlier had damaged so many parts of that beautiful city—reminded us of just how unstable the Earth's crust could be in those parts. A prearranged bus tour took us to the vicinity of Mount Cook; on to Dunedin; across the island to Te Anau; on to Milford Sound; Queenstown; the Franz Joseph Glacier; Punakaiki; back to Arthur's Pass, and then across the island again to Christchurch via the TranzAlpine train—all in just eight days! The scenery was magnificent—especially as snow had fallen recently and the mountains were all snow-capped. The beauty of God's handiwork caused us to rejoice. To complete the visit we took a hire car north to Blenheim, Picton and via the scenic route across to Nelson. We returned to Christchurch after a night at Kaikoura. During the final weekend, we visited Christchurch Corps where Ian's grandparents, George and Jennie Lonnie had been the corps officers from 1905 to 1907 and where Ian's mother was born. Ian managed to find the address where his grandparents would have been living at that time. In Christchurch we also met with our friends, Majors David and Myrtle Clark, who had been the officers at Moonee Ponds Corps when we soldiered there in 1985. Their retirement property had been badly damaged in the earthquake with a fissure producing a split-level backyard, destroying the driveway and dislocating the fencing. Amazingly, the house was habitable—for a time. Eventually, they needed to move away and relocate to the North Island.

Earlier, in August 2010, we journeyed to Dalton in New South Wales to attend the 150th anniversary of the Wesleyan (now Uniting) Church pioneered by Thomas and Sarah Brown. Like the Southwell family, they immigrated to New South Wales in 1838. The first Christian services in the district were held under a tree on their property years before a church building was constructed in the township. Thomas and Sarah's seventh child, Caroline, met and married William Southwell, Ian's great-grandfather. The young couple moved to nearby Rye Park and took up farming. We were able to visit both townships, view gravestones of ancestors and share in the Sunday celebrations. Travelling back through Yass on our way home, we visited Tom Brown's old property. Standing for a few moments under the tree where he commenced to hold services, we thanked God for godly forebears and a goodly heritage. On the way to Dalton and Rye Park, we had visited Yackandandah in north-eastern Victoria. Ian's maternal grandfather, George Lonnie, had been born there to goldmining parents in 1866. We also visited Beechworth where George made his decision to receive Christ and join The Salvation Army. Again, we thanked the Lord for his guidance and direction to our family through many years.

Although the Byways programme mentioned usually closed from early December until early February, Peter and Angela Noble and Ian, plus a few other helpers, ran a morning coffee group for those who might be at a 'loose end' during January 2011. The death by suicide of one of the Byways attendees in January 2010 had alerted us to how lonely and in need of support some people could be during the holiday season. While large numbers of people did not attend—possibly because we were not providing a bus pickup service or a full meal—those who came appreciated the opportunity. The summer season also allowed Ian time to conduct membership classes for three attendees at corps meetings who subsequently became adherents. What a worthwhile exercise that was!

From 2010 we began conducting an in-depth home Bible study on Tuesday nights at our home. This has proved to be a worthwhile time for fellowship and spiritual growth among the attendees. Our studies have continued until the time of writing, spanning Acts and Paul's letters in chronological sequence, plus Isaiah and Jeremiah. We also used a special DVD-based programme by Samuel Green entitled *Engaging With Islam* because of its relevance in Australia at this time. As we write in 2016, we have commenced a study of the Gospel of Luke.

In February 2011 we were invited, via International Headquarters and our own Territory, to visit Nigeria. That Territory wanted us to come and make some assessment of their officer training programme. They sought suggestions on upgrading the training of their officers and even having their programme accredited at university level. We had visited Nigeria previously in 2004 to conduct Servant Leadership and holiness seminars. What a thrill to be 'back into harness' doing the type of work we enjoyed when at International Headquarters with responsibility for international training and leader development! Two weeks in Nigeria were full of activity. We spoke at a divisional commanders conference, at a territorial advisory council meeting, Sunday meetings, and the training college assembly. Obviously, we needed much consultation with training and headquarters staff members, as well as possible accreditation agencies. Those observations of the college, its library and facilities, and subsequent discussions resulted in a 29-page document containing 25 recommendations. Our prayer was that Nigeria Territory would be able to implement them in the years ahead.

Commencing in 2010 the Maroondah Fellowship of Churches organised an annual Pentecost or pre-Pentecost community celebration, depending on the more suitable date. This event, which coincided with the Week of Prayer for Christian Unity, provided opportunities for the churches which were part of the fellowship to worship together. Each member-church was invited to present an item spanning about seven minutes and then hear the reason for the coming of the Holy Spirit. During the course of the afternoon we would light and blow out some candles, and cut a birthday cake decorated with the words 'Happy Birthday, Christians'. Then we would all sing, 'Happy birthday, dear Christians!' Of course, we took the opportunity to pray together before sharing in fellowship around the birthday cake and soft drinks.

Having been the guest speaker for the World Day of Prayer in 2008, Sonja became coordinator for the event in the Ringwood area from 2009 to the present. Since then, she has ensured that the event has always been a worthy and God-glorifying occasion as the venue moved from church to church in the district.

We were particularly thrilled that Ian's books published in the Stairways Series were placed on the Army's International Literature Programme subsidy list. This meant that territories and commands needing mission support could obtain them for a mere one-tenth of their normal price. Southern Africa Territory subsequently ordered 400 of the book *Born of the Spirit: Helping Seekers Enter and Grow in God's Family,* and 200 of *Prayer: The Communication of Love.* The former book was supplied to their officers, cadets and recruiting sergeants. The latter went to their officers and cadets.

As mentioned earlier, Ian had been the Chaplain to the Byways programme from 2008 to 2011. The four Byways co-leaders all felt they needed to retire at the end of 2011 and no other leader was on the horizon—other than the corps officers. Ian offered to take the leadership. His offer was accepted quickly. Sonja joined him in this work. So for the next 18 months, we coordinated teams of five to 10 volunteers in the kitchen, two or three bus drivers, nine people who served the meal and anywhere from two to eight musicians. We found this to be a wonderful ministry, with attendance numbers similar to previously. In early December, 122 attended the Christmas meal. In order to focus the attention of the volunteers on the purpose of Byways, Ian devised an easily remembered couplet: 'By food and friendship to faith in Christ'.

We thanked God for the opportunity of speaking at various corps in Victoria, at special seminars, corps meetings and companion clubs, especially about the world mission and the wonderful good news of the Gospel. Ian's fourth book in the Stairways Series, *Holiness: A Radiant Relationship* was launched late that year. The book was the fruit of many years of pastoral reflection, study and prayer, attempting to make Christian holiness understandable to the average person, in seminars, retreats and in personal counselling. Ian asked Major Norman Armistead from the United Kingdom to read the manuscript before publication. As a result, Norman invited Ian to provide articles for *The Flame*, a quarterly holiness magazine which he edited. These 600-word articles were under the series title 'Letter from Australia' and gave Ian opportunities to comment on various matters highlighting the need for Christlike living in the nation. Norman also published Max Ryan's positive review of *Holiness: A Radiant Relationship*, and Alan Bennett's equally positive review of *Prayer: The Communication of Love* in *The Flame* April–June 2013.

A highlight of 2012 was the celebration of Ian's 70th birthday. About 70 family members, colleagues and friends (approximately one for every year) spanning much of his life were drawn together because the youth hall at Ringwood Corps had limited space. It was a good opportunity for saluting God's faithfulness to our family. How delighted we were that all three of our daughters could attend. They slept at our house for at least one night—the first time together since we were based in Camberwell in 1986–89. We also had the opportunity of sharing time with Darren and Cathy as well as our grandchildren Stephanie and Nathan in April when they were on homeland furlough from New Zealand. They were moving into their fourth year of ministry at Whangarei and expected to be there for the next two years. Sharon also completed her Masters of Psychology (clinical) degree at Deakin University in Geelong. She was particularly pleased with the success of her research project into the benefits of a gratitude diary for clinically depressed patients. Jenni was also well satisfied with the work she completed during this year as a senior research officer at the Queensland Commission for Children and Young People and Child Guardian. She had written several academic papers in that area in the hope that these would be used to develop good policies to assist vulnerable young people in that state and beyond.

At the end of 2012, we asked to be relieved of being support facilitators for the Chinese corps officers cluster group. We had enjoyed the opportunity of assisting this group for five years but felt that, with our other commitments and projects, it was time to make our exit. An excellent Chinese pastor-facilitator had become leader and was doing a fine job. He knew more about Chinese thinking and culture than we did. During the early months of 2013 we still had responsibility for the Byways programme at Ringwood. The task became more challenging when the leading cook in 2012 needed to retire from the position. The Lord guided us to find alternative personnel for purchasing foodstuffs and preparing meals, allowing us to continue organising the 'front of house' volunteers and chapel services. By the middle of the year, however, we felt it was the right time to make a break from Byways and allow our new corps officers, Majors Gary and Julie Grant, to find other leaders. Ian was struggling with pains in his back and legs due to spinal problems. He could not move around the tables interacting with the attendees as before.

We were due to fly to New Zealand late in June to look after our grandchildren while Cathy and Darren went to officers fellowship. Ian was also due to have a groin hernia re-correction in July that would put him out of action for a number of weeks. Of course, we thoroughly enjoyed the visit to our family in New Zealand. Ian was able to lead a Saturday seminar at Whangarei Corps based around his book *Holiness: A Radiant Relationship*, also giving the Sunday Bible address eight days later.

Before the trip to New Zealand, Ian needed to complete papers for entry to a local private hospital in mid-July. One question asked whether he had ever experienced chest pain that radiated up to his neck and chin. He recalled he had experienced such pain prior to conducting the recent funeral of his friend and Bible study member, Alan Francis, at Ringwood. His doctor referred him to the cardiology department at Knox Hospital. After returning from New Zealand, an angiogram found that one of Ian's main coronary arteries was 90 per cent blocked. The cardiologist's attempt to insert a stent a week later was not successful because the blockage had calcified. Because Ian's cholesterol levels and treatment-modified blood pressure were in the normal range, the cardiologist decided there was nothing else that could be done at the moment other than Ian attending a cardiac rehabilitation programme. All these procedures however, delayed the hernia operation until 3 October.

The hernia correction was successful, but other complications arose due to his enlarged prostate gland and the rough insertion of a catheter to relieve bladder pressure. Subsequent bleeding led to Ian having a 'silent' heart attack on the 5 October. This was identified by an electrocardiogram and blood tests. As result he was transferred to Knox Private Hospital the next day. The hospital's leading cardiac surgeon, Mr Philip Hayward, who was due to attend a conference in Singapore on 9 October, graciously agreed to undertake surgery on Ian on the evening of 7 October. As result, Ian had three coronary artery bypasses using veins taken from his right leg and chest. He did not remember much about the following week in the intensive care and coronary care units.

A urologist who Ian had consulted previously, and worked at the same hospital, was prepared to undertake a procedure called a green light laser trans-urethral resection of the prostate (TURP) to relieve the prostate problem. This was supposed to take place on 18 October. That very day, however, Ian displayed the effects of a gastro virus afflicting some other patients and a few hospital staff. He was immediately placed in an isolation ward for three days. After he recovered, the TURP took place on 22 October. Because the procedure produced the desired results, Ian was discharged from hospital on Friday, 25 October. Cardiac rehabilitation followed at the Victorian Rehabilitation Hospital two days a week for four weeks.

Throughout all these events we were very conscious of the Lord's direction and guidance. How wonderful it was that we were able to visit New Zealand without any complications. If Ian was going to have a heart attack, what better place to have it than in a hospital! The best cardiac surgeon was available at just the right time. Even the delay in having the TURP allowed Ian to gain extra strength through having more sleep in a private room rather than shared hospital accommodation.

From 2012 on, Ian had been increasingly conscious of nagging pain in his back, hips, thighs and legs. Visits to physiotherapists had helped very little. X-rays showed that he had a slippage of his lumbar-four (L4) vertebra over his lumbar-five (L5) vertebra. In addition to the slippage, the discs between numbers of other vertebrae in the spine had degenerated to such an extent that they were rubbing on each other and irritating nerves emanating from there to various parts of the body. As one radiologist commented to Ian, 'You have a very unhappy lower spine.' Pain medication rarely provided long-term relief and the necessary doses were increasing rather than decreasing. Neither had a change of mattress, a change of office chair, nor more exercises, provided relief.

In April 2014, Mr Greg Malham, a highly skilled neurosurgeon, performed an L4/L5 fusion. This corrected the obvious slippage of the L4 vertebra over the L5 and relieved some back and right leg pain. Unfortunately, the operation did not relieve the more acute pain Ian was experiencing in his left hip and thigh. Further investigations demonstrate the cause the problems as being irritated nerves further up the spine. So in August, Mr Malham fused L1/L2 and L2/L3; and two days later reinforced the whole L1/L5 section of Ian's spine with titanium rods and screws into each of the five vertebrae. As result of these surgeries, Ian no longer needed to take large doses of slow-release pain killers. He was able to stand upright and walk so much more easily. We rejoiced every day in the months following at such answers to prayer and his new lease on life.

At the end of 2014 Sharon married Dr Greg Restall, Professor of Philosophy at the University of Melbourne, who also worshipped at the same Anglican Church she attended. At the end of the same year, Cathy and Darren completed their sixth year of a highly successful term of service in Whangarei Corps in New Zealand and returned to Victoria to take up similar appointments at the Moreland City Corps in the northern suburbs of Melbourne in 2015.

Ian had become a member of the Australian College of Educators on the basis of his qualifications, teaching experience, and recommendations by existing members in 1985. He was delighted to be recognised as a Life Member of the College in 2015.

In 2016 we were invited to return to Hong Kong for the Centenary celebrations of Salvation Army ministry to Chinese people in China, and also the 85th anniversary of The Salvation Army in Hong Kong. This was a marvellous opportunity to meet colleagues with whom we had worked from 1999 to 2003 and some we had met again when we passed through in 2008 on our way to Korea. The celebrations were led by General André Cox and Commissioner Silvia Cox. A number of former leaders and reinforcement personnel were able to visit as well, including Majors Barry and Arlene Dooley who served as General Secretary and Command Secretary for Women's Ministries respectively when we were in Hong Kong and Macau. Lieut-Colonels Ian and Wendy Swan, who had been the Training Principal and Education Officer respectively when we were in Hong Kong, were now the Command Leaders.

We shared in a full programme of events, including officers councils, a men's fellowship dinner, a women's rally, a brilliant education display by the students of the Command's schools, a stirring Sunday morning meeting at which there were many seekers, and a Chinese New Year celebration dinner with staff of the social services department. An appreciation reception at the Hong Kong Convention and Exhibition Centre gave us an opportunity to meet members of the Army's Advisory Board—including many with whom we had worked during our years there—together with some more recent supporters. We met one of these newer sponsors the following afternoon at the airport while we were leaving. He explained that he had come to support The Salvation Army because he had looked through our audited finances and was impressed by the way in which The Salvation Army used the money donated to it, and had published its accounts.

Our greatest delight, however, was to meet members of a delegation of the 'faithful remnant' of Salvationists from Mainland China. These were largely children, grandchildren and great-grandchildren of the former officers of the Army in the People's Republic of China. Amongst them was the now 19-year-old university student who we dedicated as a three-year-old in Beijing in 2000. Major Jeremy Lam, who we appointed as the Project (also pastoral) Officer for Mainland China in 2001, was now the China Development Secretary. He was obviously well-known and highly-respected by the delegates because of his coordination of our Army work in that part of the world and his caring ministry.

The year before (2015), at the prompting of Retired Bandmaster Noel Jones OF[36], who later composed a suitable tune, Ian, assisted by Sonja, wrote the following lines for a song that summarises our sense of calling and dedication over the years:

The whole world needs to hear the news[37]

The whole world needs to hear the news
Of Jesus at this hour;
The young, the old, the rich and poor
All need his love and pow'r.

Chorus after verses 1, 2 and 3

[36] The Order of the Founder (OF) is the highest Salvation Army honour for distinguished service.

[37] The song can also be sung to the meditative tune 'Spohr' (*Salvation Army Tune Book* [2015], No. 111) by adding the first two lines of the first chorus to verse one; the second two lines to verse two; the first two lines of the second chorus to verse three; and the final two lines of the second chorus to verse four.

O, who will go and take the news
Of Jesus at this hour?
O, who will dedicate themselves
To show his love and pow'r?

For there are those without the light
The Gospel message brings;
Their lives are racked by pain and grief,
Their future doomed by sins.

And others find their lives are bound
Through habits that distress;
By alcohol and drugs that wound,
With guilt they are depressed.

Our Lord can bring them hope for life,
A new start and new love;
His death and resurrection point
The way to heav'n above.

Chorus after verse 4:

Yes, we will go and take the news
Of Jesus at this hour;
Yes, we will dedicate ourselves
To show his love and pow'r.

Our hope, based on the life, death and resurrection of our Lord Jesus Christ, is that as he has led us safely to serve him here on earth, so he will lead us safely to serve him with our praise in heaven when our physical life here ends. In the meantime, our message to all our fellow believers is still: 'Bring them home!'

And this is what we pledge to do ourselves.
Yes, we will go and take the news
Of Jesus at this hour;
Yes, we will dedicate ourselves
To show his love and pow'r.

Reflections

Some suggestions

Applicable to young (and older) people, both Christians and those not yet committed to Christ.

To get the best from life and make the greatest contributions to the world, may we suggest the following as the result of our experiences over the years?

DIRECTION

1. Be guided by a moral compass. Good sources for this come from the Bible in passages such as the Ten Commandments (Exodus 20:1–17); Jesus Christ's Sermon on the Mount (Matthew chapters 5 to 7); and Jesus' summary of those two statements (Mark 12:28–31). The book of Proverbs also has good advice worth considering and applying.
2. Aim to serve others.
3. Endeavour to improve your school, university, home, place of work, community, and nation.
4. Set long-term and short-term goals for yourself. Reassess these regularly—at least annually.
5. As a student, put in your best efforts to all subject areas at school in order to discover your strengths, weaknesses, and areas of interest.
6. Develop high standards for yourself.

7. Develop a portfolio of competencies in knowledge, skills, and attitudes that you could be put to use in a variety of situations if needed. Few jobs will stay unchanged in your lifetime.
8. Have a range of interests outside of school such as music, art, a hobby, photography, church, sport, and so on.
9. If you can demonstrate you are honest, genuinely care for people, have visions for a better future, and solutions to problems they face, or the ability to guide others to solve those problems themselves, people will follow your lead.
10. If you become a leader, delegate even the things you *like* to do to others. You can coach these supporters, but let them do the work—even if what they do is not as good as you would like. This delegation will develop them, freeing you to share your visions, develop others, and recognise their successes.

ATTITUDES

1. Be thankful. Have an attitude of gratitude because most of us live in wonderful countries with great resources. If we do not live in such a country, let us be thankful that we can make a contribution to improve the situation. That may be our purpose in being alive.
2. At the same time as being thankful, ask yourself what you can do to make life easier for the many millions around the world who do not have such privileges.
3. Consider tithing (giving a tenth of) your income and also giving additional generous amounts to your church and other bodies involved in alleviating human need.
4. Be enthusiastic and positive. Communicate that you want to make a contribution whatever your role is in an organisation.
5. Be persistent and do not easily give up if you believe you are journeying in the correct direction according to your goals and moral compass.
6. On the other hand, do not be so fixed in your thinking that you cannot appreciate other people's points of view—even if you disagree with them. They may be right, partly right or actually wiser than you think.

7. Be adventurous. Think creatively. Try something new.
8. Be prepared to take a stand against injustice, violence, dishonesty, exploitation, or discrimination, wherever you find them—even if it costs you your job. Others will be glad to employ a person of high integrity.

KNOWLEDGE

1. Do not necessarily undertake a course of study because your parents or significant relatives studied in such areas. Your contribution to society could be significantly different to theirs.
2. On the other hand, the examples seen in, knowledge gained from, and networks easily accessible through, your parents or significant relatives may be immensely valuable.
3. Learn facts and understand how those facts relate to other knowledge. Try to apply the facts and ideas in new situations. Analyse and evaluate alternative opinions, and develop some positions for yourself on controversial issues.
4. Be committed to lifelong learning. The world is changing, knowledge is expanding, and technology is improving. The contributors of the future need to be abreast of these changes.
5. Carry a pocket dictionary on your smartphone or in your briefcase so you can quickly learn the meanings of new words.
6. Learn a language other than your own first language. That knowledge may be most useful in an increasingly cosmopolitan world. Carry a dictionary of that language as well as one for your own first language.
7. Mathematics and music are other languages that will help you to develop useful skills and set up different learning pathways in your brain.

NURTURING ONE'S SPIRIT

1. If you are a Christian, take time to study the Bible and pray every day, ideally in the morning. Make this a priority no matter what time you have to commence work. Because we are God's creation and he loves us, he wants to communicate with us.

2. If you are not yet a Christian, reflect and meditate for an equivalent 20 minutes or so every day. You may find God is trying to communicate with you. He loves you (See John 3:16 in the Bible).
3. Study the life of Jesus in one or more of the Gospels such as Matthew, Mark, Luke and John.
4. If you desire a personal relationship with God through Jesus Christ, the steps are relatively straightforward—almost ABC: **A**dmit to God how far you have fallen short of his standard for you, and how much you need him (Romans 3:23, Isaiah 53:6). **B**elieve (or trust) that Jesus, through his death on the cross, took the penalty you deserve for failing to achieve God's standards (Romans 6:23, Romans 5:8, 1 John 1:9). **C**ommit yourself to God now and for the rest of your life (John 1:12, John 3:36, Romans 12:1–2). Then tell someone you know who is already a committed Christian about the steps you have taken as a witness to your new-found faith (Matthew 10:32, Romans 10:9). That person (and the fellow-believers at their church) will rejoice with you, pray for you, and help you grow in your new relationship with God.
5. Read good books or e-books for ideas and inspiration.

RELATIONSHIPS

1. Aim to develop good relationships with others by being aware of them, paying attention to them, responding appropriately to them and their responses to you, and by being committed to keep the relationship growing. Relationships stagnate or break down when any one of those four steps fail.
2. Work to resolve any disagreements promptly, fairly and in a respectful, Christlike manner. Do so by continuing to be aware of the other party (or parties), paying attention to them, responding appropriately, and being committed to keep the relationship developing.
3. Seek a like-minded, compatible life partner who shares your ideals, standards, and moral compass, and with whom you would be happy to raise a family. If you are Christian, definitely pray about this matter yourself, and with any prospective life partner as your relationship develops.

4. Seek guidance from reliable people on all manner of issues. None of us has all the wisdom we need. Knowledge and experience are great teachers. The Bible and credible Christian leaders, either in person or through their writings, are good sources of such guidance.
5. Value family, friends and colleagues. They can be a wonderful support to you at every stage of your life.
6. If you have children of your own in due course, protect, nurture, and spend time with them daily whenever possible.
7. Encourage your children to keep and care for suitable pets.
8. Learn teamwork. Sing in a choir, play in a band or join a sporting team, actively participate in a church, or enlist in a service club, for instance. As USA author and pastor John Maxwell points out regularly, nothing of significance can be achieved without a team.

PLANNING

1. Plan thoroughly to achieve your goals, ideally to avoid needing to make changes of direction that could cost time, money or your reputation.
2. If you make a mistake or need to make changes to your plans, use that experience as a stepping stone toward a better future rather than a tripping stone. One mistake does not have to be final.

HEALTH

1. Take care of your health. You only have one body, ideally designed to last 70 to 90 years.
2. Eat a balanced diet, restricting the levels of fats, salt and sugars.
3. Avoid addictive substances such as tobacco, alcohol or non-prescribed drugs. They can ruin your health.
4. Exercise regularly, ideally at least 20–30 minutes a day, to assist weight control, strengthen bones and muscles and improve your blood circulation as well as burning off excess stress-producing adrenaline.

5. Take a day of rest from regular work each week, and a minimum of three weeks of holidays annually.
6. In some countries or climates, a power-nap of about 20 minutes near the middle of the day is a worthwhile investment of time. You will work better in the latter half of the day as a result.
7. Find your optimal amount of sleep (say seven or eight hours daily) and work to maintain that. You will think more clearly and make fewer mistakes if you do.
8. If you need to lift a heavy load, ask others to help. Keep the item to be lifted as close to your body as possible. If you do have to lift a heavy item on your own, protect your spine by not bending at the waist.
9. To lift something heavy, maintain your body's natural curvature by power lifting. This technique involves using the large thigh and buttock muscles through bending your knees and sticking your buttocks out to reach the height needed, keeping your head up, and maintaining the natural curvature of your back. Support your elbows on your thighs and stand up leading with your head.
10. Have regular health checks from about age 40.
11. Private hospital insurance is a worthwhile investment in Australia and some other countries (as at the time of writing).

FINANCES

1. Take care of your resources. Ensure your spending does not exceed your savings or potential to earn.
2. If you do invest, do so having gained the maximum wise advice and having a backup plan if the investment fails. If the scheme seems too good to be true, it probably *is* too good to be true—so avoid it.
3. If you receive money from the sale of property, reinvest in property otherwise your family's assets will decrease and be harder to recover.
4. Insure your major assets such as car, house and your life.
5. Be a good steward of any resources entrusted to you.

Appendix 1

Some of Ian's VISIONS (end goals: how he would like to be remembered, as at 2016)

Ian was challenged and inspired by a list of personal goals he found in the papers of his late father, Lieut-Colonel David John Southwell, in 1957 or 1958. As a result, he has compiled progressively more detailed lists for himself over the years and revised them annually. Some have been triggered by reading he had been undertaking at the time or refined by attending leader development programmes.

What follows below is his list as at 2016.

1. Totally committed to Christ in a love relationship. He (Christ) must become more important; I must become less. He is 'able to do immeasurably more than we can ask or imagine' (Ephesians 3:20). Leave it to him. Whichever way he leads, we win.
2. Balanced: relaxed yet enthusiastic, positive in attitude, joyful and physically fit.
3. Significant leader of God's people—wherever and whenever—visionary, articulate, encouraging, trusted, connector, empowerer, problem-solver, and decision-maker, who does right things.
4. One who builds and supports leaders for The Salvation Army so it will fulfil its God-given mission.
5. Inspiring Bible preacher, teacher and writer—communicating God's truths and bringing glory to Jesus.

6. Loving and loyal husband, father, grandfather, colleague, and neighbour—who works to develop good relationships with others by continually connecting with them.

Some of Ian's SPIRITUAL AND OTHER OBJECTIVES around 2016

For achieving the vision of what God wants me to be:

1. Daily aware of Christ with me. Seek significance in Christ—and him alone.
2. Keep the focus on Jesus.
3. Be courageous—try new things.
4. Consult widely and be thoughtful (rather than impulsive). Tell the emotional and intellectual truth to others—yet keep confidential matters confidential.
5. Choose well—in ways that bring glory to God—today.
6. Particularly develop self-awareness, other-awareness, emotional self-control and empathy to stop my commanding, direct style—especially when under stress—going off track and damaging morale.
7. Take time to assess if acting on an impulse is going to cost time, money, energy, health, reputation (mine or someone else's), or a relationship. If it is, then gain time needed to make a good decision by responding: 'I'd like to look into this.' Or: 'I need to think this through.' Or: 'I'd like to consider other options.'
8. Work to identify and dispel 'toxic atmospheres' in all situations.
9. Be a good listener—and smile! Encourage the speaker to 'tell me more'.
10. Trust fellow workers more. Give them more opportunities to shine. Tell them what to do (not how to do it) and allow them to show their creativity. Delegate! Empower! Thank! Recognise achievements!
11. Excite others. Make good participation (learning) wanted.
12. Look for people who will look after the details.
13. Be totally forgiving of others and of self.
14. Relax and others will relax, too. Develop an adagio speaking-style.

15. Seek always the big picture.
16. Be positive and encourage others to be positive, too. 'When you look at the sun (Son), you can't see the shadows.' (Chinese proverb, adapted).
17. Remember, I am not responsible for the expectations of others—just my attitudes, reactions, and growth.
18. Model soul-winning.
19. Include walking/exercise bike/swimming and weight exercises in my daily routine to strengthen heart, spine, and joints.
20. 'Keep the path to the cross clear by making sure all the glory goes to God.'[38]
21. Model grace by allowing people to be what God wants them to be.
22. Persevere despite opposition. Be strong in the Lord and in the power of his might.
23. Enjoy the journey—and show it!
24. Claim the promise: 'Not by might or by power but by my Spirit' and move forward with the Holy Spirit—and in faith.
25. When the unexpected happens, listen for the Lord's comforting words: 'It is I; do not be afraid.' Blockages can lead to blessings.
26. Develop more sermon illustrations.
27. Practise **ESERC** to get the best out of the people I work with. **Envision** what has to be done. **Select** the right people to do it. **Empower** them to do it (provide the right environment and resources). **Recognise** their achievements. **Celebrate** with them.
28. Attend to the cross. Open heart and mind to what Jesus did for me (and all other people) on the cross. Haunt Calvary. Linger there.
29. As an extrovert working with introverts, preface comments by saying: 'These are my first thoughts...'
30. Practise **MPL**: **Match** (the posture and actions of the one you are trying to influence); **Pace** (get in step with them); and then **Lead** them where you want to go.

[38] Corps Sergeant-Major Ken Heffernan, of Sydney Congress Hall, speaking during a Zonal Conference in Korea in 1999.

31. Continue to develop emotional intelligence **ABCD**:

    Awareness skills: Emotional self-awareness; Emotional management; Assertiveness; Self-actualisation; Optimism.

    Behaviour skills: Independence; Stress management; Impulse control; Conflict management.

    Contact skills: Relationship-building; Empathy; Social responsibility.

    Decision-making skills: Problem identification; Creativity; Selecting solutions; Reality testing.

32. When I feel stress, take time to analyse the real reasons, the real issues—the hidden message. Determine whether to fight, forget or re-frame. Use assertive 'I-statements' to express how I feel.
33. Continue collecting material for various specific writing projects and polish what has already been written by editing and rewriting.
34. Sort and simplify library and filing system.
35. Encourage people to share their stories: 'Tell me more.'
36. Continue to master smartphone, digital camera, e-book reader(s), scanner, slide scanner, computer and webcam for efficient use and transfer of data. In a leadership role, leave such details to others and let them get on with it—or let them seek help to do so. Ask, 'Who can best help you with this?'
37. Help Maroondah Fellowship of Churches (MFC) gain new member churches, and have a clear focus and direction. **Affirm** fellow believers; **Inform** about ecumenical activities; **Motivate** uncommitted people toward faith in Christ as they see us working together; and **Support** churches in encouraging spiritual growth and social justice.

Some Leadership Objectives

Ian developed the following specific personal leadership objectives for himself inspired by the writings of John Maxwell, Stephen Covey and others.

1. A leader's core functions are: to articulate the vision, keep the momentum going, organise his followers (build a team), empower his followers, coach his people, pastor his people, keep his people secure and prepare successors.
2. **CARE:** **C**ommunicate **A**ppreciation **R**ecognition and **E**ncouragement
3. Create positive change.
4. Love your work. See it as an adventure.
5. 'Listen, dream, have integrity, be so well prepared, so well organised and so madly enthusiastic that the team wants to be there.' (Heard from one-time Carlton Football Team coach, David Parkin).
6. Take responsibility for everything done under my leadership.
7. Give straight answers to even the most difficult questions.
8. Make it easy for others to approach you.
9. Keep growing. Be teachable.
10. Aim to get the best out of the people you work with.
11. Remember occasions when too much adrenaline led to clouded judgment, triggering over-activity and eventual exhaustion. Seek God's guidance, slow down breathing, and relax.

Ian's own summary of leadership requirements for organisations or communities:

Vision, energy, availability, integrity, credibility, reliability and suitability.

Leaders provide visions to set directions, and energy to encourage others to follow. Without leaders being available, credible and reliable, energy wanes, momentum fades and organisations become directionless before collapsing.

Appendix 2

Sample competency list for Salvation Army officers

This sample list was drawn up at the South Asia Training Leaders Conferences in 2004 and 2005. At least 85 per cent of these competencies would be common for Salvation Army officers anywhere in the world—especially in the areas of spirituality and attitude.

As with all the lists prepared in consultation with territorial leaders, training leaders, corps leaders, and representative local officers around the world during 2003–2007, this one reflects a few specific needs and cultural factors that needed to be taken into account especially in India, Sri Lanka, Pakistan, and Bangladesh at that time. We have marked the obvious ones with asterisks.*

COMPETENCIES FOR SALVATION ARMY OFFICERS IN SOUTH ASIA

Based on the vision of confident, competent and Christlike leaders, we propose the following competencies for those to be commissioned as Salvation Army officers in South Asia.

Knowledge

Upon completion of the Course, cadets will be able to:

- Express in speaking and writing a wide knowledge and sound understanding of the Bible and its teaching.
- Explain the doctrines of The Salvation Army in the context of Christian ministry.
- Demonstrate knowledge of tools needed for effective biblical interpretation.
- Demonstrate a clear understanding of Salvation Army ethos, along with its traditions and history, so that the Army can be shown as relevant to cultural issues.
- Explain the role of the officer in relation to the mission and structure of The Salvation Army, identifying and explaining the biblically based principles of our mission.
- Demonstrate knowledge of the principles and procedures of Salvation Army orders and regulations, and how to apply them in various situations.
- Demonstrate a wide knowledge of Christian thought, including the areas of church history, world religions, Christian ethics and missiology.
- Explain verbally and in writing existing local and South Asian cultural practices (rituals, ceremonies) and ethics in relation to biblical teaching.*
- Demonstrate understanding of South Asian anthropology, sociology and psychology in relation to Christian teaching. *
- Explain the norms, customs, and conventions of existing cultures and ethnic groups in the territory to prepare officers for cross-cultural ministry.*
- Demonstrate Christian values in family and community.
- Demonstrate knowledge of both Salvation Army and government regulations and procedures in regard to property and its management.
- Demonstrate a clear understanding of current world and national politics that may affect Salvation Army management and procedures.

- Demonstrate an understanding of social trends within society and The Salvation Army's ongoing social welfare community programs and emergency services.
- Demonstrate knowledge of the regulations and procedures for public relations work, fund-raising, the Annual Appeal, and the best use of media.
- Demonstrate a clear understanding of basic health care and hygiene.*
- Demonstrate a working knowledge of the impact of HIV/AIDS on communities.*
- Demonstrate knowledge of community counselling techniques and psycho/social support mechanisms available for AIDS orphans.*
- Demonstrate knowledge of church growth principles.
- Exhibit an understanding of music and its role in worship.
- Demonstrate a working knowledge of the English language.*
- Demonstrate knowledge of quality hospitality.
- Demonstrate knowledge of the best methods of working with various groups of people (for example, women, children and youth).*

Skills

Upon completion of the course, cadets will be able to:

- Prepare and present effective Bible messages on salvation and holiness, relevant to the life and ministry of the congregation.
- Demonstrate ability to lead balanced and creative Salvation Army worship.
- Lead unsaved persons to Christ and disciple them in holiness.
- Demonstrate ability to teach principles and concepts of Christian thought.
- Speak confidently and competently in public.
- Demonstrate understanding of Christian ethics and missiology.
- Study independently as a basis for lifelong learning.
- Outline and apply the various Christian disciplines (e.g. to develop personal devotional time) in his/her life.

- Demonstrate the ability to be a Christian leader and take creative roles.
- Demonstrate the ability to operate as a member of a team.
- Apply Christian values in private and family life.
- Publicly witness to a personal assurance of salvation and a conviction about his/her calling.
- Apply spiritual disciplines and be an effective manager of self and time, property and finance.
- Apply human behaviour theories, and offer appropriate pastoral counselling.
- Identify causes of conflict and facilitate win-win solutions.
- Exercise pastoral roles in leading worship, visitation and pastoral care, and conducting Salvation Army ceremonies (e.g. weddings, funerals, etc.).
- Apply the skills and methods of pastoral care and counselling.
- Demonstrate people motivation and management in a variety of situations.
- Initiate and manage corps and social services programmes.
- Demonstrate financial management and accountability in a corps/social centre.
- Demonstrate basic skills in quarters' maintenance and property repairs.
- Demonstrate practical skills relevant to the total life of the community, for example, literacy, home management, health, agriculture, household repairs, tailoring, embroidery, cookery and handicraft.*
- Demonstrate skills in managing community development projects from sponsoring organisations.*
- Show quality hospitality to every visitor.
- Communicate effectively with a diverse range of people (e.g. age and culture).
- Demonstrate understanding of the history of the local church.
- Demonstrate knowledge of local cultures and languages and ability to adapt to different cultures and cultural settings.*
- Apply church growth principles sensitively to specific and varied situations.

- Interpret and apply Salvation Army orders and regulations (principles and procedures) to various situations.
- Perform various public (community) relations activities, negotiating with the local authorities and non-government organisations, and using the media effectively.
- Demonstrate cleanliness and hygiene, and teach health care and disease prevention.
- Demonstrate ability to deal with both emergency and ongoing social welfare needs.
- Apply and teach counselling techniques, as well as offering spiritual support to the congregation and community.
- Offer spiritual counselling to members of the congregation, and especially psycho/social support to HIV/AIDS orphans and families, using government-sponsored networks as appropriate.*
- Act independently of un-Christlike, family or traditional influences, and can challenge these influences.*
- Demonstrate the ability to use the latest means of communication such as the computer and the internet.
- Demonstrate the ability to maintain historical records of the local corps.
- Coordinate effectively fundraising activities.
- Demonstrate the ability to work with different groups of people (especially women, youth and children).*

Spirituality and attitude

Upon completion of the course, cadets should reflect the following spirituality and attitudes:

- A personal assurance of salvation.
- Commitment to a meaningful and consistent prayer-life.
- A life that is increasingly guided by God the Holy Spirit and reflecting the 'fruit of the Spirit' (Galatians 5:22).
- A life of true commitment to Christian faith, behaviour, and values.

- Conviction about his/her calling to a lifetime commitment to God and The Salvation Army as an officer.
- Commitment to be available to serve the Lord and the Army wherever needed.
- Loyalty to God and loyalty to The Salvation Army, its leaders, and its people.
- A determination to be a person of absolute integrity and honesty in all aspects of life and service.
- A strong purpose (passion) to lead people into the Kingdom of God and to build up the body of Christ, in The Salvation Army.
- Compassion and concern, openness and acceptance in relation to others and to self.
- Self-discipline and motivated initiative.
- Commitment to ongoing development of personal spiritual life.
- Commitment to independent study as a basis for ongoing, lifelong learning to increase his/her effectiveness as a Salvation Army officer.
- Commitment to team ministry.
- Commitment to stewardship in regard to time, finance and property.
- Commitment to pursue self-support in regard to financial resources.
- Commitment to learn the languages, cultures and religions in the area to which they may be appointed.
- Commitment to be a servant-leader.
- Total commitment to the Lord in all circumstances.

Appendix 3

Glossary of some Salvation Army Terms and Abbreviations used in this book[39]

Advisory Board: A group of influential citizens who, believing in the Army's programme of spiritual, moral and physical rehabilitation and amelioration, assist in promoting and supporting Army projects.

Articles of War: Earlier name for the Soldier's Covenant (see below).

'Blood and Fire': The Army's motto: refers to the blood of Jesus Christ and the fire of the Holy Spirit.

Cadet: A Salvationist who is in training for officership.

Candidate: A soldier who has been accepted for officer training.

Census Board: See Pastoral Care Council.

Chief of the Staff (CoS): The officer second-in-command of the Army throughout the world.

Chief Secretary (CS): The officer second-in-command of the Army in a territory.

---

[39] Definitions adapted from *The Salvation Army Year Book 2016* (London, UK; Salvation Books, The Salvation Army International Headquarters; 2015), pp. 18-20; also 12, 34–36 with permission of The General of The Salvation Army.

Command: A type of small territory.

Commission: A document presented publicly, authorising an officer, or local officer to fulfil a specified ministry.

Congress: Central gathering is often held annually and attended by most officers and many soldiers of the territory, command, region or division.

Corps: A Salvation Army unit established for the preaching of the gospel, worship, teaching and fellowship and to provide Christian-motivated service in the community. Corps is The Salvation Army term for a church or congregation.

Dedication Service: A public presentation of infants to the Lord. This differs from christening or infant baptism in that the main emphasis is upon specific vows made by the parents concerning the child's upbringing.

Corps Cadet (CC): A young Salvationist who undertakes a course of study and practical training in a corps with a view to becoming effective in Salvation Army service.

Corps Sergeant-Major (CSM): The chief local officer for public work who assists the corps officer with meetings and usually takes command in his/her absence.

Envoy: A Salvationist whose duty it is to visit corps, societies and outposts, for the purpose of conducting meetings. An envoy may be appointed in charge of any such unit.

General: The officer elected to the supreme command of the Army throughout the world. All appointments are made and all regulations issued under the General's authority.

General Secretary (GS): The officer second in charge of the Army in a Command.

Home League (HL): Part of the Women's Ministries of The Salvation Army in which Christian influence is exerted and practical help given for the benefit of the individual, the family and the nation.

International Headquarters (IHQ): The offices in which the business connected with the command of the worldwide Army is transacted based in London, UK.

International Secretary (IS): A position at IHQ with responsibility for the oversight and coordination of the work in a specific geographical zone or functional category and for advising the General on zonal and worldwide issues and policies.

Junior Soldier (JS): A boy or girl who, having accepted Jesus as their Saviour, has signed the Junior Soldier's Promise and become a Salvationist.

Local Officer: A soldier appointed to a position of responsibility and authority in the corps; carries out the duties of the appointment without being separated from regular employment or receiving remuneration from the Army.

Mercy Seat: A bench provided as a place where people can kneel to pray, seeking salvation or sanctification, or making a special consecration to God's will and service. The mercy seat is usually situated between the platform and main area of Army halls and is the focal point to remind all of God's reconciling and redeeming presence.

Officer: A Salvationist who has been trained, commissioned and ordained to service and leadership in response to God's call. An officer is a recognised minister of religion.

Officer Commanding (OC): The officer in charge of the Army in a Command.

Order of the Founder (OF): The highest Salvation Army honour for distinguished service.

Outpost: A locality in which Army work is carried out and where it is hoped a society or corps will develop.

Pastoral Care Council (PCC; previously known as the Census Board): Established in each corps for the care of soldiers, etc., and maintenance of membership rolls.

Promotion to Glory (pG): The Army's description of the death of Salvationists.

Ranks of Officers: Lieutenant, captain, major, lieut-colonel, colonel, commissioner, General. *Previous ranks* have included: ensign, adjutant, staff-captain, field-major, senior-captain, senior-major, brigadier and lieut-commissioner.

Red Shield: A symbol saying 'The Salvation Army' in the local language, identifying personnel, buildings, equipment, mobile units, and emergency services.

Salvation: The work of grace which God accomplishes in a repentant person whose trust is in Christ as Saviour, forgiving sin, giving new direction to life, and strength to live as God desires.

Self-Denial Appeal (SD or SDA): An annual effort by Salvationists and friends to raise funds for the Army's worldwide operations.

Sergeant: A local officer appointed for specific duty, usually in a corps.

Society: A company of soldiers who work together regularly in a district, without an officer.

Soldier: A converted person of at least 14 years of age who has, with the approval of the Senior Pastoral Care Council, been enrolled as a member of The Salvation Army after signing the Soldier's Covenant.

Soldier's Covenant: The statement of beliefs and promises which every intending soldier is required to sign before enrolment. Previously called the 'Articles of War'.

Territorial Commander (TC): The officer in command of the Army in a Territory.

Territory: A country, part of a country or several countries combined, in which Salvation Army work is organised under a territorial commander.

Young People's Sergeant-Major (YPSM): A local officer responsible for young people's work in a corps, under the commanding officer.